The Beans *and*

the Dreams

*Strategic Management from an International
and Holistic Perspective*

Reader's Edition

Stephen A. Engelking

Published by

The Hugh & Helene Schonfield World Service Trust

Johannesstrasse 12, D-78609 Tuningen, Germany

www.schonfield.org

Copyright ©2013 Stephen A. Engelking MBA, BSc, CertEd,
FCMI, FCIM

ISBN: 978-1-9998691-7-5

Contents

Part Three

The Organization, Entrepreneurship and Change

Part Four

A New World

Appendix

List of Illustrations and Tables

Introduction

Management science has become like theology, dominated by respected gurus and a body of accepted teachings. However, the pressures of a rapidly changing business environment are making managers and leaders more and more aware of the need for a broader scope of ideas to help in decision-making and the encouragement of innovation. Here I have attempted to combine conventional theories of management with concepts and writers outside of the conventional and accepted orthodoxy at the danger of being burned at the management stake for heresy.

Yet, the original source of this work on strategic management was inspired by the need to provide students of the subject at bachelor and masters level with a basic script to guide their studies and was first published as a series of four books. This was of course accompanied by face-to-face lectures and many discussions and term papers. It is the author's intention to here provide a simple framework that managers and leaders as well as students and teachers of management can use as a basis for provoking thought and intention. It was because of many requests to provide the four sections in the form of one book as a reader for managers and others interested in strategy that inspired me to produce this reader's edition.

It is impossible to learn management purely in theory and only by combining theory with practice can a deep and spontaneous ability to make informed decisions be achieved. As we would wish to include the modern thinking on evidence-based management, many of the activities here include the need for readers to carry out their own research.

There are four general parts to this presentation of strategic management. In the first we will deal with the individual, starting with the reader themselves, the fundamental ideas and qualities required in a manager and the roles played by individuals in organizations. The discussion continues on the quality of leadership and leadership styles.

The second part will concern itself with the issues involved in groups, the forming of teams and the empowerment of individuals in an organization.

The third part is about organizations, culture and structure. It will take a look at how organizations are created and developed through the perspective of entrepreneurship.

The final section will deal with the management of change in organizations and strategies from the viewpoint that organizations are playing an increasing role in the formation of society.

It is important to note at this point that we have an additional aim in presenting this material: Many readers will be non-native speakers and it is hoped that you will gain some additional practice in working with texts in English. For that reason you may expect the inclusion of some radical and unusual ideas that stretch beyond the bounds of day-to-day management and should present a framework for discussion.

A number of activities are provided which should be carried out when time permits. This should help in a deepening of understanding and aims to provoke a critical engagement with the subject material.

It is the conviction and experience of the author that if you aspire to the highest in mankind, you will also achieve the great-

est success for your organization – thus the title of this book –
the 'Beans *and* the Dreams'. Go out and fulfill your dreams!

S.A.E.

Acknowledgements

At this stage I must acknowledge my indebtedness to all the institutions with which I have worked. I must admit to having been very much influenced by ideas gleaned from my studies and later tutor position with a number of universities both in the UK and in Germany. The materials and learning have become so internalized that they are now an integral part of my thinking and have considerably influenced my work here. Additionally, I am particularly indebted to the University of Baden-Württemberg, especially the faculty offering studies in Small and Medium-Sized Enterprise under the direction of Professor Dr. Lothar Wildmann in Villingen-Schwenningen, who gave me the scope to develop and teach these ideas on holistic management, and was always encouraging and positive in his approach to the needs of students and organizations alike.

My work with the Steinbeis University Berlin was also a splendid opportunity to share ideas and experiences with mature students of business at various locations. With some of these ladies and gentlemen, I was able to found the International Leadership and Business Society (www.ilbs.org) to encourage the sharing of knowledge.

Working with the Open University in the UK has also been an enriching experience and the contact to some of the most mature and intelligent students studying their finals in the MBA was both a challenge and a source of new learning. It is such a pity that this university seems to be departing from its original vision of providing the best education to the needy in society and exchanging the dreams for the beans. Let it be a warning to all of us when we feel too comfortable with our consciences. In fact, presenting my ideas of advocacy management to the alumni of this university gave me the encouragement to start work on this book.

Of course my wife's support over the years and the encouragement from my seven children and the understanding that a father may not always spend as much time with his children as he should, have helped me achieve what I could.

The great personalities that have become close friends and who have obviously influenced this work, amongst others are Willi Haller (the inventor of flexible working hours, who was responsible for me seeing that people are what matters in the organization), Hugh Schonfield (I have also authored his biography entitled "A Life for Mankind"[1]) and his idea of a servant-nation as well as Arun Gandhi. Both Willi and Hugh are no longer with us but I would hope through this humble contribution, to continue their work and thinking so that others may profit from it in the future. Arun Gandhi continues to be a source of inspiration as he travels the world passing on the things he learnt from his grandfather, who may yet be proven as the person, who amongst other things, knew best what business was about.

About the Author

I would just like to share a few words about myself so that the reader might understand a little of my background.

I grew up in England with an English mother and a Texan Father. I didn't have it too easy as a youngster and finally left grammar school to take up an apprenticeship with Royal Dutch Shell as an instrument mechanic. I later became a sales engineer for Honeywell Controls and other organizations. Having married at the age of 19, my wife has been my life-long companion and we have lived a busy and adventurous life. In our young years, we decided jointly to become teachers and took a teaching degree at London University. She majored in mathematics (so she has always looked after the 'beans') and I in religious studies (the dreams). It was during this time that I met Hugh Schonfield and worked with him on his vision of a new society based on equity and justice. Another of his associates was Willi Haller. We became close friends with him and his family. Together we founded a community school in London to experiment with practice-oriented education for school dodgers. Later we joined Willi in Germany at the founding of his company Interflex where I became materials manager (so I did my fair share of managing beans too). Some ten years later, I founded my own electronics company, which was finally passed on to my son Amos a couple of years ago and continues to grow, before setting to write down these thoughts. I have also founded the Arun and Sunanda Gandhi Educational Institute in Germany with Arun Gandhi whilst at a conference in Nepal as a delegate from the International Leadership and Business Society of which I am chairman.

I have been lecturing strategic management and marketing to students from a wide variety of universities in both English and German for well over a decade now. One learns a lot from the interaction with others and many students bring a lot of their experience into the process. I am also a council member of the historical Sack Family Foundation, which means that I travel and interact with the most interesting people across the globe from all walks of life.

All these experiences have been very enriching for me and I hope you will join us in the quest for deeper knowledge and understanding.   *S.A.E.*

Part One

The Individual

How do Managers Learn?

Henry Mintzberg's (2004, p. ix)[2], in his monumental work, 'Managers not MBAs', utters the unthinkable statement:

I was simply finding too much of a disconnect between the practice of managing that was becoming clearer to me and what went on in classrooms, my own included, intended to develop those managers.

In these feelings, I have found myself not alone. Over the years, I asked colleagues all over the world and especially in the United States what they thought about teaching conventional MBA students. I have been surprised by how many agreed with me. A well-kept secret of business schools is how many of their faculty have had it with teaching MBAs.

So a dispute about the effectiveness of management learning has been breaking out amongst business schools and managers the world over. In the meantime, there is even a magazine under the title of Management Learning devoted to just this subject.

It is not my intention to go into the subject of learning theory at this stage but there are some basic principles, an understanding of which can help when thinking about one's own learning.

We could have a long discussion as to whether management is an art or a science, but let us assume for a moment that it is certainly a bit of both. Managers would therefore require both tacit (hands on — from practical experience) and explicit (from theory, research and experience shared by others). This all needs to be combined to form a body of intrinsically perceived knowledge that can lead to action and decision-making. This is certainly a rather long-winded, reiterative procedure and may need a lifetime to attain. We hope to be able to help you join us in this quest for managerial enlightenment!

There are three principles in a man's being and life, the principle of thought, the principle of speech, and the principle of action. The ori gin of all conflict between me and my fellow men is that I do not say what I mean and I don't do what I say. Martin Buber (1878 – 1965).

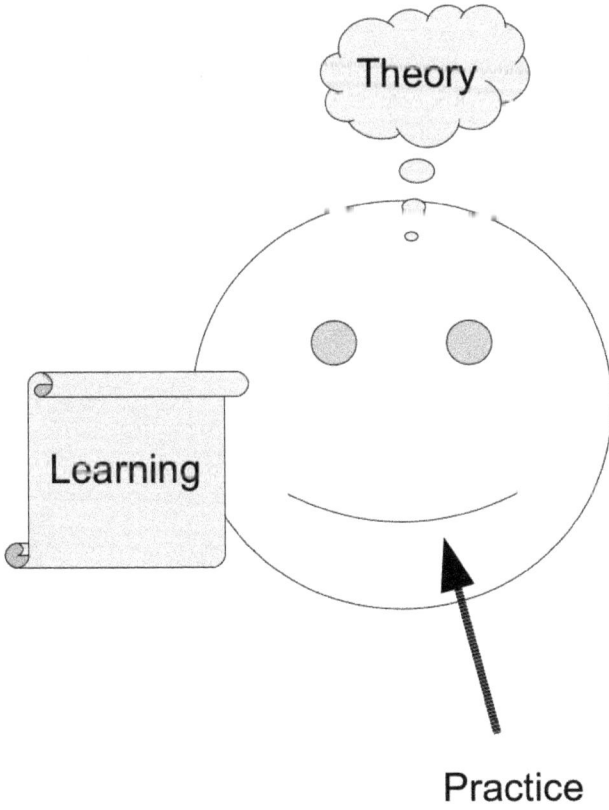

Fig. 1: Theory, Practice and Learning

Definitions and Purpose

The purpose of taking a holistic approach to management and strategy is to enhance and fertilize the ability to integrate strategic concerns across the organization, society and the environment (macro) while at the same time paying attention to and realizing the significance of issues at the individual and group levels (micro). This can partly be demonstrated by the well-known saying, 'think global, act local' while some situations will require managers to 'think local and act global'

At the same time, it pays attention to the functional and technical levels and the mechanics of survival (basic needs) while integrating spiritual and ethical needs into the strategic planning process — **the beans *and* the dreams[3].**

In the same manner it also has an historic perspective. Glancing back to the 'caveman' we are reminded of the need to provide for basic needs which has driven man forward through to the eschatological vision of a world of peace and harmony which has always served as the ultimate motivator to pull man on towards his destiny. This latter is very relevant in strategy because it is essentially a predictive science. As Clausewitz (1832)[4] states, strategy is about winning the war. Tactics on the other hand, also a requirement in management, are to do with winning battles and this is where we are concerned with the here and now and what we can learn from past experience.

Thus, a holistic view of strategic thinking is essential for the propagation of creativity and innovation not only in our orga-

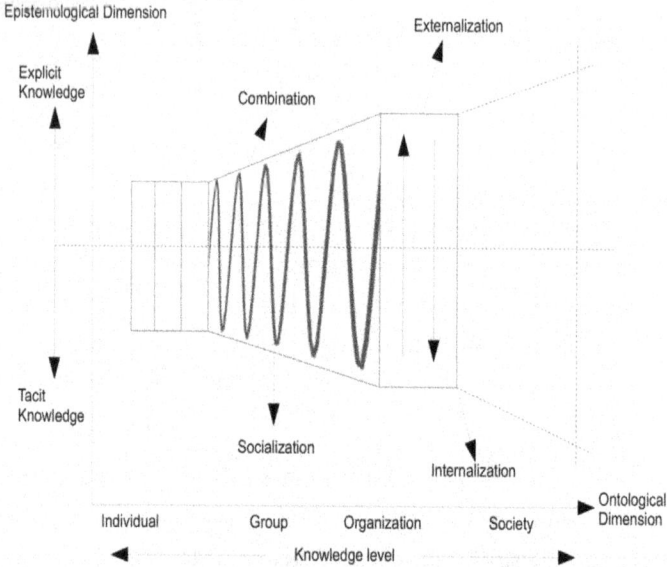

Fig. 2: The Knowledge Spiral (Nonaka and Takeuchi, 1995)

nizations but for us as individuals and in our society as a whole. How else can we meet the challenge proposed by an ever faster changing business and social environment? Knowledge management ideas have embraced a considerable amount of holistic thinking as demonstrated by Nonaka and Takeuchi (1995)[5] in their concept of knowledge sharing. Seen as a spiral where there is a continual exchange between tacit and explicit knowledge and between the individual and his environment we are confronted by the fact that this knowledge sharing process has to include all kinds of knowledge. We are forced to the realization that beyond knowledge lies a stable state where we can apply the word 'wisdom'. Past societies have had their wise men and women who have been able to read the oracles and who have had the insight and foresight to make decisions on behalf of those they represented. Wisdom cannot be inherited but is both a talent and the product of the knowledge sharing process. In the famous story of Solomon, we note that when given the choice by God, Solomon chose wisdom. This gift makes him become one of the most influential and successful rulers of his time, we are told. We talk of the knowledgeable individual, the knowledge-based organization and the knowledge society. The gurus have long striven for individual wisdom. Should we perhaps be striving for *wise* organizations, as Charles Handy often remarks, and even the *wise* society? In the diagram below, the four elements of 'Individual, Group, Organization and Inter-Organizational' (I have replaced this last element with the word 'Society' to broaden the perspective as will be discussed later) are clearly seen in the knowledge sharing process.

Activity

How would you see the development of thinking in business based on your own experience? Is the growth of knowledge encouraged in your organization? Collect any examples of this and make a list. How does this happen?

Competition and gaining competitive advantage have been traditionally seen as the drivers of business. Our strategies have generally been focused on gaining competitive advantage through superior marketing or innovation or through more cost-effective production. This is generally still the main striving of organizations in a market economy. Undoubtedly, man has often had to compete against the elements and nature in order to survive. Sometimes he has competed against his neighbors for scarce resources that has even led, in its most extreme forms, to fighting and wars. We have tended to apply this thinking to our organizations, seeing them competing for scarce resources. We use the language of war in our strategic thinking, building upon General von Clausewitz (1780-1831) and Sun Tzu (544-496 BCE). In the advent of the knowledge society, however relevant these ideas still are, we are increasingly involved in the search of a resource (knowledge) which is theoretically unlimited and in fact can only be unleashed in its shared form. This implies the need for co-operation rather than competition. Thus the term co-opetition has been coined, which allows for the positive aspects of fair competition with the idea of co-operation where possible. At the same time, some organizations like 'The Body Shop' have been finding new ways of competing, using holistic concerns (such as avoiding animal testing) to appeal to the values held by its customers. In Germany, we are drawn to the DM drugstore chain, which appeals to higher values to gain customer and employee loyalty and which has been a secret of their booming success. The privatization of public domain service industries such as hospitals is challenging traditional thinking about the meaning of 'the firm'. The stakeholder view of management also pays attention to the relationship with all those involved with the organization—including the competitors. Such a view requires wisdom to deal with these often seemingly conflicting interests. Here, the realization that organizations are also made up of individuals can help clarify our thinking by referring us to the probable agendas held by the members of the groups and organizations with which we are dealing. It helps us not only to consider the 'beans' but also remember the dreams of those involved. Successful organizations are those that are able to pay the necessary to attention to both. The good strategist of the future will need to have his feet on the ground and his head in the clouds.

Activity

What opportunities do you see for your organization to cooperate with competitors which as yet remain untapped? What evidence can you collect on this issue? Do you see any dangers in doing this and what are they?

Can you think of any examples of organizations who have been able to apply a more holistic approach in their business strategy? Trying doing some Internet research and see what evidence you can come up with.

Another buzzword of our managerial age is sustainability. A holistic strategy is very much concerned with the environment. The movement for holistic management in farming, which integrates a concern for the soil and the environment as perquisite for sustainable growth and long-term business success, has a documented history of success. A further development is the work of James Lovelock (1988)[6] and his Gaia hypothesis that includes:

> *Living organisms that grow vigorously, exploiting any environmental opportunities that open.*

> *Organisms that are subject to the rules of Darwinian natural selection: the species of organisms that leave the most progeny survive.*

Organisms that affect their physical and chemical environment...

The existence of constraints or bounds that establish the limits of life.

These ideas are gradually spreading into other business areas as managers realize that they are dependent both directly and indirectly on the environment. The growing awareness of the public in the affluent societies for environmental issues has led to the development of successful organizations such as Greenpeace, providing a powerful lobby and spokesman for nature. Some large companies have ignored this at their peril and we are seeing growing initiatives in the form of quality standards for environmental care as well as concepts such as social auditing being practiced by large organizations and reputable consultants.

While the informed reader will already be aware of and in agreement with most of these points, we are confronted by the exploding complexity of simultaneously having to address all these various demands on our strategic thinking. It is with this in mind that concepts of holistic management and strategy are being developed in an attempt to break down this complexity into units of more bounded rationality but which includes devices for avoiding myopia for the big picture.

'One of the biggest problems ... is that most people don't see the organization as a whole. They see fragments. Because of this you get localized optimism, many wrong decisions and much miscommunication' (Eli Goldratt, 1984)[7][8]

All of this is however not just a question of method it is also one of motive. Adolf Knapp (1999)[9] has come up with 4 I's:

Integrity: *honesty, fairness, reliability, transparency*

Intention: *alignment of external and internal motivation*

Inspiration: *Integrating, vision and wisdom, spirituality*

Intuition: *empathy, sensibility, open-mindedness, emotional intelligence*

This calls not just for new strategic models but also for a new breed of leader.

Activity

What are the prevalent attitudes in your business? Is there a general interest in and regard for environmental issues? Do discussions take place between employees about environmental and social issues? If so, are these interests shared by management?

See if you can create a short questionnaire for collecting qualitative data and circulate it amongst some of your colleagues. What does their response tell you?

A Broader View of

Strategy

One of the inspirations for this current work was Charles Handy's (1999)[10] book 'The Hungry Spirit'. In discussing Maslow's (1987)[11] pyramid with respect to motivation, Handy says that upon Maslow's pyramid we could mount a spire, just as a church spire. Upon this he would set vision, stating that, if our highest aspirations are only self-actualization, we are liable to end up with individuals, organizations and a society of self-centered egocentrics. People, organizations and society need a vision and a mission beyond the realization of self-satisfaction. This provokes the thought that the demise of our companies and society itself may be due, at least partly, to a lack of vision and an inordinate amount of egocentricity.

Norman Maxfield (2001)[12] pointed out that there may be something which can motivate us even beyond vision. He suggested the lines of Maslow's pyramid be extended to make two arms opening out into infinity? Within these arms, Norman would place enlightenment. This is the wisdom of age.

Could it be that management thinkers are today's seekers after truth? In ancient Israel there were prophets who would tell the people when they were erring or forewarn them of impending danger. It was the prophet that was often responsible for breaking societal mindset. Even a king would fear his or

her words. During the anarchistic theocracy of the early He-
brews there was a period described as the 'Time of the Judges'.
The judges were persons (sometimes men, sometimes women)
who were respected and thus appointed by the people in un-
spoken consensus as trustworthy in judgment Their office was
prophetic in nature and the last of them, when the trust in
providence had ebbed, possessed the authority to appoint military rulers and kings. Today, one sees management thinkers
elevated to prophetic heights and even referred to, in a surprisingly non-cynical manner, as 'gurus'.

The modern manager, in fact, is expected to have the wisdom
of a prophet. Certainly, when things go wrong, he or she is the
first to be stoned as a false prophet. The dichotomy is, that one
expects the manager to behave like a prophet and always to
have the foresight to make the right decisions for the future.
When the future turns out to be less rosy than expected (and
everyone was only too happy at the time to believe that good
fortune would prevail), the manager is suddenly exhorted to,
so to speak, don animal skins, become a caveman and club
those superfluous and expensive employees out of the way.

In fact, we can trace an historic *Maslowic* 'progression' in societal thinking from the concern for providing the material ne-
cessities of food, clothing and shelter through to the solid, self-
actualizing innovating heroes of the last decades. Our heroes
were, for a long time, white clad scientists and midnight-oil-
burning inventors who were promising us the unending
heaven-on-earth of brilliant consumables to fulfill all the
needs and desires of the world's population. But one day, the
world woke up to stinking pollution, dwindling resources, ex-
panding poverty and unceasing war and strife. As the Dalai
Lama[13] has stated:

Today's problems rest on centuries of negligence, centuries of pain and unresolved interactions. We are ignoring spirituality. Forget organized religion if need be--just talk about ethics, about how the basic quest for human happiness cannot be achieved by people who don't understand karma, that all actions have consequences. Furthermore, as people see clearly their predicament, that our fates are inextricably tied together, that life is a mutually interdependent web of relations, then universal responsibility becomes the only sane choice for thinking people.

Around this time, one or two management investigators started to talk of 'sustainability'. It was no longer enough to think in terms of short-term profits and heaps of cheap-to-produce PVC commodities. Back in the 1960's and 1970's, books like 'The Waste makers' by Vance Packard (1960)[14] were appearing and E. F. Schumacher (1975)[15] wrote his moving work, 'Small is Beautiful'. Companies could no longer live lives governed alone by the ethics of financial gain but were beginning to realize that suffocating, poisoned or starving customers did not necessarily hold the potential for increasing returns. Without resources, prices would climb astronomically and consumables become extortionately expensive. Businesses destroyed by natural catastrophes due to global warming would not provide the backbone to an economy. Companies would have to subscribe to a global and societal vision if they were to maintain prosperity. The saturation of existing markets, as western consumers reached the top of the motivational pyramid, meant that new markets needed to be accessed. This would necessitate some balancing and sharing of the world's wealth.

Even though some of the horror scenarios painted fortunately have not manifested themselves extremely to date, sustainability has become an important part of management science.

Because world politicians seem incapable of reaching agreement on measures to be taken, the responsibility of individuals and organizations is even more of importance. Ecology has become an ethical issue.

Activity

In this section we are trying to cross the disciplinary boundaries in order to see what we can learn from areas from religion and philosophy that will help understand the broader managerial issues. What ideas from your education and experience do you think you could apply and which are not found in traditional management literature?

The micro-economic and societal challenges were also no less. It has become apparent that we are finding ourselves catapulted from the industrial society into the knowledge society. Knowledge requires intrinsically motivated human minds. Old models of the organization as a well-oiled machine become increasingly obsolete. Knowledge workers respond poorly to financial incentives and increasingly need to believe in their organizations. Many state-run organizations are being privatized in an attempt to make them more efficient and the demands of not-for-profit organizations, which generally rely heavily on human resources, are feeding back into management theory and business schools.

In fact, much of management thinking and business education in the past has been dominated by thinking centered on the power of money. Speculators were able to reap huge profits on the shares of companies in the IT and other 'new economy' businesses. Soon, it was symbolic of some kind of new democracy that even those on social security would spend their last pennies buying shares in some telecommunication company bound to boom in the next few months. It wasn't long before the bubble burst and the houses built upon sand collapsed. The result was that millions of naive investors lost their savings and the cash landed in the pockets of banks and other investors with insider knowledge. The whole concept of earning by speculating and compound interest are morally and economically questionable as models for an ethically successful society. Tobin, as cited by Brainard and Nordhaus (1991)[16], recognized this in his call for a tax on currency speculation as a means of discouraging this activity.

A Gallup International global survey[17], conducted across more than 65 countries and which interviewed in excess of 50,000 people between May and July 2005

> *Poverty or the gap between rich and poor is considered the main problem facing the world. A quarter of the world population interviewed (26%) mentions poverty/the gap between rich and poor as the main problem the world currently faces.*
>
> *Poverty is the problem concentrating most mentions across all regions and all socio-demographic groups.*
>
> *It was the most mentioned problem in 60 of the 68 countries that participated in the survey.*
>
> *Far behind, with around one in ten mentions, people cite terrorism, unemployment and wars and conflicts as problems the world is facing.*
>
> *Hunger, one of the oldest humanitarian enemies continues to threaten the world in the 21st Century.*

A third of those interviewed say there have been times in the last 12 months when they and their families have not had enough to eat.

'The Gallup International Association' based in Switzerland and founded by George Horace Gallup (November 18, 1901-July 26, 1984) and now run by Gallup's son is interested in public opinion research on such issues as hunger and poverty, United Nations, etc., such as the survey quoted above. Their mission statement is:

The right to speak out vigorously on governmental and corporate policies is one of the most staunchly defended freedoms of the Western World. The advent of modern public opinion polls, dealing as they do with important political, social and economic issues of the day help to provide an opportunity to let government officials, public and private institutions, and the public itself know where the people stand on these issues. The usefulness of this mode of public expression is attested to by the fact that every important democracy in the world has now one or more competent public opinion research organization.

It is difficult to see how any concept of management or leadership can ignore these issues but it would seem that the dichotomy is observable in the two widely differing Gallup organizations that exist. The other Gallup, 'The Gallup Organization' based in Washington DC under CEO Jim Clifton aims at improving shareholder values through increased profits. In this paradigm there seems no place for principles and social responsibility as a driver for the organization.

This Gallup Organization's mission is summarized in 'The Gallup Path':

1. *Identify strengths*

2. *The right fit*

3. *Great managers*

4. *Engaged employees*

5. *Engaged customers*

6. *Sustainable growth*

7. *Real profit increase*

8. *Stock increase*

At first sight these two paradigms may appear to be in irrevocable conflict. The aim of a holistic view of strategy and management is to find ways to mold them together. In fact, what we are observing is merely the strong representation of a particular group of stakeholder interests. Taking sides will not take us forward, only the promotion of collaboration is able to achieve that.

In fact, we find confirmation in this when it is understood that the Gallup Organization bases a considerable amount of its thinking on Csiksentsmihalyi's idea of flow (basically, being thoroughly absorbed in what one does) in its program. Interestingly enough, that author is in fact a disciple of the Jesuit paleontologist Teilhard de Chardin (1881-1955). Csiksentmihalyi (2002)[18] states:

> *In a sense, flow is what drives this human need for going beyond what we have. In creativity or optimal experience, I have found that it is always a struggle, and the struggle has to do with essentially opening yourself up and yet delving deeply into yourself. Here are these two processes — differentiation*

and integration – which have to go hand in hand for complexity to evolve. So I see flow as a very important dynamic in the evolution of complexity. It gives you the incentive, the motivation, the reward for going beyond what you have. But it does not give you an ethical direction, so I would say it has to be flow with soul.[19]

In fact, he may not at all be happy with the use of the theory of flow just for growth and profit, shareholder value and the bottom line, to quote again:

Well, I think the great religions were all pretty good at pointing this out, whether we're talking about the five precepts of Buddhism or the capital sins of Christianity. You find that those are pretty much on target, in the sense that they all have to do with things like greed – whether it's gluttony or envy – with wanting things for yourself, trying to get things for free from others by stealing, robbing, cheating, or depriving others of their opportunity to lead a good life. So all these things psychologically go against the development of the soul or the development of complexity because they reduce the person back to his or her biological needs or the conventions of the culture, and they don't allow growth[20]

Activity

The diagram on the following page is an attempt to present the idea of holistic thinking based on the famous Maslow pyramid. Undoubtedly, you can think of better ways of presenting it and may not agree with all the ideas included in this diagram. Try to construct your own diagram to gain a better understanding of all the issues facing our businesses and our world.

From caveman to angel – the holistic and historic scope of strategy

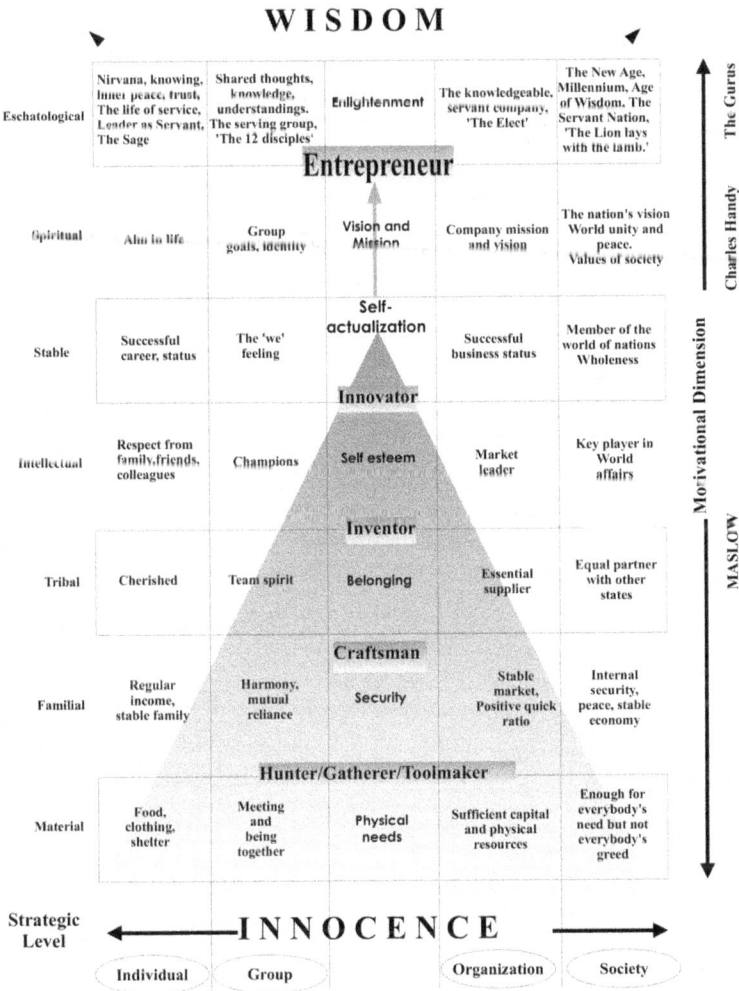

			WISDOM			
Eschatological	Nirvana, knowing, Inner peace, trust, The life of service, Leader as Servant, The Sage	Shared thoughts, knowledge, understandings. The serving group, 'The 12 disciples'	Enlightenment	The knowledgeable, servant company, 'The Elect'	The New Age, Millennium, Age of Wisdom. The Servant Nation, 'The Lion lays with the lamb.'	
			Entrepreneur			
Spiritual	Aim in life	Group goals, identity	Vision and Mission	Company mission and vision	The nation's vision World unity and peace. Values of society	
Stable	Successful career, status	The 'we' feeling	Self-actualization	Successful business status	Member of the world of nations Wholeness	
			Innovator			
Intellectual	Respect from family, friends, colleagues	Champions	Self esteem	Market leader	Key player in World affairs	
			Inventor			
Tribal	Cherished	Team spirit	Belonging	Essential supplier	Equal partner with other states	
			Craftsman			
Familial	Regular income, stable family	Harmony, mutual reliance	Security	Stable market, Positive quick ratio	Internal security, peace, stable economy	
			Hunter/Gatherer/Toolmaker			
Material	Food, clothing, shelter	Meeting and being together	Physical needs	Sufficient capital and physical resources	Enough for everybody's need but not everybody's greed	
Strategic Level	← **INNOCENCE** →					
	Individual	Group		Organization	Society	

Fig. 3: Fig. 3: The Holistic Scope of Strategy

Finding a Framework for

a Holistic Strategy

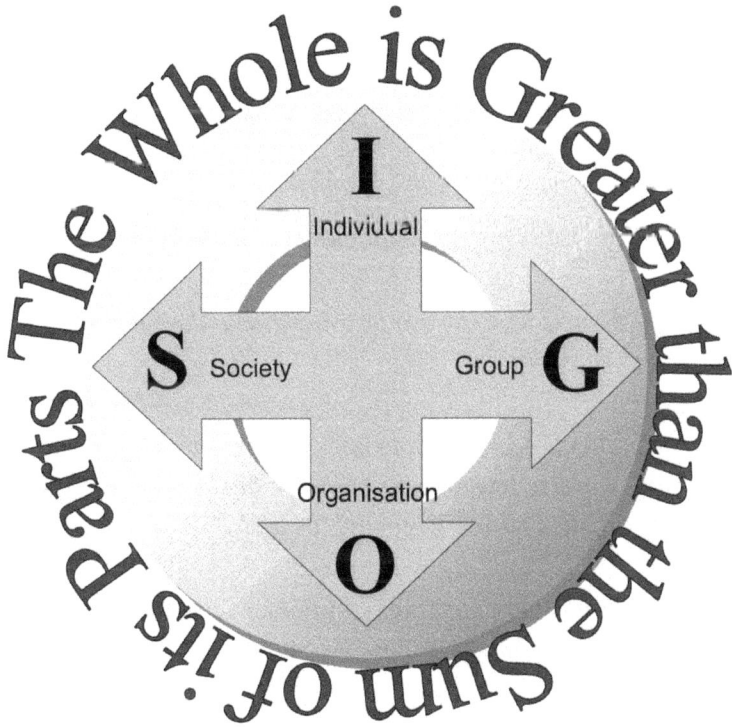

Fig. 4: The IGOS

To remind ourselves of the basis of a holistic approach to management and strategy discussed at the outset of our study, our very simple model referred to as the 'IGOS' (Individual, Group, Organization and Society), is presented in diagrammatic form. Later it will be discussed in more detail and will be discovered as a thread throughout this work.

Activity

This section contained many theoretical ideas and you may feel that the approach was too philosophical. This probably depends on your view of the role of management. Before moving on to the next section, try answering the following questions:

Make a list of five things that you think state the main jobs a manager should do.

What do you think are the main means of motivation?

How would you deal with an employee who does not seem to be enjoying his work?

How would you deal with an employee (or yourself for that matter) who seems to be enjoying his work but is nevertheless obviously dissatisfied with himself and his life?

What could your organization do in order to create a more holistic approach to its tasks?

Spiral Dynamics

Spiral Dynamics looks at leadership and how ethical decisions and actions are based on values. Ulrich et al (1999)[21] state that decisions are best made by leaders with a clear set of values. Furthermore, leaders who do not have clear values wander from one goal to another. Beck & Cowan (1996)[22], building on the research of the Psychologist Clare Graves, illustrate these values by the spiral dynamics of eight zones each describing the various leadership states and stages of human development using colors to describe the respective stages.

Activity

What similarities are there between the holistic matrix, the ideas of Maslow and the idea of Spiral Dynamics as shown in the following diagram?

Vmeme Level	Color	Target	Thinking	Orientation Behaviors	Lifestyle	Stress Type
First Tier ᵛMemes						
1	Beige	Me	Instinctive	**Wild** — food, water, shelter, safety, sleep, mating	Lives for survival	Vulnerability
2	Purple	Us	Animistic	**Social** — family tribe, honor, respect elders, ancestors, spirits	Lives for past	Tradition
3	Red	Me	Egocentric	**Psychological** power-driven, exploitative, privilege	Lives for now	Fear
4	Blue	Us	Absolutistic	**Abstract** purposeful, authoritarian, dualistic, dogmatic	Lives for future	Stagnation
5	Orange	Me	Materialistic	**Entrepreneurial** strategic, growth & success-driven, acquisitive	Lives for gain	Emptiness
6	Green	Us	Humanistic	**Community** harmony, liberty, equality, fraternity, relativistic	Lives for cause	Plurality
Second Tier ᵛMemes						
7	Yellow	Me	Systemic	**Flexibility** spontaneity, competence, uncertainty, balance	Lives for synergy	Isolation
8	Turquoise	All	Holarchic	**Compassionate** transpersonal, intuitive, interconnected	Lives for wisdom	Contentment
9	Coral	All	Infinite	**Imaginative** otherworldly, transcendent, enlightened	Lives for others	Unknown

Fig. 5: The Structure of the Spiral Dynamics World

Functions of Management

Firstly, take a few minutes to write down some ideas and answers to these questions:

> *What do you think a manager is?*

> *What is an organization?*

> *What is your aim in life?*

> *What is the aim of your Organization?*

> *What is the aim of your college?*

Most traditional views of strategic management to date have tended to look at strategy from the point of view of the organization. The newly developing holistic approach is an attempt to look at strategy at all levels. In this unit we are concentrating on looking from the perspective of the individual and from the dimension of basic needs to spiritual and emotional needs.

Different Views of the Role and Purpose of Management

The classical view

Although now over 80 years old, the idea of management as expressed by the Frenchman Henri Fayol in 1916 and quoted by Pugh & Hickson (1989)[23] still provides the basis of the definition of management used today:

To forecast and plan

To organize

To command

To co-ordinate

To control

Activity

Do you agree with this definition? Think of the people in authority over you – your boss, perhaps, your professors, etc. How do you see them fitting in with this definition? What are the weaknesses in this definition? In what type of organization would you expect to see this kind of managerial behavior?

This is a very rational approach[24] and we will develop it further. Planning seems to be at the core of the idea but managers are not always in control of all the circumstances that affect decision-making. In order to make sure that there is a consistency in the way decisions are made throughout the organization, it is necessary to make a distinction between the short-term and the long-term objectives of the organization. We are reminded again of Clausewitz's differentiation between strategy and tactics. Strategy is the 'war' we wish to win, whereas tactics are the 'battles' we fight.

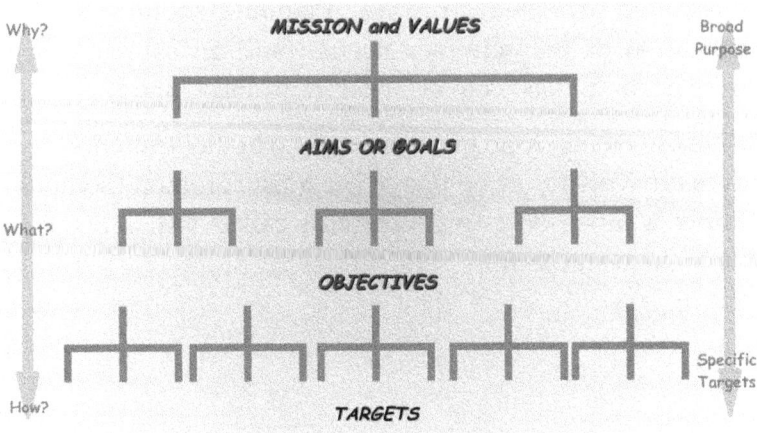

Fig. 6: The Pyramid of Purposes OU (1995)

Planning

Thus, for the sake of planning, it is necessary to develop a hierarchy of objectives as illustrated below:

Pardey (2006, p.132)[25] differentiates between aims—'the general direction being headed for'—and objectives—'specific and focused on achievement in the medium term'.

Objectives need to be clearly defined and you need to know how you want to achieve them.

> Are they realistic?

> Are they attainable?

> Have you got or can you obtain the resources to achieve them?

You will find yourself soon going round in circles. We cannot do everything we want because we do not have the resources. Then we have to gain the resources, which means planning new objectives and so on. This process of going round in circles is called an *iterative* process. Planning should include a specification of the activities needed and an estimate of resources needed. Who is to do what, how and when?

To give ourselves some guidance as to whether our chosen objectives are realistic, often one of the most common methods is to apply a mnemonic (memory aid) called **SMART** (Doran, 1981)[26] which stands for

> *Specific,*
>
> *Measurable,*
>
> *Achievable,*
>
> *Relevant and*
>
> *Timely*

or the **SMARTER** framework which adds

> *Evaluate and*
>
> *Revaluate to make the model more cyclic.*

Within this framework you would normally insert further theories or concepts and link to the relevant evidence. One widely used framework, for example, is another mnemonic called the **5 W's and H**, which stands for

> *What,*
>
> *Who,*
>
> *Where,*
>
> *Why,*

When and

How.

This idea was made famous by the author Rudyard Kipling (1902)[27] with this poem:

> *I keep six honest serving-men*
> *(They taught me all I knew);*
> *Their names are What and Why and When*
> *And How and Where and Who.*

Activity:

Take a few moments now to reflect on your own life and aims. Draw a pyramid of your own life concept. Ask yourself, 'will it look the same if I draw it in in 10 years time?' What does the answer to this question suggest to you? Are your aims SMART? Make a table showing this and include some evidence for your observations. What are the shortcomings of these models? Do plans always work out as expected? Can you find any discussions on this subject? Then consider the ethical aspects—does the aim always justify the means, providing it is a good aim?

The Rational Approach to Decision-Making

Whilst our approach to management and strategy has been clearly stated as 'holistic', it is important to take a look at the alternative and classical approach, the so-called 'rational approach to decision-making. This is a step-by-step method where quantitative data obtained through observation or statistical is used to make long-term decisions. In order to make choices that are going to work using this approach, we need to know on what basis and what criteria are relevant from that choice.

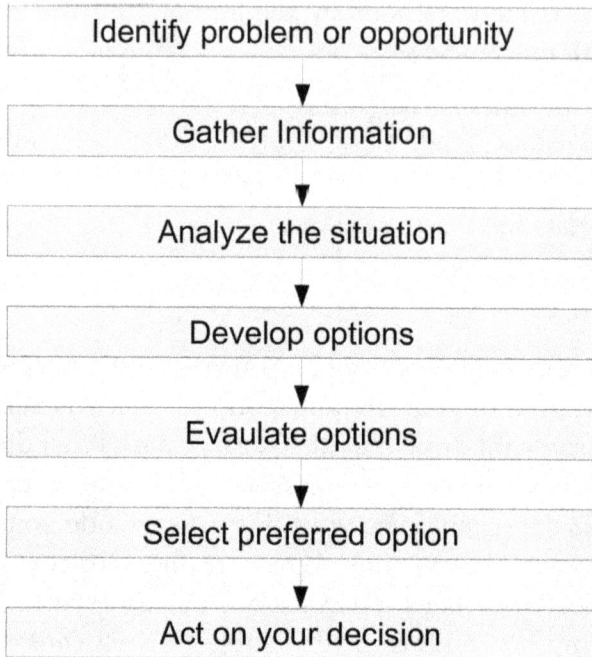

```
┌─────────────────────────────────────────┐
│       Identify problem or opportunity     │
└─────────────────────────────────────────┘
                    ▼
┌─────────────────────────────────────────┐
│             Gather Information            │
└─────────────────────────────────────────┘
                    ▼
┌─────────────────────────────────────────┐
│           Analyze the situation           │
└─────────────────────────────────────────┘
                    ▼
┌─────────────────────────────────────────┐
│             Develop options               │
└─────────────────────────────────────────┘
                    ▼
┌─────────────────────────────────────────┐
│             Evaulate options              │
└─────────────────────────────────────────┘
                    ▼
┌─────────────────────────────────────────┐
│           Select preferred option         │
└─────────────────────────────────────────┘
                    ▼
┌─────────────────────────────────────────┐
│            Act on your decision           │
└─────────────────────────────────────────┘
```

Fig. 7: The Rational Decision-Making Process

This means that we need sufficient information in order to be able to consider all possibilities. This is summed up in the diagram above.

Activity:

> *Think of a decision you need to make in the near future and cre-*
> *ate a diagram similar to the one above to illustrate it. What are*
> *the weaknesses of this concept? When would you use this ap-*
> *proach? Think of a personal decision you need to make and try to*
> *apply this approach. Could you additionally apply any of the*
> *other theories we have discussed previously?*

But do things actually happen like this in practice? Are all the decisions we make totally rational? Do we have all the facts and can we foretell the future? What are the strengths and weaknesses of this model?

But do we actually make all our decisions logically? How much of what we decide is governed by our own characters and the results of our upbringing and environment. Can we learn to make better decisions? This is an endless theme for discussion and psychologists spend a lot of their time debating it. It is often referred to as the 'Nature−Nurture' debate. Cognitive psychology is concerned with how human beings deal with the information around them. In the meantime, it is recognized that all humans have their own cognitive 'style'. How they arrived at it−nurture or nature−is only relevant in as far as it may affect whether and how our traits (inherent attributes) can be styled to enable the behavior necessary for us to play our role.

For the purposes of our discussion, taking style for granted, we can only say that differing styles tackle problem solving in different ways. There is no *right* way of doing things and we have to learn that differing styles are an essential part of organizational life. Also, the approach we apply may depend on the situation−whether the problem has bounded rationality or is a complex issue. The processes that people apply to problem solving can be described thus:

Perception processes—how we see the world. Complexity vs. simplicity. The means we use to communicate and develop understanding: visualizing, verbalizing, imagery, etc.

Problem solving processes—how much information is used: scanning, focusing. It governs how much of the information is employed, dealing incrementally or the broad picture: serialism, holism. Kirton (1989) [28] has categorized people into adaptors or innovators—those who prefer to use established solutions and those who prefer to find new ones.

Task process—this is the way in which we approach particular jobs. Constricted vs. flexible, impulsive vs. reflective, uncertainty acceptance vs. caution.

	Score		Score
Like solving simple problems		Like solving comlex problems	
I need to see them written down first		I can visualize problems	
It is better to focus on one problem at a time		It is better to scan all the problems before making a decision	
It is better to move on one step at a time and take fewer risks		You need to know the whole picture in order to make decisions	
Tried and tested solutions are the best		We need to find new ways of solving problems—just because a solution worked before doesn't mean it will work a second time	
Before making decisions, you should sleep over it		Snap decisions are the best	
One should be careful before taking a big decision		Don't worry, it'll all work out in the end	
TOTAL		TOTAL	

Fig. 8: What's your style?

Activity:

Using the cognitive styles above, fill in each box of the table below, giving yourself marks out of 10 for each attribute:

Now add up your score for each column. If your score on the left hand column is higher than the right, you probably tend to have an 'adaptor' style. Otherwise, you are likely to have an 'innovator' style.

What do you think about the above questions? Make yourself a set of questions to try to classify into the two styles. Ask someone to complete it. Is the result you get what you expected?

The style differences of Adaptors and Innovators can be roughly defined as[29]:

Adapters	Innovators
Do it better	Do it differently
Work withing existing frames	Challenge, reframe
Fewer, more acceptable solutions	Many solutions
Prefer well-established situations	Set new policy, structure
Essential for on-going functions	Essential in times of change

Fig. 9: Style Differences (Henry, 2001)

Control and the Control Loop

The word control and particularly, in recent times, 'Controlling', are words often used particularly in the German style of management. This is perhaps due to what Geert Hofstede refers to as a high Power-Distance indicator in the German business culture. We will come back to this research later. In many ways it is a much-misused word and certainly has negative connotations when it is applied to the controlling of people. Interestingly, although an English word, you will spend a long time looking for jobs with the title 'Controller' in an American or English newspaper because the term in English is 'Comptroller'. The sense in which we use it here is in the sense of the controlling of decision-making processes and the meaning of the word is nearer to 'test' or 'check' rather than the German word *steuern*. In fact, the word 'process control' in English is used technically for measurement and control equipment which has a feedback and correction loop.

The process of control requires that I:

> *Know what I want to achieve*

> *Have the information on how the process is running*

> *Can influence the process by taking corrections based on accurate data.*

Imagine a room thermostat. You set the dial to 20°C while the room is at 15°C. The heating switches on and starts to heat the room. The thermostat registers the temperature and switches off the heating when it reaches 20°C. The room cools down and the heating switches on again. This is very simplistic, of course. What happens in reality is that there will be hysteresis and the thermostat will have a switching offset, say between

19 and 21°C so if you drew a graph of the room temperature, it would be a wavy line. Also, because heating is slow to react, there would be considerable overshoot and the room temperature could possibly rise to 24°C and drop to 17°C, for example. To solve this problem, you would have to be preemptive, i.e., based on experience of the conditions in the room (insulation, etc.) you would include logic into your control system which would forecast the effects of switching the heating on and how long it took to reach the temperature set. Then you could switch off the heating before it reached 20°C, and so on.

Thus, taking remedial action when plans are not working as expected may require preemptive action based on previous experience. You can find some more useful information on this subject by visiting the Wikipedia page on control theory (but you should not quote this as a source when writing an academic paper of course).

The control loop[30] below, illustrates the controlling process:

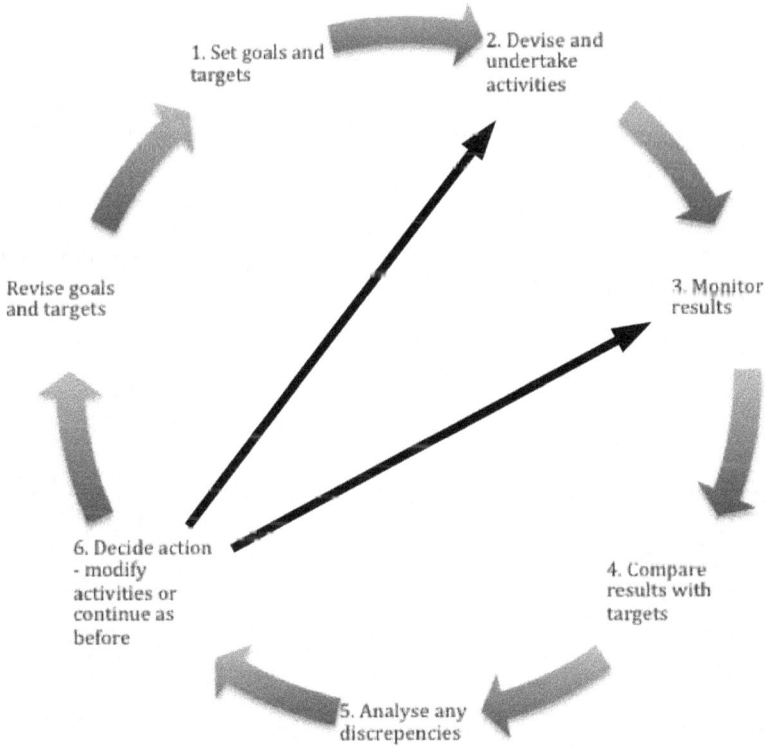

Fig. 10: The Control Loop

The Holistic Approach

As previously stated in the introduction, the holistic approach to strategic management takes the point of view that the whole is greater than the sum of its parts and that any strategy that does not take account of all the anthropological components of society, that is the individual, the group or team, the organization and society, and does not pay attention to all the motivational dimensions is not likely to lead to sustainable success. Applying this idea now to yourself as an individual, we can move up to the more esoteric dimensions of human personality. Since the days of F.W. Taylor and Henry Ford, managers have felt that it is not appropriate to consider these aspects. The worker is a resource to be used for the benefit of the company. The advent of the knowledge society and the growing need for creativity and entrepreneurship have led to increasing awareness for what is sometimes referred to as emotional or spiritual intelligence. Certainly, none of us today wish to be considered as cogs in a machine and the importance of the individual is something held up high by our society.

So how can we develop this area? Charles Handy (1991)[31] talks of three underlying principles:

Curiosity

Forgiveness

Love

and Henry (2000)[32] adds:

A sense of direction

Back in the period after the Second World War, the moralist Frank Buchman[33] called for businessmen to live according to four principles:

Absolute love

Absolute purity

Absolute honesty

Absolute unselfishness

These concepts are based on ideas that go back to the 'Sermon on the Mount' and are to be found in most religions. Many businessmen would still say that this is no basis to run a business. They would contend that you have to have a different set of ethics for the business world than in your private life and such notions are not likely to lead to a concentration on profitability. In times of dwindling resources, pollution and a world where our would-be consumers are largely living in poverty, it is questionable whether we can afford to take such a restrictive view. Also, we have much to learn from the teachings of the sages. It may be pertinent to remember that the inauguration and growth of our capitalist society as we know it, was founded very much on the beliefs which the protestant movement encouraged, such as hard work, honesty and fair dealing. It should be made clear that making a profit is not a sin as long as it is used for the benefit of the organization, society and those within it. It is however questionable whether the quest for profit will actually long term succeed in achieving that aim, a matter which will be further discussed. Gandhi and others have criticized the accumulation of wealth through share and currency speculation, which practice may in fact have a long-term detrimental effect on economies. The current financial crisis at the time of writing has clearly been the result of this approach to business and finance to the point at which financial manners have had more in common with those of a black jack player than of a logically thinking financier.

However you think about it, the point of all these writers is that managers should become 'reflective practitioners' of their art. If we treat medical practitioners as 'gods in white', why should we not expect high moral and ethical standards from our managers? After all, a wrong decision by a manager could cause people to lose their jobs with all manner of personal and family consequences. The responsibility of management should not be treated lightly and this is one of the important reasons why the demands for highly qualified professionals in our organizations are increasing. This is the challenge made to you as a student or practitioner of management and an area worth searching for personal excellence.

Activity

Why not try out the above notion on yourself now? Take a piece of clean paper and stop for a moment to consider yourself and your behavior in relation to the above standards. Write down anything that occurs to you. Be willing to be self-critical in this. Think about things you did yesterday – are there any things which do not live up to those standards or which you could have done better?

How could you build these ideas into your control loop? What do you understand by these terms? – discuss.

Keeping a daily log

There are several reasons and methods of keeping a daily log or reflective diary of your management practice and life behavior. It is a kind of diary but not one where you just write a list of what you did that day. Firstly you should decide what medium is best for you. Some people prefer to use a program like Evernote, a free tool that allows you make notes and save snippets of information like web pages or documents. These can be shared across your various devices and are automatically synchronized. Some people prefer to use something like a diary app or a word processor, whereas many still feel happier with a small notebook and pencil.

Whichever method you choose, this should become a perpetual habit. Allocate a specific time each day when you take say 10-15 minutes out time and jot down the thoughts that come to you. Base your 'meditation' on some framework like I have suggested above and try to be reflective. On the other hand, be honest with yourself but not overly critical. It is better to concentrate on what you can learn out of situations and to build on your strengths.

Additionally, it is best when you have access to your log during the day so that you can jot down anything that occurs to you spontaneously.

It is at this point when you should start to think how you can apply the theories you are reading about here and through your own research and reading. You could make yourself a table with one column for the issue, one column for your general thoughts, another for say the 4 principles of Handy and another for relevant theory.

These are only suggestions. There is quite a bit of material available on this subject including a Wikipedia article and an excellent book entitled 'The New Diary" by Tristine Rainer (2004)[34].

Complexity and Bounded Rationality

The Management Experience

Continuing our discussion around yourself as an individual, how do you manage to cope with the everyday pressures of life and how do you react to others around you when you are 'in stress'?

The Superficiality Trap

Henry Mintzberg (1998)[35] states that a manager is a 'person with a perpetual occupation'. That means his job never comes to an end and there is always something that needs doing. It is easy for a person to feel overloaded and short-tempered in this situation and, no doubt, you will have experienced this yourself, at least in situations where it has seemed that you had too little time to complete the work you had to do before a particular deadline. In England, before the days of the emancipated view of woman and where the idealized view of woman was the ideal housewife, there was a saying that went, 'a woman's work is never done'. In those days, a woman was seen as (if not respected for) a manager of the household. In the same way managers are often in a similar position.

Some may regard this a virtue and you will often hear managers and bosses boasting about how hard they work. However, the down side is that it leads to a certain superficiality. It is thus that we talk of the manager being in the 'superficiality trap'.

Mintzberg's research of managerial behavior demonstrated that:

There are no evident patterns of activity behavior except that work occurred in very short bursts

There is little free time. Breaks are rare

Work was highly fragmented

Work was frequently interrupted

Periods of work were short

Verbal contacts and media are preferred over written

Scheduled meetings eat up managerial time

Managers as boundary managers, link his/her own organization with outside networks

Managers seldom 'tour' yet WTJ (walking the job) enhances 'visibility' & understanding of the actuality of work and production/service methods, standards and problems.

Managers control little of what they do. Self-control over their initial commitments enables them to unlock the activity trap and orientate themselves to extracting information, exercising leadership

He said that managers condition themselves to a pattern of being overloaded with work and prefer not to get involved too deeply in any particular issue. He suggests that managers become proficient in their superficiality.

Bounded Rationality

In order to cope with this situation, an alternative model of decision-making has evolved referred to as 'bounded rationality'. This is an attempt to restore rational decision-making processes. It assumes that perfect decisions are not always possible and hopes to find acceptable solutions that meet the criteria 'good is good enough'. If it is not possible to find satisfactory solutions, the manager lowers his aspirations and settles for less. Although it can be also accused of a certain tendency to superficiality, it manages at least to retain some elements of rationality[36].

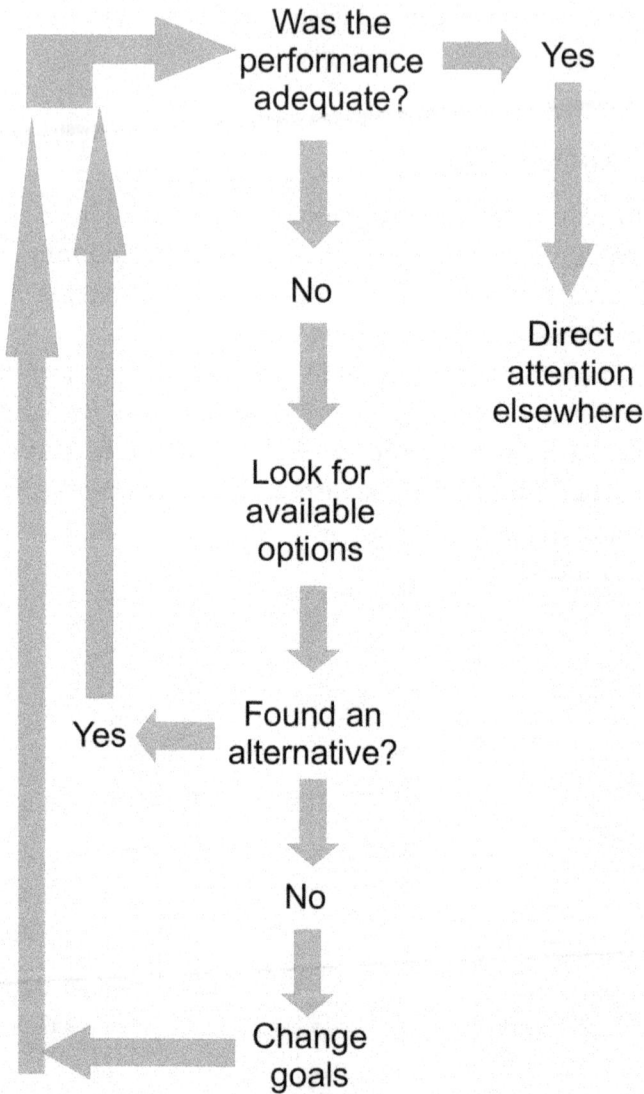

Fig. 11: The Process of Decision-Making using Bounded Rationality

---

Activity

Think of some situations where you have observed superficiality or made decisions yourself under such circumstances.

Imagine you wish to buy a car and have to decide between a new car and a second-hand one or any other big decision you can imagine making. Draw a diagram as above but add the decisions and items into the box. Do you find this approach helpful at clarifying your thinking?

Bounded rationality may work best when there is a:

> *limited time scale*
>
> *priorities are clear*
>
> *implications of decisions are limited*
>
> *the problem can be treated as a separate matter*
>
> *there are a limited number of people involved*
>
> *it is known what needs to be done,*
>
> *it is known exactly what the problem is*
>
> *or it is known what the solution would be*

The alternative to bounded rationality is logically **unbounded rationality,** which is used to deal with situations referred to as *messes.*

Messes

The symptoms of messes have a:

> *longer, uncertain time scale*

> *priorities can be called into question*

> *uncertain, but greater the implications are worrying*

> *can't be disentangled from the context*

> *there are more people involved*

> *it is not known what needs the be known*

> *one is not sure what the problem is*

> *there are in fact no 'solutions'!*

Successful vs. Effective managers

Fred Luthans (1988)[37] talks about the difference between so-called *good* and *getting-ahead* managers. The getting-ahead manager is notable for:

> *building tacit alliances*

> *discretely lobbying of the powerful*

> *editing and glossing what he says*

Activity

Do you know a colleague or fellow student who behaves like one of Luthan's getting-ahead managers? What do you feel about it – is it justified and is it in the interests of the organizations? Recall a situation where you perhaps have behaved in a similar manner. Sometimes, we might confuse this with a justifiably ambitious attitude.

Time Management[38]

In order to avoid a tendency to the superficiality trap and the fire-fighting syndrome, it is useful to find techniques that will help us cope with the pressures of everyday life. This can be just as important to the student with a heavy load of academic studies as well as the manager with his 'perpetual occupation'. The feeling that the workload just does not go away can lead to frustration and ultimately to health problems. Often there are responsibilities pulling us in different directions and we might feel that we are not adequately coping with any areas of our lives.

One of the ways of alleviating this is one of the ways of coping with this. Unfortunately, we do not do find it easy to apply in practice but an analysis of the basics may help us. Firstly, we may wish to look at the ways in which we misuse time:

Three ways of misusing time:

> *By suffering from the fire-fighting syndrom*

> *One is surprised by deadlines*

You cannot find your documents

You do work which would be better done by others

One neglects routine paperwork

You do not explain things properly to others

You go to meetings without being properly prepared

By allowing yourself to be stressed

Tiredness impairs your judgment

Little things seem disproportionally important

One is over-optimistic about what can be done in a given time

The result is that one is overloaded, works longer hours and ends up being more stressed

Confusing what is urgent with what is important

This one usually even catches the well-organized manager out and is usually caused by:

Being too responsive to inputs

Having a short-term outlook

Activity

Take a look at your own approach to work. Write down a list of things under the above headings which are either true examples or show that they do not apply to yourself.

How to Manage Time

Below are some suggestions on how you can manage your time better:

Spend time to save time

Create systems or procedures to handle particular matters. You may even have to write down a list of the things you need to do. Even if you feel 'stressed' it is worth taking time out to get yourself better organized.

Decide on priorities

Be clear about what you want to achieve. You can use the above list to decide on your priorities by numbering the items of 'things to do'. You may have to decide that you are not going to be able to do certain things.

Stand back and identify key work areas. Linking the tasks that need to be done with respect to the broader vision and objectives may help to weed out less important tasks. It may help to break the tasks down into categories so that you can get a clearer picture of priorities.

Structure your time

Break time up into blocks.

Certain tasks may need periods of concentration. It is useful to plan these for the times when such circumstances are more favorable so that the work is carried out more effectively.

Schedule regular exercise and relaxation

Making sure that you set time aside for relaxation and exercise is also important. These are the moments when we are often reflective and discover solutions to insoluble problems. They are certainly not 'a waste of time'.

Take holidays

By making yourself dispensable you may create an additional effect but you need to have time away and with other people to give yourself refreshment.

Negotiate commitments

Saying "no" if necessary

It is not always easy to say no but it is much better than breaking your promise or producing slipshod work. Maybe the person wishing to load you with work has no idea of what your workload already is or what your responsibilities are. Saying 'no' may be one way of getting the message over.

Help people making demands understand your work

Maybe the person wishing to load you with work has no idea of what your workload already is or what your responsibilities are. Saying 'no' may be one way of getting the message over.

Be realistic about what you can undertake.

Regular work planning

You might find it helpful to use of personal organizers, project planning software or other tools. It will not solve all your problems but it helps give you a feeling of more control and helps you to consider priorities. It may help you be more realistic about what you can fit in. It is not a disaster if things do not work out and you have to change your plans. This has to be accepted as a part of everyday business life.

Time-saving tips

Delegation (up, sideways or down)

"Do it now!"

"Good is good enough"

Avoid temptation to waste time

'Is it good or is it bad"

The Holistic Approach

In our busy times we have tended to have lost the ability to meditate. Remembering Siddhartha's secret to success in Hermann Hesse's famous book of the same name, we can re-iterate an attitude that can be regularly practiced in moments of stress:

I can fast. *(that is, I can do without something for a while — it won't kill me!)*

I can think. *Spending time to meditate and mull over problems rather than immediately getting involved in action.*

I can wait. *This may not be the right moment for a particular activity. It may be better postponed to a more opportune time. It may be better not to do something at all if we feel under extreme pressure.*

Also, it might be important to remember that we are not alone on this planet. We are not the center of the universe and there are other issues than just what we need (or think we need) to do at this moment. Maybe there are issues of much greater importance that in fact we are neglecting. Getting things in proportion maybe one of the main issues in time management. A moment of stress may be the time to ask, 'what would you do if you knew you only had six months to live?'

Another device that holistically oriented managers can use to help cope with stress is meditation. This does not necessarily mean practicing Yoga or Zen meditation (although these would certainly do no harm) but one can take 5 minutes at the beginning of the day and maybe just a few minutes once or twice during the day to meditate on the four principles of love, unselfishness, purity and honesty or another similar model which appeals to you. This could be part of running a daily log as mentioned above. Also, we might wish to consider our own personal vision and mission as well as that of our organization and reflect on the compatibility of our actions. These tools can give us renewed inspiration and energy to help make difficult decisions and set priorities.

Roles

Mintzberg's (1973)[39] Managerial Roles

Mintzberg defines 10 managerial roles that he groups into 3 areas:

Interpersonal roles

These are the relationships between a manager and the people working with him.

> *Figurehead* – *the manager is automatically a figurehead because of his position*

> *Leader* – *he or she represents the needs of the organization. One is also reminded of Greenleaf's idea again of the leader as servant – serving the organization and its stakeholders.*

> *Liaison* – *the manager is involved in maintaining a network of relationships within and outside of the organization. As organizations start more and more to resemble Handy's shamrock organizations, this becomes an increasingly important role and skill.*

Informational Roles

> *Monitoring* – *the manager has to know what is going on and report back.*

Dissemination – passing on information of all kinds including perceived information.

Spokesperson – This is the manager as the public voice of the organization and in addressing stakeholders

Decisional Roles

This is often considered the most important role of the manager. Mintzberg sees four different classes of decision-making.

Entrepreneur – involved in change processes in the organizers and as initiator of change – usually on their own volition.

Disturbance handler – these are the things that are not planned and where the manager is required to take spontaneous action. This is one of the areas where the managers is particularly required to possess wisdom.

Resource allocator – this can be everything from money and people to time and involves planning and authorizations

Negotiator – the manager is often required to negotiate for resources and as part of the decision-making process.

Thus management is seen as an art and classifying the roles should help the manager reflect on situations and his or her responsibilities.

Role Sources

People in any organization are pulled in different directions where they are required to fulfill different roles.

Task and Role

Often the employee is pulled towards the demands of a particular task or project and may have tight deadlines to meet, even if the other routine jobs and demands stay the same.

Organization and Role

There can be expectations from the organization and those around the manager which make demands. Also, he may not always know what is expected of him. Anyone who has started a new job will know the feeling of not knowing what one is supposed to do until one 'gets to know the ropes'. Sometimes, in representing the organization's point of view, the manager may come into a conflict of loyalties situation where, in representing the views of higher management, trust and comradeship with peers and subordinates may be called into question. Then we can call this whole idea of management hierarchy into question. Gary Hammel (2011)[40] asks how necessary it is to have all these levels of people managing people and how can we continue to finance all this and put up with the slow decision-making process. Maybe the call is for everybody to become a leader and make decisions within their own area of responsibility. Hamel goes on to say that 'management is the least efficient activity in your organization'. He calculates that management accounts for 33% of the cost of an organization. Maybe that is why small and medium size enterprises tend to be so effective and innovative. He talks of what he calls the 'cost of tyranny' with the result that you 'Narrow an individual's scope of authority, and you shrink the incentive to dream, imagine, and contribute'.

Activity

Compare this with Mintzberg's 'spokesperson' role. Who do you take sides with?

Person and Role

The way you respond to the role you have to play depends very much on you yourself as a person. Some people do not like giving orders whereas others are able to encourage consensus. How you react under stress or in a crisis depends also on your personality. It will also depend on how you think about yourself. You may be aware that people resent you being authoritarian and on the other hand, if you are unable to be decisive, you may be considered to be too weak. This will depend also on the make-up of the people around you and how much you adapt to their expectations.

The Inner Child

Missildine (1987)[41] talks of the fact that a manager is involved with the 'inner child of the past' of each of those in his group or team. Each of us has a past which includes relationships with adults — parents, siblings, grandparents, teachers, etc. — and we learnt specific manners of behavior in order to cope with these relationships. These coping mechanisms are usually retained into adulthood and are triggered by certain situations — e.g. The student in the lecture! Thus, it is important for the manager to recognize this.

Activity

*Consider the way you behave under situations where you are
confronted by authority. How do you behave? What about people
around you? Give some examples where you see the hidden child
coming to the surface. Ask a friend to comment on you – if you
can hear it. What can you learn from this?*

The Emotional Underground Organization

Under the surface of the organization's day-to-day functions is
an underground organization which is rich in emotional dialog. People have psychological needs that are either met or not
met by the organization. We are all aware of those 'decisive'
managers who always seem to know what to do and to have
their feet on the ground. They often avoid meetings, seeing
them as a waste of time. People are often impressed by his
seeming efficiency – others are to blame when things don not
run smoothly. The subordinates of such a manager are likely
to display the 'hidden child' syndrome and depend on the decisive manager for their sense of direction. This becomes a
self-fulfilling prophecy, confirming the decisive manager in
his fundamental belief. In fact, the behavior of the decisive
manager may only be a cover for feelings of uncertainty.

Negative Capability

Charles Handy (2002)[42] has come up with the idea of negative
capability as a means of coping with the complexities involved in management. It is important that we accept our mistakes, avoid being a party to building a culture of blame and
be willing to accept the future whatever it brings.

Handy (1990, pp 54-56)[43], was citing Keats definition of 'negative capability' in his letters of 1817, where he stated that it is as 'when a man is capable of being in uncertainties, mysteries, and doubts'. He went on to say, "I would extend the meaning to include the capacity to live with mistakes and failures without being downhearted or dismayed. We will never know enough about any unknown to be certain of the result. We will get it wrong some of the time. Doubt and mistakes must not be allowed to disturb us because it is from them that we learn ..."

He went on to say, "Entrepreneurs, the successful ones, have on average nine failures for every success. It is only the successes that you will hear about, the failures they credit to experience. Oil companies expect to drill nine empty wells for every one that flows. Getting it wrong is part of getting it right ... Negative capability is an attitude of mind which learners need to cultivate, to help them to write off their mistakes as experience. It helps to get your first failures early on; the later ones are then less painful. Those who have a gilded youth, in which success leads on to success, are sometimes the least experimental and the most conservative as they grow older because the fear of failure looms larger ...

"We learn by our mistakes, as we always tell ourselves, not from our successes; but perhaps we do not really believe it. We should, for we change by exploration not by retracing well-known paths. We start our learning with uncertainties and doubts, with questions to be resolved.

"We grow older wondering who we will be and what we will do. For organizations as for individuals life is a book still to be written. If we cannot live with these uncertainties we will not learn and change will always be an unpleasant surprise."

It may be linked with the spiritual idea of faith in God or faith in providence.

From the above, we can only give the following advice on acceptable role behavior:

> *Don't slip out of your role*
>
> *Implicit negotiation – create successive understandings. Practice tacit role negotiation by feeling the way carefully in discussions. Accept that misunderstandings can help clarify and lead to understanding of roles.*
>
> *Reflect on your roles – sharing and testing perceptions with others can be helpful*
>
> *Recognize and acknowledge others' feelings – this provides a safe setting where emotions can be expressed – containment*
>
> *Recognize also currents of warmth, joy and excitement as well as anxiety and hostility.*

Gifford Pinchot (1985)[44], who first coined the word 'intrepreneur', came up with ten ways a manager should behave:

> *1. Come to work each day willing to be fired*
>
> *2. Circumvent any orders aimed at stopping your dream*
>
> *3. Do any job needed to make your project work, regardless of your job description*
>
> *4. Find people to help you*
>
> *5. Follow your intuition about the people you choose and work only with the best*
>
> *6. Work underground as long as you can – publicity triggers the corporate immune system.*

7. Never bet on a race unless you are running in it.

8. Remember it is easier to ask for forgiveness than permission

9. Be true to your goals but be realistic about the ways to achieve them.

10.Honor your sponsors.

Leadership and Ethics

As Rosabeth Moss Kanter (1983)[45] says, in future the role of leaders will be to inspire their employees with their vision, empowering them to make decisions for themselves. Having a strong vision and clear principles is the basis of all good leadership and particularly so in the case of a holistic strategy. This vision needs to take account of all stakeholder interests, has to be empowering, and have clear guidelines so that colleagues know what the expectations are.

This is echoed in the ideas of Lawler (1991)[46] when he talks of 'the high commitment organization', which he defines as:

1. *Leadership style rather than management*

2. *Great attention to employee selection and training*

3. *Motivating employees through vision*

4. *Empowerment*

5. *Willingness to change*

6. *Egalitarian environment*

7. *Intensity, challenge, caring, passion*

8. *Employees having a strong feeling that they are making a contribution*

9. *Frequent use of images, slogans, social events, rewards.*

A strong vision must be capable of firing stakeholders with an unquenchable enthusiasm. This is difficult if the vision is only about the bottom line or about shareholder value. This may go towards answering the question of why not-for-profit organizations like Greenpeace are so successful, not only in terms of achieving their idealistic goals but in terms of financial viability.

In the book "Leading at the Edge: Leadership Lessons from the Extraordinary Saga of Shackleton's Antarctic Expedition", Dennis Perkins (2000)[47] defines 10 leadership principles which he uses to describe why Shackleton's leadership was so effective:

1. *Never lose sight of the ultimate goal, and focus energy on short-term objectives.*

2. *Set a personal example with visible, memorable symbols and behaviors.*

3. *Instill optimism and self-confidence, but stay grounded in reality.*

4. *Take care of yourself: Maintain your stamina and let go of guilt.*

5. *Reinforce the team message constantly: "We are one – we live or die together."*

6. *Minimize status differences and insist on courtesy and mutual respect.*

7. *Master conflict – deal with anger in small doses, engage dissidents, and avoid needless power struggles.*

8. *Find something to celebrate and something to laugh about.*

9. *Be willing to take the Big Risk.*

10. *Never give up – there's always another move.*

Another aspect of good leadership—and maybe the most important—is what Dorothy Marcic (1997)[48] calls 'managing with the wisdom of love' in her book of the same name. She quotes Hawley (1993)[49] who identifies five dimensions of work:

1. *Physical: Concerned with physical life issues, such as buildings, equipment, comfort, safety, and adequate pay.*

2. *Intellectual: Includes the collective intelligence of employees plus their continuing drive for further development and learning, as well as abilities to effectively use available resources, to plan productively, and to be on the cutting edge.*

3. *Emotional: Involves the interpersonal work environment, how well people get along with each other and how effectively they can be a team. Research shows that effective teams usually need members to be concerned with the process skills of support, listening, positive feedback, and lack of defensiveness, all of which require members with mature emotional development.*

4. *Volitional: The desire or will to change for the better. We may know that some other behavior would be healthier but we may lack the will to change it. One psychiatrist wrote that the hardest thing for his patients was not to change but to decide to change. Once the will was there, change was relatively easy.*

5. *Spiritual: Concerned with moral issues, such as justice and respect, and working toward empathy. Understands each member to be a unique human being, a sacred soul with dignity.*

Activity

Think of the leaders around you or with whom you have associated in the past. What attributes do you consider made them good or bad leaders? What famous leader can you think of? What makes him or her great in your opinion?

Torbert's (2004) Ideas on Leadership

The interest in the theme of leadership has come out of research which seems to demonstrate that there is a link between leaders and the success of the organizations they lead (Rooke and Torbert, 2004)[50]. This concept is based on the notion that leaders are made and not born. How they develop being critical for organizational change.

Thus the discussion evolves into the matter of leadership development. Torbert's seven leadership attributes (see table below) classify the characteristics of managers or leaders who display each attribute. The ultimate goal is for a leader to develop to the attribute (action logic) of Alchemist yet only 1% of leaders on their survey had this profile!

Attribute	Characteristics	Strengths
Opportunist	Wins anyway possible. Self-oriented. Manipulates.	Good in emergency situations and sales opportunities.
Diplomat	Avoids overt conflict. Wants to belong; obeys group norms; rarely rocks the boat.	Good as supportive glue within an office; helps bring people together.
Expert	Rules by logic and	Good as an individ-

Attribute	Characteristics	Strengths
	expertise. Seeks rational efficiency.	ual contributor.
Achiever	Meets strategic goals. Effectively achieves goals through teams	Well suited to managerial roles.
Individualist	Interweaves competing personal and company action logics. Creates unique structures to resolve gaps between strategy and performance.	Effective in venture and consulting roles.
Strategist	Generates organization and personal transformations. Exercises the power of mutual inquiry. Vigilance and vulnerability short and long term.	Effective as a transformational leader.
Alchemist	Generates social transformations. Integrates material, spiritual and social transformation.	Good at leading society-wide transformations.

Fig. 12: Torbert's (2004) Leadership Attributes

Peter Senge and Leadership Types

In his classic book, 'The Fifth Discipline', Peter Senge (1990)[51] asks the question, 'what does it take to lead a learning organization? Stating that learning organizations require a new type of leader, he observes that the traditional type of leader can be defined as 'giving clear directions and well intentioned manipulation to get people to work together towards common goals'. He states that this concept of leadership is rooted in our Western view which is individualistic and non systemic where leaders arise as heroes in times of crisis.

In a learning organization such hero roles are out of place as the leader is responsible for organizational learning and building the organization In stating this, he identifies three basic leadership roles:

1.   Leader as designer

2.   Leader as steward

3.   Leader as teacher

Important in Senge's view is that a leader should take a firm stand for the building of a learning organization. He sees this as the first step in inspiring the vision, so that it becomes more than a model or technique, but rather the creation of something new.

Leader as designer

This is where Senge introduces his metaphor of the ocean liner. When asked what the role of the leader is, people usually come up with all sorts of ideas, such as captain, navigator, helmsman or engineer. Rarely does anybody mention the role of designer. The designer, in fact, has more influence on the performance of the ship than the others. They can only fulfill their roles if he has done his job properly. At this point, he quotes the saying of Lao-tzu:

> The bad leader is he who the people despise.

The good leader is he who the people praise.

The great leader is he who the people say, 'We did it our-
selves'.

The first task of the designer is to design the purpose, vision
and core values of the organization. This is necessary in order
to construct a shared vision, which leads to long-term thinking, essential for learning. This is entails what Senge calls 'personal mastery' on the part of the leader and demonstrates a
commitment to the truth. The task of the leader is carried out
through mentoring, coaching and helping people to learn.

Leader as Steward

This has to do with the skill of telling what he calls, 'the overarching story', relating the big picture to people and explaining to others the reason why they do things. They should be
showing how the organization needs to evolve and how this
fits in with something bigger. These qualities of leadership include a 'we' that 'goes beyond the organization itself to hu-
mankind more broadly'. In other words, as we have stated
elsewhere, Senge also sees the learning organization as one
that is a vehicle for bringing change and learning into society
as a whole.

In this context, the leader becomes the steward of the vision.
In this interactive process, the leader learns also to progress
from the possession of their own personal vision to becoming
part of a vision much bigger than themselves.

Senge, a master in drawing on a wide range of sources to support his arguments quotes George Bernard Shaw[52], which necessity calls for repetition here:

This is the true joy in life, the being used for a purpose recognized by yourself as a mighty one.... the being a force in nature instead of a feverish, selfish little clod of ailments and grievances complaining that the world will not devote itself to making you happy.

Leader as Teacher

The role of a leader as teacher is seen in helping people to understand reality. Senge sees four different levels of reality:

1. Events

2. Patterns of behavior

3. Systemic structures

4. Purpose story

Leaders in learning organizations should focus particularly on purpose and systemic structures. He points out that this role is not about teaching people how to realize a vision but getting everybody in the organization involved in learning and helping them develop their 'systemic understandings'. He sees this as the only antidote to losing the commitment to the truth.

Senge concludes this section of his book with the observation that the choices we make in the future will be decisive. Learning organizations can only be built by those who freely choose to do so and who 'put their life spirit into the task'[53].

Activity

Would you describe your organization as a 'learning organization'? How does a learning organization differ from a conven-

tional one? How do the ideas of Senge correspond to the ideas of a
holistic view of management? Can you find any evidence of in-
tentional learning in your organization?

At this point, it may be of interest to look inside and outside
the boundaries of management and to allow our mindsets to
be shaken by varying views on leadership.

Martin Buber — Types of Leadership

In the fundamental thinking of the German philosopher Martin Buber (1928)[54] amongst his discussions of bible leaders, he
comes to the conclusion that true leaders are chosen and that
the term is reserved for those who actually begin something
new. In the business context, the word leader for Buber seems
similar to the meaning of the word 'entrepreneur'.

He identifies five basic types of leader. The leadership style is
contingent and relevant for the particular time in history. We
may be able to draw parallels between this idea and management leadership styles as they have developed over the last
century or so. Whereas Taylorism, Scientific Management and
the ideas of Henri Fayol may have been relevant in their era of
industrial development, the knowledge society of today may
require a different style of leadership. At the same time, we
can apply this concept to the different types of leadership that
may be required during the course of the development of an
organization

Buber's 5 types of leader are:

The Patriarch (e.g. Abraham)

At the beginning there are no people to lead. Leaders have to be 'fathers' and have to 'beget a people'.

This is often the role a leader plays in the early development of a firm. Often such leaders find it difficult to break away from this style of leadership and it may be necessary for the next generation to provide a new kind of leader who will create a new culture. This issue is very much connected with the problems associated with a generation change in an organization. Understanding the role of leadership and recognizing leadership style can be an important tool in facilitating organizational change.

The Leader in the Original Sense (e.g. Moses)

This is the leader who literally leads the way for a people in bondage who need to be led to freedom. This type of leader does not function as a king but may the precursor to a kingdom. Haller (1990)[55] states that the Commandments and the Law of Moses provided the basis for an economic and social order based on God's directive but that this can only be understood in the context of the freedom from the bondage of Egypt and later Babylon. And this fact is contained in the preamble to the Ten Commandments. This is both an inner and external freedom. As Haller, using non-religious language, expresses it: 'actually right from the beginning a society free from domination'.[56]

It may we worth reflecting at this juncture that freedom comes with duty, as Chappell (1993)[57] states, most people tend to think of absolute freedom as freedom from constraints but, he says: "I've learned that the most rewarding kind of freedom is *responsibility* – the duty to help others and the community" (Chappell, 1993, p. 161).

Thus this type of leadership role may be the one played by a charismatic personality who leads people out of an existing stifling company environment to create a new company with those employees (as Wilhelm Haller cited above, actually did).

The Judge (e.g. Samuel)

The idea of the Hebrew Judge is leadership based on voluntarism. The aim is to 'make right'. This can often be disappointing because 'men (and women) are what they are'. This type of leadership tends to be temporary and is preparatory for the king leader.

This could be the type of leader who has gained his position due to charismatic power. He will often be disappointed when employees act on their own behalf from selfish motives rather than for the good of the company as a whole. It may be that the employees see him as a weak leader and will also then call for a strong leader when they feel threatened. Such leaders have a strong sense of fairness and justice and are often respected for this.

In the Hebrew tradition, according to Haller (1990)[58], the demand made upon Samuel to appoint a king is seen as the first and greatest betrayal of the task set for the people. This had come about by the desire of the people to be 'like all other peoples'. A firm under this kind of leadership might have a strong call from employees to become a 'real firm'.

The King — the Founder of a Dynasty (e.g. David)

A king has to be anointed but also has to live up to the task. The failure of kings to do this gave birth to the idea of Messianism — the king who lives up to his anointing.

This is the tough leader who demands that things are done his way. Employees will except his decisions out of necessity and may fear to question them or to make their own suggestions, either out of fear or respect. Unfortunately, most of these leaders are privately criticized because they do not always have the interests of the employees at heart and may be tempted to exploiting the organization for their own interests. The stakeholders are also looking for the messianic kind of leader who only has their interests at heart.

Adair (2002)[59] quotes an example of this type of leader in an exemplary form in the person of King Alfred of England. According to Adair, this king changed the culture of England, combining strong leadership with spirituality and learning and was himself an intellectual, modeling himself on King David. In English legend, King Arthur is another messianic figure; who with his round table, where every member had the same status, there is no 'head of the table'. This seems to combine the idea of King with the ideal type of leader we discuss next.

The Prophet (e.g. Isaiah)

This leadership idea is contrary to history because he is appointed (from Above) to oppose the king and even the people. The idea of the 'suffering' servant because often rejected by king and people starts to develop, an idea we will further develop later. Being a prophet means being powerless and his function is to remind those in power of their responsibility.

This is also a special leadership role to be found in business and may be the most important. This kind of leader accepts the current status quo but is critical and openly opposes the hypocrisy and self-interest of the king as well as the dishonest and unfair ways of the stakeholders. If he is too loud in his protest, he is likely to suffer for it. He himself must be impeccable and have no interest in personal power. In a modern management setting, one could conceive a position in the organization derived for just this purpose with the necessary immunity. On the other hand, I am often asked by students, 'I haven't got any say in our organization—I have no power to change things'. Yet everybody can become a prophet leader and lead from the 'shadows'. This requires a deep understanding of power.

Activity

How helpful do you find the application of Buber's thinking on leadership?

How would you categorize the leaders in your company? What is your own leadership style in terms of Buber's styles?

The Leadership Concept is Concerned with Dialog: I —Thou

According to Buber, who favors the prophet-leader style, the true leader allows himself to be led by a higher force and must accept the position offered to him taking upon himself the responsibility entrusted to him—'making it real with the free will of his own being, in the autonomy of his person'.

Process of Leadership

The leader is taken out of the community by cutting himself off from natural ties. The real work is done in the shadows. This can be referred to as a 'secret' or 'hidden' leadership and the results often not being ascribed to the leader and often becoming apparent much later. The true leader is thus willing to work without reward, glory or recognition from his or her peers.

Comparison of the Ideas of Plato with Those of Isaiah

Buber goes on to compare these ideas with the thinking of Plato who has two ways of identifying leaders:

> *The philosopher himself comes to power or,*

> *The philosopher has to educate those in power to conduct their lives as philosophers.*

Plato's idea	Isaiah's idea
Spirit is the possession of man. Power is man's possession. (Idea repudiated by Kant: 'the wielding of power inevitably destroys the free judgment of reason').	Spirit invades and seizes a man—power is not his possession. Power is given to man to enable him to discharge his duties as God's lieutenant. If he abuses this power it destroys him.
Believes his soul to be perfect	Recognizes himself as essentially unclean
Wishes to establish an institution (the Republic)	Isaiah only wishes to transmit a message
Utopian	Contingent

Fig. 13: Comparison of Plato's to Isaiah's Thinking

A Sixth Kind of Leadership—the Priest

However, the theocratic idea of Isaiah is the direct rule of God in men's hearts, not the rule of priests, which Buber states has been described as 'the most unfree form of society' (ibid, p.157) because it abuses the highest known to man for the sake of power.

This form of leadership is often found in religious sects where the members are relieved of their own will to make decisions. Thus the members basically 'sell their soul' to the leader who claims to be able to interpret the will of God for the people. It has no justifiable use in business but will no doubt be found there all too often. None but the powerless can speak the king's will.

The future society is seen as a true people where all the people in the community are genuinely governed by God through (ibid.):

> *honesty without compulsion*
>
> *kindness without hypocrisy*
>
> *brotherliness of those passionately devoted to their divine leader.*

Where there is social inequality and distinctions between the free and the unfree, splits the community and creates chasms between its members. He goes on to say, 'when Isaiah speaks of justice, he is not talking about institutions but about you and me, because without you and me the most glorious institution becomes a lie (ibid).

For Buber, as for others such as Schonfield, the ultimate leadership is found in the messianic concept—the idea of an anointed king who also has the attributes of the prophet as well as fulfilling the other concepts of leadership in an ideal way and whose humility is his source of power as servant of his people. In Schonfield's utopian 'Mondcivitan Republic (Commonwealth of World Citizens)' a people is created, not linked to a specific race, who live out the ideals as a 'guinea pig' of their own experiment as an arbitrational model. We find this concept in modern management theory in such ideas as Robert K. Greenleaf's servant leadership ideas. This can be developed into the idea of 'guinea pig management' where organizations are created with the express purpose of experimenting with the implementation of new management ideas.

The aim of leadership in our organizations should be to create such models that can be prototypes for society at large. This may be the true purpose of business per se. The true leader in business may have to embody the different types of leadership from time to time as necessary and the true quality of leadership may be in just this ability to recognize the situations and adapt to them. This compares well with Fiedler's (1967)[60] contingency theory of management that claims that leadership effectiveness depends on the situation at hand (contingency) because of two factors—'leadership style' and 'situational favorableness'.

An inherent part of Buber's thinking is his 'I-Thou' theory of dialog that has also influenced gestalt theory. The importance of dialog between oneself and the 'higher authority' and the dialog that takes place between human beings is an essential part of effective leadership and stands in contrast to the individualism of our society.

Activity

Can we afford to take the risk of using our company as a laboratory? What are the dangers of doing this and what are the opportunities? Is the idea contrary to the profit drive of an organization?

Stephen Covey — Principle Centered Leadership

The management writer, Stephen R. Covey (1991)[61] talks of 'principle centered leadership' and argues that there are natural laws which cannot be ignored and upon which we can base principles which give us a clear sense of direction in decision making. Principles, unlike laws do not change with fashion but are basic concepts upon which we can agree. While not in conflict with religion, they can be embraced by those of any religious or non-religious persuasion. Covey believes that principles are central to our thinking and living. According to Covey, centering on any one of these areas disorients and confuses us, whereas centering on principles gives us a sense of direction and balance. In the same way, this can be related to organizational life. In our businesses we tend to focus on individual aspects or groups of persons or on particular problems. Sometimes we get so worked up by our competitors or get so angry with suppliers that we lose our sense of perspective. Orienting our businesses on principles, once again, can help everybody in the organization to focus on the real issues and to help us avoid fire-fighting tactics.

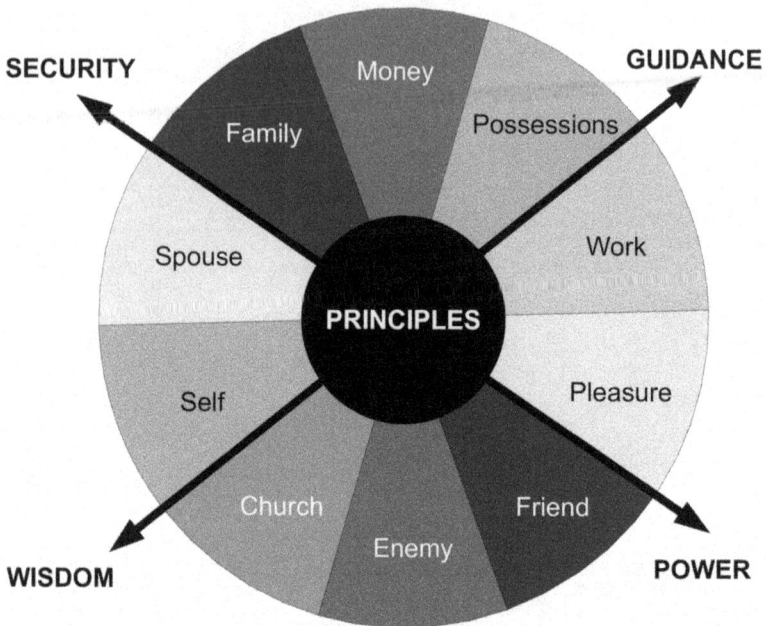

Fig. 14: Alternate Life Centers (Covey, 1991)

Activity

Due to space, it is only possible to briefly mention Covey's important ideas. Take a few moments and see what you can find in Internet. How could principled living affect not only our companies but also society as a whole?

Mahatma Gandhi — Natural Law

You might find it interesting after the above discussion to consider Gandhi's (2001)[62] ideas on types of person and ask yourself how you fit into these descriptions and the way people you know fit to them. What do you think would be the ideal state for a leader or manager and how would you try to achieve it?

1. *Tamasic*   one who works in a mechanical fashion

2. *Rajasic*   one who rides too many horses always restless, doing something or other

3. *Sattvic*   the one who works with peace in his mind

It is possible to identify other principles by which one can live. In essence, however, all ideas seem to revert to the basis of natural law. Mahatma Gandhi expressed principles in terms of what negative modes of behavior can be counteracted by antidotes based on natural law principles in his 'seven deadly sins'[63]:

Wealth without work	Getting something for nothing — speculation, gambling, etc. Deming (1982, p. 99) points out that the 'pursuit of the quarterly dividend and short-term profit defeat constancy of purpose'[64].
Pleasure without conscience	Just doing what you want regardless of the cost to others
Knowledge without character	Business and all education should not ignore character building. Building knowledge in the organization today is one of the most important tasks of management but this is useless unless combined with strong personal and corporate principles
Business without ethics	'The end justifies the means'. The desire for profitability — or even survival — can lead to a blurring of ethical boundaries unless we relate to strong principles
Science without humanity	The last century was often witness to the results of this. In our technological developments we need to bear in mind who we are actually serving.
Religion without sacrifice	Humility is a hallmark of great leaders. It often means backing down and letting others make mistakes. Better no religion than one which is a pure palliative.
Politics without principle	This may be the reason we make little headway in solving the most urgent problems in society.

Fig. 15: The Seven Deadly Sins

His grandson, Arun Gandhi told me that he would add an eighth deadly sin: *freedom without responsibility*. They go hand in hand and things go badly wrong when freedom is detached from being responsible.

Judgment

A very important point, which should be made at this juncture, is that the fundamental difference between principles and laws is that laws are intended for the judgment of others, whereas principles are the way we measure our own personal behavior. Using principles to point the finger at others would be missing the point of principle-guided leadership. The judgment of others has to be consequentially avoided.

History

There have been many attempts to define these 'natural laws' or principles. Typical examples are the 'Ten Commandments' (The Mosaic Law), which are aimed at providing a set of guiding principles for society rather than laws in the sense of modern justice. By the time of Jesus the Nazarene, Judaism had developed concepts, which reduced these 'laws' down to the basic principles contained in the 'Sermon on the Mount'. Other religions also developed similar guidelines and principles because it became evident that it was necessary for people to agree on a common set of ideals if society was going to function amicably.

Activity

Together with members of your family or colleagues, try to agree on a set of principles which could be a sort of code of conduct for behavior in the group.

Cremer, Wells and Schonfield — World Peace and Justice

At the end of the 19th century a British member of parliament, Sir William Randal Cremer, was working with other parliamentarians on means to encourage world peace and justice. He developed ideas of arbitration that laid the foundations of modern diplomacy. He also saw the need for an international court of justice with recognition of and above the nation states and which was finally realized in the ICJ in The Hague. He received the Nobel Peace Prize in recognition of his work in 1903. His organization (The International Arbitration League) continued with its mission and was instrumental in the foundation of the United Nations.

Amongst his disciples was a famous historian, Hugh J. Schonfield, a friend of H.G. Wells, who, together with other idealists took over the work of Cremer's organization after the Second World War and attempted to create a mediating servant nation. This nation defined a set of universal principles for individual, group, organizational and societal life that formed the basis of the principles of the International Leadership and Business Society of which I am currently chairman. Unfortunately, Schonfield's servant nation, after an initial success and much recognition, faded into obscurity by the 1980's. Its failure is probably due to the then still prevalent concept of top-down thinking and the changes in the international landscape which made such an ambitious initiative difficult to realize. Nevertheless, it had a strong formative influence on such people as John Lennon[65], Wilhelm Haller (human resource management pioneer), Joseph Abileah (Israel/Palestinian arbitrator) and Sir Richard St. Barbe Baker (Men of the Trees—which has been responsible for the planting of least 26 trillion trees internationally, by some estimates). These people, amongst others, were all adherents of the Schonfieldian idea.

The idea of servant leadership was developed by Robert Greenleaf (1904-1990) and his movement. It sees servant leadership in business and organizations as the kernel for change and has influenced great management thinkers such as Peter Senge (Learning Organization) and continues to be active to this day. Senge (1990) sees both the need for compassion and a commitment to the whole in his discipline of 'personal mastery'.

Jonathan Sacks in a circular email of 15th January 2014 stated, in discussing the meaning of the word or name 'Cohen'::

> *Faced with this problem, the commentators offer two solutions. The word cohanim, "priests," may mean "princes" or "leaders" (Rashi, Rashbam). Or it may mean "servants" (Ibn Ezra, Ramban). But this is precisely the point. The Israelites were called on to be a nation of servant-leaders. They were the people called on, by virtue of the covenant, to accept responsibility not only for themselves and their families, but for the moral-spiritual state of the nation as a whole. This is the principle that later became known as the idea that kol Yisrael arevin zeh ba-zeh, "All Israelites are responsible for one another." Jews were the people who did not leave leadership to a single individual, however holy or exalted, or to an elite. They were the people every one of whom was expected to be both a prince and a servant, that is to say, every one of whom was*

called on to be a leader. *Never was leadership more profoundly democratized.*

The principles formulated by Schonfield are as follows:

Principle 1: No-one is an Enemy

To acknowledge no-one as an enemy no matter what he or she should do; for to admit the existence of an enemy is to create a barrier, darkening understanding, breeding hatred, and giving encouragement and license to cruelty and inhumanity.

At first glance this statement appears radical and may shock our fundamental notions of the world. Naturally, people generally have a tendency to sort 'wolves from sheep' and to put people into categories. Our competitors may be seen as our 'enemies', which it is our duty as good businessmen and women to fight and, if possible, destroy. However, we must ask ourselves if this paradigm is particularly helpful. Without competitors, we would, for example, be unlikely to develop and effectively market products that are of real benefit to customers. Also, competitors help us develop the market and we may be better off sharing a big market with others than having to make the whole effort of educating people of the advantages of having such a product as we monopolize. The difficulties of being first to market demonstrate the problems attached to this. There could be times, in fact when we even can find it advantageous to actually cooperate with our competitors (co-opetition) — e.g. when building new foreign markets or sharing development costs on new products.

At the same time, this principle challenges our thinking on war scenarios where the creation of a *Feindbild* is part of the psychology used to gain mass acceptance of the restraints and demands made upon citizens in such a situation. But we all know the consequences of this mode of thinking — it ends up just as the principle states, in the 'giving encouragement and license to cruelty and inhumanity'. Unfortunately, it would seem that even religions and ideologies need a *Feindbild* for their success, which led John Lennon (1971)[66] to include the idea of a world without organized religion in his prophetic idea of a brotherhood of man.

Also we are drawn once again to ask ourselves the fundamental question, which we will be addressing many times, of what is the purpose of business? Whatever view we have of the need or purpose of businesses to make a 'profit' (something which begs definition), it seems impossible by any stretch of the imagination that it would in any way be beneficial to take up the alternative credo of 'some are enemies' or even 'all are enemies'. Often, however, it is considered that the creation of a picture of a competitor as an enemy will act as a driver and motivator. Unfortunately, this creates a lot of negative energy that may hinder genuine creativity in the organization. If the purpose of business, on the other hand, is the creation of 'competitive advantage' or 'the creation of value' as promulgated by many modern management scientists, then our attention is not focused on a particular enemy but only the general admonishment to simply do things better. To do that we need to be surrounded by competitors who are also actively trying to do this.

On the personal level, we have to ask ourselves what effect enmity has upon our own well-being. Such negative attitudes can build up a 'power of negative thinking', which destroys our own capability to think logically and objectively.

Principle 2: No-one is a Foreigner

To recognize no one as a foreigner, or of a lower dignity, since all belong to the same human race determining to treat all, whether fellows or not, in a way which is founded on reverence for the human personality.

In the meantime, national laws have caught up with this principle to some extent in the form of anti-discrimination laws, But the matter goes much deeper. As individuals, we find it very difficult to treat those from different cultures really impartially. The only way to move in this direction may be by seeing the advantages of cultural diversity and what this can add to the innovation of an organization and society. Certainly, those we treat as foreigners would perhaps treat us as such if were in their country. The point is that we are all in fact foreigners when we are abroad!

As racialism has a destructive history in society, it is not conducive to our personal wellbeing or to that of our businesses. In this sense, businesses have a clear responsibility to reducing animosity between races. The matter goes further however. As this principle states, it is about reverence for the human personality. We can only build this respect and reverence by actively trying to learn about and understand other cultures. That is why cultural studies should be an integral part of management and individual education. And 'foreigner' is not just restricted to people from other countries but as we have disaggregated cultures, e.g. social class differences, misunderstanding can lead to a destructive process.

Principle 3: Service to All

Ever promoting and actively assisting all measures which are for the welfare and equitable unification of mankind, and at all times responding to the extent of ones ability to any call for aid in an emergency, catastrophe or apparent need.

Let the greatest among you become as the youngest, and the leader as one who serves[67]

At this juncture, we come to what is probably one of the key principles of leadership. Service is one of the most important attributes of a mature manager. Also, an organization which orients its thinking around service is most likely to be successful in as much as service includes:

> *Service to customers — organizations that put customers first and are truly marketing-oriented are likely to be successful.*

> *Service to employees — one of the purposes of businesses is to serve the interests of employees within the economic restraints imposed upon us. This links again to the above two principles. This includes empowering and trusting our colleagues with the right and expectation to make decisions and carry responsibility — another part of the reverence for the individual as mentioned above.*

> *Service to suppliers — we depend on our suppliers and we should treat them rather like customers (supplier marketing), trying to inspire them with our vision and treating them as partners rather than with an attitude of power. Finally, we may be dependent on their services to us. An attitude of cooperation is more likely to help us in time of need than arrogance.*

> *Service to shareholders and owners — persons investing money in the organization have expectations too. It may be somewhat difficult to motivate employees and customers with 'maximum return on investment' but shareholders may also have other expectations. They may be investing their funds because they want the organization to reach spe-*

cific goals and because they can identify with the mission of the organization. It is necessary for the people in the organization to respect and understand these issues. As traditional banking withdraws its support for business, organizations will be forced to look at alternatives. It may be possible to attract capital from sources hitherto not involved in the financing process as exemplified by the Schumacher organization's SHARE scheme[68].

Robert K. Greenleaf described servant leadership as follows[69]:

The servant-leader is servant first... It begins with the natural feeling that one wants to serve, to serve first. Then conscious choice brings one to aspire to lead. He or she is sharply different from the person who is leader first, perhaps because of the need to assuage an unusual power drive or to acquire material possessions. For such it will be a later choice to serve — after leadership is established. The leader-first and the servant-first are two extreme types. Between them there are shadings and blends that are part of the infinite variety of human nature.

"The difference manifest itself in the care taken by the servant-first to make sure that other people's highest priority needs are being served. The best test, and difficult to administer, is: do those served grow as persons; do they, while being served, become healthier, wiser, freer, more autonomous, more likely themselves to become servants? And, what is the effect on the least privileged in society; will they benefit, or, at least, will they not be further deprived?

This principle also calls for a social responsibility in times of need or catastrophes. Undoubtedly it includes our attitude to the environment and the issues of social responsibility. At a personal level, we can ask ourselves about such things as our role and attitudes in the family and amongst friends.

It should be pointed out that this is not to be seen as some kind of 'don't kick the cat' altruism but requires courage and bravery. Be aware that taking this stance may be seen as a sign of weakness by others and that they may try to exploit it to their own advantage. There is a big difference between actively being a servant leader and being a sucker!

Principles of Servant-Leadership

Butler University Minneapolis[70] states, "After carefully considering Greenleaf's original writings, Larry Spears, CEO of the Greenleaf Center has identified a set of 10 characteristics that he views as being critical to the development of servant-leaders. These 10 are by no means exhaustive. However, they serve to communicate the power and promise that this concept offers:

Listening	Empathy	Healing	Awareness	Persuasion
Conceptu-alization	Foresight	Steward-ship	Commit-ment	Community

Fig. 16: Principles of Servant Leadership

1. Listening

Traditionally, leaders have been valued for their communication and decision making skills. Servant-leaders must reinforce these important skills by making a deep commitment to listening intently to others. Servant-leaders seek to identify and clarify the will of a group. They seek to listen receptively to what is being and said (and not said). Listening also encompasses getting in touch with one's inner voice, and seeking to understand what one's body, spirit, and mind are communicating.

2. Empathy

Servant-leaders strive to understand and empathize with others. People need to be accepted and recognized for their special and unique spirit. One must assume the good intentions of coworkers and not reject them as people, even when forced to reject their behavior or performance.

3. Healing

Learning to heal is a powerful force for transformation and integration. One of the great strengths of servant-leadership is the potential for healing one's self and others. In "The Servant as Leader", Greenleaf writes, "There is something subtle communicated to one who is being served and led if, implicit in the compact between the servant-leader and led is the understanding that the search for wholeness is something that they have."

4. Awareness

General awareness, and especially self-awareness, strengthens the servant-leader. Making a commitment to foster awareness can be scary--one never knows that one may discover! As Greenleaf observed, "Awareness is not a giver of solace — it's just the opposite. It disturbed. They are not seekers of solace. They have their own inner security."

5. Persuasion

Servant-leaders rely on persuasion, rather than positional authority in making decisions. Servant-leaders seek to convince others, rather than coerce compliance. This particular element offers one of the clearest distinctions between the traditional authoritarian model and that of servant-leadership. The servant-leader is effective at building consensus within groups.

6. Conceptualization

Servant-leaders seek to nurture their abilities to "dream great dreams." The ability to look at a problem (or an organization) from a conceptualizing perspective means that one must think beyond day-to-day realities. Servant-leaders must seek a delicate balance between conceptualization and day-to-day focus.

7. Foresight

Foresight is a characteristic that enables servant-leaders to understand lessons from the past, the realities of the present, and the likely consequence of a decision in the future. It is deeply rooted in the intuitive mind.

8. Stewardship

Robert Greenleaf's view of all institutions was one in which CEO's, staff, directors, and trustees all play significance roles in holding their institutions in trust for the great good of society.

9. Commitment to the Growth of People

Servant-leaders believe that people have an intrinsic value beyond their tangible contributions as workers. As such, Servant-leaders are deeply committed to a personal, professional, and spiritual growth of each and every individual within the organization.

10. Building Community

Servant-leaders are aware that the shift from local communities to large institutions as the primary shaper of human lives has changed our perceptions and caused a send of loss. Servant-leaders seek to identify a means for building community among those who work within a given institution."

The idea of servant leadership is not only found in the example of Jesus of Nazareth. It can also be found in eastern religions such as the Lao Tzu[71]:

'How did the great rivers and seas get their kingship over the hundred lesser streams?

Through the merit of being lower than they; that was how they got their kingship.

Therefore the sage, in order to be above the people, must speak as though he were lower than they, in order to guide them he must put himself behind them.

Thus when he is above the people he has no burden, when he is ahead they feel no hurt.

Thus everything under heaven is glad to be directed by him and does not find his guidance irksome.

The sage does not enter into competition and thus no one competes with him.'

And from Africa in the words of Nelson Mandela:

'*I intend to be a servant not a leader, as one above others. I pledge to use all my strength and ability to live up to the world's expectation of me.*[72]'

Important attributes of the servant leader are humility and listening.

Activity

What observations can you make about the leaders you know. How do you think you would live up to these ideals?

What steps can a leader take in order to build community? Give a few examples.

How does the idea of 'Growth of People' tie in with ideas on employee motivation and other leadership ideas in this section? What other similar ideas can you discover or know about?

Principle 4: Complete Impartiality

Under no circumstances to engage in aggression, oppression or willful misrepresentation to avoid all such behavior To hold oneself free of all alliances, agreements and contractual obligations, whether open or secret, which can have the effect of favoring any group, party, section or state, or any interests whatever, to the hurt or detriment of others.

Impartiality is difficult enough; complete impartiality is a very high demand on the individual. This principle gives us a clue, however, how perhaps we can make steps towards achieving this:

Aggression:

One way of staying impartial is not to get involved in aggressive behavior in the first place. Once we have been identified as being aggressively in favor of something, it will be hard to convince others that we are truly impartial. But companies and societies can behave aggressively also. Sometimes, in fact aggressive behavior is praised in the organization—'aggressive salesman'. We can ask ourselves how good long-term relationships with customers are when they are founded on aggressive sales.

Oppression:

We need to take a hard look at the way we produce goods. Cheap labor in low wage countries can usually only be made possible by oppressive regimes or situations. Trying to extract work from human beings by oppression is the very opposite of empowerment and democracy. On the one hand, we may be proclaiming self-determination and empowerment in our organizations at home for our privileged affluent only made available at the cost of work obtained by oppression abroad.

In the family there can be no place for oppression. Unfortunately, this still happens. Husbands oppress wives, parents oppress children, teachers oppress pupils, etc. Sometimes it may be in the small things that we have been accustomed to take for granted.

Again, how can we talk of impartiality under this climate?

Willful misrepresentation:

This is certainly not uncommon. If we intentionally 'bear false witness' we are demonstrating partiality. Even in our dealings with facts, we may misrepresent them in order to underpin our argument. We are then not behaving objectively and certainly not in the best interests of our organizations. It is not always easy to behave truthfully, in our dealings with banks, customers, etc., but it is certainly the best long-term policy.

Don't make agreements at the cost of others:

This would certainly include price cartels. It may call into question the whole idea of making exclusive agreements, but this would be a matter of interpretation. Remember, that these are principles and not laws. The point here is that if we make such agreements we are not displaying true impartiality.

Principle 5: And Work for Peace

Studying to be impartial and humane in all relationships and judgments and laboring in the cause of mediation and reconciliation.

This is very similar to the above principle but rather stresses the positive aspects. Rather than desisting from partiality, here we are actively called to work for peace. We may ask ourselves how we can get involved in the processes of mediation and become known as an organization for our impartiality and humanity. In our businesses we should be striving to reconcile strife and ensuring that we do not encourage it. For example, if someone is talking about someone else in their absence and making negative comments, we do not have to agree but should find gentle ways of steering opinion towards third parties' positive attributes. We should also encourage open criticism face to face rather than backbiting. Again, this is an issue in our families and amongst our friends.

Principle 6: True Democracy

Working in the interests of true democracy in a cooperative spirit, based on mutual service and respect, holding all persons in honor in public and private.

This principle is a blueprint for our workplaces. True democracy is not the will of the majority at the cost of the minority.

Good managers will be vigilant for the interests of the voice-less minorities. Decision-making which is cooperative and which includes everybody's opinion, seeking consensus, is more likely to carried by all the organization. True democracy in our families may sometimes seem difficult to achieve but we also have the need for decision-making amongst unequals. In both situations it is not that it is always because one person wants to exert power over others but perhaps from a genuine belief to be acting in their best interests. This sometimes requires a lot of patience. Probably the issue of mobbing falls under this category and we need to be on the lookout that we do not find ourselves encouraging such behavior, which is at best cowardly.

Holding people in honor is a high demand and we need to critically assess our own behavior in this respect. Companies should learn to behave this way also when talking about customers or competitors. We have perhaps learnt to be nice to customers on the phone, but our attitude may change once we have hung up!

Customers should not be cheated by selling products that are known not to live up to their claims. This is part of honoring the psychological contract we have with our customers and treating them with due respect.

Principle 7: Equity and Justice

Continually seeking to cultivate and display those standards of conduct, both in public and private life, which are equitable and just.

This is a key issue. It is known from equity theory that a feeling of not being treated equitably can be a strong de-motivator. Much of the dissatisfaction amongst employees comes from such feelings. People have a strong inbuilt sense of justice but this can often be misdirected by lack of real information. Openness in the firm is a big issue, but being open and offering adequate opportunity for discussing things can help iron out some of the misunderstandings.

In our families we can attempt to be equitable and just. We will not always be able to treat people the same but we can try to be equitable.

The Gift of Equality

'He who treats as equals those who are far below him in strength really makes them a gift of the equality of human beings, of which fate had denied them...'

(Simone Weil[73])

Noetic Science — Willis Harman (1978)[74]

Willis Harman (1978) defined Noetic science in the following way:

A new science is arising; a science of the human mind much broader than psychology has been to date. We have called it 'Noetic' science, after the Greek word for intuitive knowing.

In human history, Harman sees two basic developments:

1. The rise of modern materialistic science — where objective knowledge should be empirically based and publicly verifiable rather than the prerogative of an elite priesthood.

2. The creation of a secondary knowledge level, still empirically based and publicly verifiable but this time in the area of subjective experience, including the wisdom of the great religions and gnostic groups.

Harman believed that our belief systems create our reality — not just psychologically but fundamentally. He believed that these principles can be used in business and societal decision making processes as one is both cause and creator of one's destiny. He sees industrial society at a crisis point because:

> *Uncomfortable trade-offs are required in areas such as energy, environment, employment, etc.*

> *The decline of the Judeo-Christian ethic since the industrial revolution.*

> *Nation after nation is retreating from democracy.*

Thus the crises we are experiencing are reflections of the moral and spiritual crises of the industrial society, which has to be resolved. Harman believed that we are on this earth to learn and that is fundamentally the purpose of life. We can learn by looking inward and by looking outward and if one looks inward, one will discover that one is here to learn from and serve the whole.

Activity

Which ideas discussed above would you say are related to Harman's ideas? Which ones and why do you say that?

Five Guiding principles or laws — Leo Tolstoy

Tolstoy bases his ideas on the Beatitudes (Sermon on the Mount) of Jesus of Nazareth. Although his beliefs are very much based on the individual and individual behavior, he sees this as the basis of the new society.

This, in common with other writers, he sets in contrast to the Ten Commandments or the Mosaic Law. His ideas are founded on the principle of Natural Law, sometimes referred to as Noachide Laws. His thinking can be summarized as follows:

Do not be be angry with your brother	Anger is never justifiable. Pardon without restriction. Do not be abusive or call another 'fool' (because this is an attempt to relieve ourselves of another's humanity. Reconciliation. Be at peace with everyone. True religion is the extinction of enmity amongst men.
Never abandon your life-partner	Tolstoy sees condemnation of libertarianism. This is the source of many of the world's problems. Many people today would have serious problems accepting his thinking on monogamy and divorce but it is difficult to fault the logic of his argumentation.
Take no oath	The taking of oaths should be avoided in all circumstances. He also refutes the idea of judgment, capital punishment and imprisonment.
Resist not evil	This is the most important for Tolstoy and the key to the Messianic idea. It is the departure from the eye for an eye and revenge thinking, which is the way society works. He sees it as the alternative to the societal status quo — an idea that turns everything on its head.

Do not use violence as a means of dealing with violence. It requires considerable courage but is the only way to reverse the destructive order of things. We see the practice of this concept by such persons as Gandhi, Abileah, Martin Luther King, just to name a famous few. These people created miracles of change when they reversed the prevalent order of thinking.

Love your enemies

And bless those that curse you (not just love your neighbor and hate your enemies). Humans have the same fundamental worth even when they behave in an evil fashion. 'Neighbor' in Hebrew actually means a fellow Hebrew i.e., a compatriot. In this case an 'enemy' is also a foreigner (as in German), literally 'hostile people'. Love without distinction of nationality. Takes away all the excuses for nationalism and armies and 'organized state murder', as he describes war.

Fig. 17: Tolstoy, The Five Guiding Principles

Application in business

Activity

Are Tolstoy's ideas too radical to be of application in business? Or rather, the fundamental question, which Tolstoy and others have asked, is business an area of human endeavor where morals, ethics and principles have no place?

The early industrial or Victorian era espoused an ethic which said that you should endeavor to maximize profit in your organization in order to make donations to charity, thus separating business from private ethics. What do you think about this idea?

Tolstoy argues that while the risks and costs involved in living to these laws is undoubtedly high at first glance, it may in fact be less than the price we are paying for living the other way. For example, a strict pacifist may get thrown into jail for refusing military service and be parted from his family and not be able to provide for them. On the other hand, it is accepted that a man should be a soldier where he will also be separated from his family and possibly even killed. Below, I have tried to combine Tolstoy's ideas with Lewin's Forcefield Analysis (1943)[7576].

The Dignity of Difference

This section is based on the ideas of Jonathan Sacks (2002)[77] and is intended as food for thought on some of today's ethical and globalization issues.

Globalization

In discussing globalization and its relation to politics, business and economics Sacks observes that

'The prophets of Israel were the first to think globally, to conceive of a God transcending place and national boundaries and of a humanity as a single moral community by a **covenant of mutual responsibility** (the covenant with Noah after the Flood). (p.12-13). He points out that dangers arise in social transformation when any one institution exceeds its proper bounds. (p.15-16). Historical examples are:

> *Middle Ages – Religion*
>
> *18th Century – Science*
>
> *19th/20th Centuries – Politics*
>
> *21st Century – The Market – monetary exchange is appropriate for some transactions but not all.*

His suggestion is that under conditions of maximal uncertainty we are best guided by relatively simple moral principles (p.17) – the six C's:

The Dignity of Difference

This section is based on the ideas of Jonathan Sacks (2002)[77] and is intended as food for thought on some of today's ethical and globalization issues.

Globalization

In discussing globalization and its relation to politics, business and economics Sacks observes that

'The prophets of Israel were the first to think globally, to conceive of a God transcending place and national boundaries and of a humanity as a single moral community by a **covenant of mutual responsibility** (the covenant with Noah after the Flood). (p.12-13). He points out that dangers arise in social transformation when any one institution exceeds its proper bounds. (p.15-16). Historical examples are:

> *Middle Ages – Religion*
>
> *18th Century – Science*
>
> *19th/20th Centuries – Politics*
>
> *21st Century – The Market – monetary exchange is appropriate for some transactions but not all.*

His suggestion is that under conditions of maximal uncertainty we are best guided by relatively simple moral principles (p.17) – the six C's:

Control

Contribution

Creativity

Co-operation

Compassion

Conservation

These should be the prelude to a seventh principle: A new global covenant of human solidarity. There is also a need a sense of direction in society and economic systems are to be judged on their impact on human dignity. Society should make space for otherness allowing people not to feel diminished but enlarged in the dialog with people of other persuasions.

Globalization divides as much as it unites; it divides as it unites – the causes of division being identical with those which promote the uniformity of the globe (Zygmunt Bauman (1998)[78]).

He foresees two possible scenarios:

Year 2020 – Scenario 1

Global prosperity

ICT systems have doubled real income in 20 years

Birth control spreads and reduces risk of overpopulation

Genetically modified crops etc. increased food production – starvation a thing of the past.

Using Internet, etc, education to Western standards has become available even to the remotest African village

International agreements put an end to child labor and exploitation

AIDS and TB brought under control through low cost medical treatment

Genetic intervention breaks many hereditary diseases.

Genome research into aging bears fruit bringing a life expectancy of 120 years.

Humanity in the midst of a new golden age.

Year 2020 – Scenario 2

Latest terrorist attack on New York spreading nuclear waste over areas of Manhattan affecting up to 20 million people.

Coordinated attack on Subway systems on various cities using chemicals released in crowded stations – thousands of casualties.

Air travel at a standstill due to a series of hijackings.

Vicious local wars in Africa after the breakdown of government.

Revolutions in Egypt, Jordan, Algeria and Saudi Arabia bring dominance of fundamentalist regimes in the Middle East.

Global economy at the point of collapse. Unemployment at a record high.

City centers have become no-go areas due to criminality, homelessness, drugs, etc.

Freak weather conditions killing hundreds of thousands annually.

Pollution levels require the

Fig. 19: Possible Scenarios (p.24-25)

There has been a change in the appreciation of the time span for change. Once it was longer than a single human life now it is considerably shorter and continually decreasing (White-head, 1942)[79]. Global capitalism, whilst a blessing to many also creates vast inequalities and destabilizing effects (p.28):

The average North American consumes:

> *5 times more than a Mexican*
>
> *10 times more than a Chinese*
>
> *30 times more than an Indian*

1.3 billion — 22% of world population live below the poverty line

> *841 million malnourished*
>
> *880 million without access to medical care.*
>
> *One billion lack shelter*
>
> *1.3 billion no access to safe drinking water*
>
> *2.6 billion without sanitation (Held, 2000)[80]*

Among children:

> *113 million (2/3 are girls) go without schooling*
>
> *150 million are malnourished*
>
> *30,000 die daily from preventable disease (Brown, 2002)[81]*
>
> *Top fifth of the worlds population has 86% of the GDP*

Bottom fifth has 1%.

*Assets of the three richest billionaires more than the com-
bined wealth of the 600 million inhabitants of the least developed counlies. (Held & McGrew, 2000)[82].*

Globalization is not only economic (p.30) but also cultural
— 'McWorld' (Barber, 1992)[83]. There were in fact early concerns
about the effects of globalization — Schumpeter (1947): *Capitalism creates a critical frame of mind which, after having destroyed
the moral authority of so many institutions, in the end turns against
its own.*[84] The symptoms of this are obvious in the last generation with a 3–10 times increase in stress related problems.

The market-dominated market has changed the way we think.
We talk increasingly about efficiency (how to get what you
want) and therapy (how to not feel bad about what you want),
which are marketing concepts (which Sacks defines as the
stimulation and satisfaction of desire). We tend not to talk
about **what ought we to desire.** It is about autonomy and
rights ruling out the possibility for objective choice.

Markets are transactional and are about prices not values.
Government has become procedural and managerial. Of the
100 largest economies today, 51 are companies and only 49 na-
tion-states! (p.34). Companies do not necessarily have a wider
responsibility than to contribute to shareholder value. Also
there is no direct connection between the owners of wealth
and its producers. The companies do not live in the countries
where they produce, like the industrialists of old but global
executives often travel the world while staying within their
own culture of international hotels, food and people.

Sacks concludes that markets have subverted institutions like
the family, community and the bonds which link members to
a common fate.

Exorcising Plato's ghost

Politicians at international forums may reiterate a thousand times that the basis of the new world order must be universal respect for human rights, but it will mean nothing as long as the imperative does not derive from respect for the miracle of Being.... It must be rooted in self-transcendence: transcendence as a hand reaching out to those close to us, to foreigners, to the human community, to all living creatures, to nature, to the universe: transcendence as a deeply and joyously experienced need to be in harmony even with what we ourselves are not, with what we do not understand, with what seems distant from us in time and space, but with which we are mysteriously linked because, together with us, all this consti-tutes a single world; transcendence as the only real alternative to ex-tinction. (Vaclav Havel (1998), *The Art of the Impossible*)[85].

Sacks argues that in the Hebrew Bible vs. Plato's ideas, univer-salism is the first rather than the last step in the growth of moral imagination. Babel is seen as a kind of totalitarianism —'the attempt to impose an artificial unity on divinely created diversity' (p.52). God, the creator of humanity, having made a covenant with all humanity, then turns to one people and commands them to be different.

Philosophical Ethics	Biblical Ethics
Based on Plato and focuses on what we have in common — things we share in virtue of our universality — belong to Man not to men	Dual nature of moral situation — membership of the universal human family and the Noachide covenant
Rationality (Kant)	We learn to love humanity by loving specific human beings.
Emotion (Hume)	
Desire for pleasure / aversion to pain (Bentham)	Sanctity of life
Duty	Dignity of the human person
Obligation	The right to be free — no man's slave or the object of someone else's violence
Sympathy	
Solidarity	At the same time we are members of specific context-bound moralities — loyalties to our community that go beyond mere justice.

Fig. Philosophical ethics vs. Biblical Ethic (p. 56)

Judaism has historically been a living alternative to empires, because imperialism and its latter day successors, totalitarianism and fundamentalism are attempts to impose a single regime on a plural world. To reduce men to Man, cultures to a single culture, to eliminate diversity in the name of a single sociopolitical order (p.60).

Five universalistic cultures can be observed in the history of the West:

1. The Alexandrian Empire

2. Ancient Rome

3. Medieval Christianity

4. Islam

5. The Enlightenment

All of these did not acknowledge the dignity of difference. No one civilization can cover all the spiritual, ethical and artistic expressions of mankind.

Control: The Imperative of Responsibility

There seem to be conflicting messages between the Market and life and the social sciences. Markets maximize choice. Contrary to the teaching of Spinoza, Marc, Durkheim and Freud, we have not chosen but are the result of social structure, economic forces, historical inevitability of early childhood conditioning. According to Darwin, our actions are only the result of our unconscious struggle for survival and dominance. Thus we could talk of life as a series of givens.

Markets and representative democracy in the new economic order should give the individual the ability to make choices but in the meantime it has developed into consumer cultures with artificially created and temporarily satisfied desires.

As Oscar Wilde stated, 'A cynic is one who knows the price of everything but the value of nothing'. Values such as love, loyalty, altruism, faithfulness are not marketable, earned not bought and part of what we are — not what we own. What we buy has now transferred to services — 'paying for attention'. (p.77).

The Relationship to
Holistic Management

To the reader, some of these ideas may seem too extreme or indeed irrelevant for management. However, we are challenged by the fact that any future-looking view of strategy has to have a strong ethical basis if it is going to lead to a sustainable economy. Some things businesses will not be able to change but managers can be catalysts for change both in their own organizations and thus in society as a whole. We can no longer afford to restrict our view of strategy to the organization alone, it must include concern for each individual, the groups of individuals who work together, their organizations and the society in which they all share their existence with the other creatures of this planet. Too long has it been an ethic of business not to have an ethic. Morals, spirituality, the virtues of meekness and kindness have too long been taboos for the businessman.

Nor is the concept Gnostic; it is not a question of spirit is good, matter is evil but of holistic fulfillment.

For this reason, the term 'holistic strategic management' is employed. While in some sense eschatological, this view does not see strategy just from an historic point of view. It is not purely a natural historic progression from sin to salvation but, not being bound to time, consists of two fundamental dimensions or levels.

The Motivational Dimension

Strategy moves conceptually from the lowest point on Maslow's pyramid to the highest, going beyond to find vision and finally (we hope) enlightenment. At this point it would be dangerous to imagine that this is a purely historical process or that we are naturally progressing upwards. The process is continually moving across the dimensions in the course of daily events. Just as the individual has a need for food at the lowest level and may reach a deeper understanding of the world in another moment of inspiration, the two cannot be divorced from each other. Therefore, the processes are simultaneous and we cannot have a successful company, even in the not-for-profit sector, if there is not a solid financial basis. The company thus has physical needs, which we usually refer to as physical resources and assets. This has to be balanced with the more ethereal attributes, particularly knowledge and human resources that are referred to as intangible assets.

The Strategic Level

The word 'level' is used here rather than dimension to highlight the fact that these levels co-exist and ranges from the individual to society. Humans remain individuals when they are in a group or company environments and are always living in society, even at those times when one would wish one were not! People play a role in a group of colleagues, family and friends and have tasks to perform in organizations. This interaction of the four levels is what makes for complexity. Decision-making requires a full view of both these dimensions and at all levels together. The historical element is thus only a backdrop, which can be considered for the purposes of understanding and learning from experience, but we are not autonomously and automatically growing to ever-greater heights. The recognition of the effectiveness of management teams and that the whole is greater than the sum of the parts are integral components of the holistic view of human involvement. Man is a lone individual with basic needs on the one side while being part of the Brotherhood of Man on the other. Gandhi seemed to understand this as he fought with his own personal weaknesses, which did not prevent him from having a vision and fighting for the rights of his people.

Everyone hopes for a better future but our 'Kingdom of God' has to be very much amongst us. In the holistic strategy matrix above (fig.2), this progression is displayed rather as one from innocence (rather than ignorance) to wisdom which can be compared with the utopian idea of the historical progression from primitive man in pre-society to the perfect being in the post-society. This is, of course the stuff for dreamers and no manager wants to be accused of that. While the caveman and the angel co-exist in us simultaneously we are nevertheless exhorted by the words of John Lennon, 'I may be a dreamer but I'm not the only one' and we have to admit that great organizations have been built and the world only ever been changed by visionaries.

Our view of strategy has to reflect this. Just as Clausewitz[86] defined strategy as winning the war and tactics as winning the battle, we are required in our businesses to keep a clear view of the war we want to win while fighting our battles. Of course, as humans, we cope better with bounded rationality and it is thus important for us to concentrate on defining winnable battles on a day-to-day basis. However, our businesses and indeed ourselves and our society seem to have lost a vision of where we want to go. We have contented ourselves with the battles we find we have to fight and have long forgotten what the war is. Many managers are fighting their own private Vietnam. In extreme cases, there is the picture of the manager with a perpetual pre-occupation involved in fire-fighting exercises. No longer has he extinguished one fire than another springs up to draw his attention but he never makes any real progress towards creating an organization where the problems do not occur. He never gets to the source of the fire and he may personally burn out in the attempt.

Encouraging reflective Managerial Thinking and Challenging Mindsets

In western countries, the Christian ethic has given way to vague ideas of the social market economy as the paramount virtue. Since the fall of the Soviet system, western economies have been declining and the funding of social systems becomes less and less viable. An aging population and increasing unemployment make demands, which cannot comfortably be borne by taxation systems. It begins to look as if our social market economy is about to lose its social tag, which was only perhaps expedient as long as there was a 'guerrilla in the basement'. Left without a Samaritan moral base, weak concepts of honesty and purity of motives, 'business as usual' may be difficult to sustain. We are already seeing the fruits of this in the revelation of false balance sheets to hoodwink investors, corruption at all levels and environmental scandals as the result of falsely placed profit motives.

So what purpose does this idea serve and what is the point of our discussion?

Managerial thinking is trapped in a mindset based on taboos, which relegate any mention of morals, ethics, spirituality or the like to hippy, otherworldly nonsense. In amalgamating those Maslowic dimensions and seeing them as part of an integrative whole spreading through to the visionary and the esoteric, management is challenged to take a more realistic view of the individual's place in the organization and the organization's role in society. The aim is to break mindset and allow creativity and entrepreneurial spirit to grow and thrive. There is much talk of the 'knowledge society' in management circles and knowledge management courses are thriving in management training. But a little knowledge is a dangerous thing. What is required is the *desire* for wisdom. Wisdom differs from knowledge in that it requires a deeper understanding of the interplay at all levels. Often seen as an instinctive quality, it is the ability to make judgments, to find the 'best' solution. Knowledge may help us in this but it will not necessarily make us wise. Only wise decisions are the right and lasting decisions.

A further and practical purpose of this approach is also to provide a useful framework for strategic analysis and planning. Planning here is to be understood, not as a rigid set of tasks to be consecutively carried out but rather a means getting a broad picture and to be able to detect the effect of change in order to adjust strategies and tactics to realize the vision.

Many will be familiar with the story of King Solomon. Asked by God what he most wished to have, he chose wisdom. Wisdom made him rich and brought him respect. His 'company', became extremely powerful and successful, not because he sought riches but because he sought wisdom. An example of that wisdom is in the story of the two women who, fighting over the ownership of a child, come to Solomon for judgment.

Solomon suggests cutting the child in half and giving one half
to each woman. This gruesome suggestion would often suit
our mode of thinking today and is typical of the sort of compromises we find ourselves making. However, Solomon knew
what effect this could have. The true mother gave up her
claim. The life of her child was more important than ownership. The true entrepreneur will often display this behavior.
Often the continuing existence of his enterprise is more important than his ownership. Ricardo Semmler[87] saved the jobs that
his organization had provided by giving up his possession of
employees and processes with his 'Amoeba Principle'. Thus
Semco was able to ride the storm of many political upheavals
and economic crises.

Our attitude to the world has to reveal the same wisdom. Our
love for our organization and its stakeholders has to be
greater than our desire for ownership and control 'of the
means of production'. Our love for the world has to be greater
than our desire to become rich at the cost of others. These are
the qualities of the true entrepreneur and the effective strategist.

Activity

*We have discussed a number of various ideas, which could influ-
ence our personal approach to our organization and the groups
with which we work. What new ideas could you bring into your
organization or life, which would really make a difference to
things? Make a list and discuss this with someone whom you
trust. What was their reaction?*

Cultivate harmony within yourself, and harmony becomes real;

Cultivate harmony within your family, and harmony becomes fertile;

Cultivate harmony within your community, and harmony becomes abundant;

Cultivate harmony within your culture, and harmony becomes enduring;

Cultivate harmony within the world, and harmony becomes ubiquitous.

Live with a person to understand that person; Live with a family to understand that family; Live with a community to understand that community;

Live with a culture to understand that culture; Live with the world to understand the world.

How can I live with the world?

By accepting.

Fig. 20: Tao te Ching – Lao Tse

Part Two

The Group

Pushing control down the organization

Bearing in mind our discussions in my previous book; it would seem to be paramount to effectively push control 'down' the organization. If people are allowed to control themselves and reflectively correct their own ways of working, then there will be fewer requirements for them to be 'managed' from above. This leads to greater efficiency, more motivation and a higher level of creativity. The role of management becomes a mentoring, guiding and teaching role, where the communication of vision and values are paramount. One of the terms used for this is 'self-directed teams' or 'SDT's'. We will discuss these ideas at a later point in more detail.

Certain issues, of course, will be beyond the scope of the individuals at team level. Basic fundamental issues of policy, making resources available for teams to be able to carry out their tasks and making sure that SDT's do not work against each other and the interests of the organization are important roles. The aim in this approach, however, is to arrive at a flatter organization where decisions are made at the most relevant level.

It is with respect to this, that the behavior of each individual becomes increasingly important. It is the responsibility of management to encourage individuals through visionary leadership to take a clear ethical stance relating to the four levels of the holistic view of business, here each illustrated by a quotation from the ancient Hindu Bhagavad-gïtä to demonstrate that 'there is nothing new under the sun':

The individual

Accepting differences in culture, gender, age, race or religion and seeing these differences as a clear advantage to teamwork, the organization and the building of a creative society. Acknowledging the responsibility of each individual to play an active part in the work of the organization as part of a greater mission and a contribution to the present and future societies.

The individual has to be accountable for his actions but not in a culture of blame. Rather, the individual is in a learning process that needs to be encouraged by managers who are willing to discuss mistakes in an open and empathetic manner in order to encourage the individual to discover corrective action. However, this is in contrast to an attitude of ignoring incorrect actions that would have the effect of encouraging sloppy attitudes. Individuals need to learn to meditate on their actions and their attitudes in an optimistic approach to personal change.

One who performs his duty without attachment, surrendering the results unto the supreme God, is not affected by sinful action, as the lotus leaf is untouched by water. (Bhagavad-gïtä)

The team or group

Recognizing the team as an important social construct and as a nest of innovation for the organization. Teams need different styles of people that are complimentary and not hostile — both adaptors and innovators. Teams also have to be accountable for their actions. This can be measured not only against the corporate vision but also against societal values. The work of the team has to be in the spirit of 'fair play' and not in an attitude of competition with other teams. The team wishes to work with others to fulfill the corporate mission. Work has to be carried out with due respect to ecological and environmental considerations. For some it may be tempting for the team to be used as a substitute for meeting basic needs as in a family. This should, however not be confused and it is not possible for the management team to fulfill this function. However, teams can become personally supporting and may be helpful (sometimes, alas harmful). No doubt, encouraging stable family culture is positive for the efficient running of organizations. The Japanese companies who sometimes operate like large welfare organizations demonstrate this effectively.

By the evil deeds of the destroyers of family tradition, all kinds of community projects and family welfare activities are devastated. (Bhagavad-gïtä)

The organization

The organization has to consider the requirements of its stakeholders. These include those providing the capital for the operation of the organization (basic needs) but also society and future generations as a whole. The interests of the individuals in the organization and of the self directed teams have to be integrated by organizational management to form a whole that is serving the corporate vision and mission.

I do not see how any good can come from killing my own kinsmen in this battle. (Bhagavad-gïtä)

Society

Neither individuals, nor teams or organizations can afford to ignore their responsibility to and dependence upon society. In the interests of sustainable strategies, it is necessary to nurture attitudes that are in line with the needs of society as a whole. This is not limited to basic moral attitudes, such as honesty, avoidance of corruption and fair dealing but extends to the interests of the environment, the wise use of resources and so on. This underlines the need for pro-active attitudes to societal responsibility as organizations aim to live into future generations. No organization can afford the scandals resulting from ignoring these basic fundamentals as is witnessed by the demise of many organizations so exposed.

The bewildered spirit soul, under the influence of the three modes of nature, thinks himself to be the doer of activities that are in actuality carried out by nature. (Bhagavad-gïtä)

Activity

Can you recall any scandals involving large organizations in recent times? What has been the effect on the organization? What was the public's attitude? Do you think that we should have different standards in business to what we expect privately?

Do you think managers are prepared well for the responsibilities
of pushing control down the organization? If not, what changes
do we need to make in our education systems and what systems
can we operate in our organizations to improve the situation?

Control processes

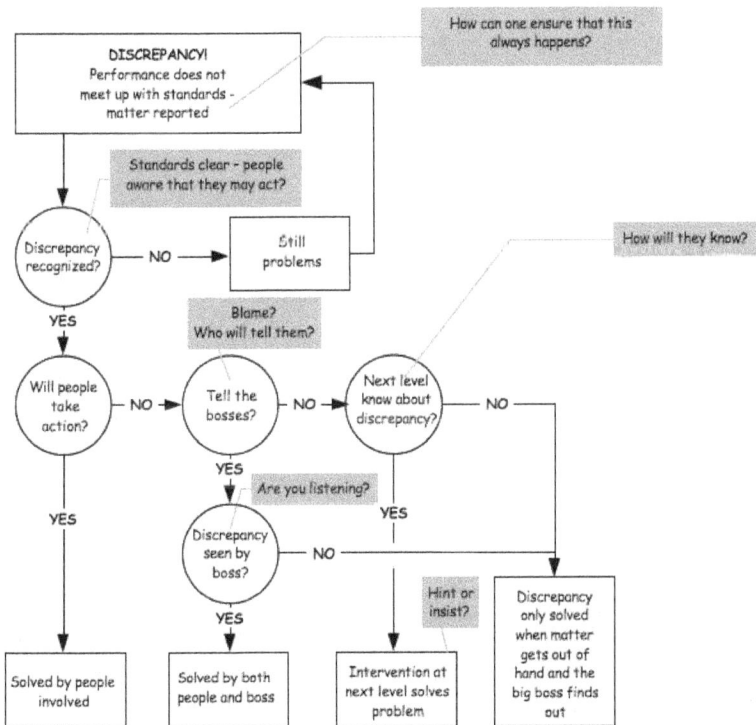

Fig. 21: Passing Control Down the Organization

Activity

How would you go about making sure that corrective action is taken at the lowest possible level? What things should be in place in the organization to make sure this happens?

Directing or
Empowerment?

So far, we have been looking at the organization mainly from the point of view of the individual. But individuals do not usually work alone. The traditional view of management sees managers as making decisions and controlling things, as we have described above. This is the hierarchical approach to management which is still prevalent. However, we could take a different view of people working in organizations and be more concerned with how effective they work.

Considering the holistic placing of the individual in the organization and society, we have to acknowledge that we have to build environments which:

Enable effective action

Are influencing rather than directing

Encourage team working

Create intra-organizational networks

Create inter-organizational networks

This concept is termed *empowerment* and was clearly formulated by Rosabeth Moss Kanter (1989)[88] in a famous article entitled 'The new managerial work'.

There are considerable changes taking place to such an extent that management and leaders are having to rethink their profession. It seems that hierarchy is slowly disappearing and power structures crumbling. Working has become much more complex and motivating people does not work according to the old adages.

This is being caused by increased competition which is making organizations have to be more flexible in their approach and adaption to markets. This is acerbated by takeovers and mergers, management buyouts as well as organizations which have not adapted going to the wall. In some countries there are extensive structures and laws for encouraging worker participation and in some cultures, having a share in decision-making is a basic expectancy.

It is also becoming more usual to cooperate with other companies and even one's competitors as the need for fast to market becomes an important success factor. Employees are increasingly required to think out of the box and come up with novel entrepreneurial ideas (we will be dealing with this in more detail in the next volume).

Market pressures are forcing organizations both in the for-profit and the not-for-profit sectors to be lean and cost conscious, leaving no room for top heavy administration structures. The border between the two sectors is becoming more and more fuzzy. Into this process the concept of 'Open Source' has appeared which is confusing the establishment and calling the whole question of extrinsic rewards into question.

This is pretty hard for some managers to stomach because it would seem as if the very basis for their existence is being eroded. Fayol's (1916)[89] roles of a manager, with such terms as 'Command', are slowly hard to align. Once, an ex-army officer would have been welcomed into that culture with open arms, having been trained in the 'commanding of men'. Today, modern organizations might see this rather as a disqualification. Thus many persons are now taking MBA and management courses to prepare them for commercial life when they retire from military service. This is effecting change even within those organizations.

So now, the question of 'how do we motivate our people to give their best?' becomes the main issue in organizations. Human capital cannot be kept in a bank deposit but has to be treated with care for what it is—a collection of real human beings, each with their own private agenda.

So in these new organizations we start to talk of *lateral* relations and horizontal structures opposed to *vertical* relations based on monitoring and directing.

Criticisms

There are critics of Moss Kanter's view points, of course. One of these is Elliott Jaques (1917-2003)[90]. For Jacques, the hierarchy is a natural form of a social organization which enables an elegant solution to the problem of the integration of the individual aspirations of people with diverse skills and knowledge. He insists on the primacy of hierarchical accountability in the formation of socially just and productive organizations. Theorists who emphasized the importance of teamwork, employee participation, democratic management models and flat hierarchies, have accused him of elitist thinking.

Seeing the need for accountability in organizations, he argues that if managers and employees are not called to account for their decisions, then management is shirking its responsibility. Also, people are employed individually and thus managerial hierarchy is essential. Firms are unlikely to be competitive if there is no clear authority and managers cannot be called to account for their actions. It should be noted, however, that 'hierarchy' is sometimes confused with 'autocratic'. Jaques thinks that fostering networks undermines the duty of managers to mediate between subordinates and that the individual can only develop under authority and leadership.

It can also be argued that empowerment tends often to be used to serve the interests of the organization rather than the employees. In practice, the actual power structures of the elite in the organization remain unchanged and empowerment is only implemented when it suits upper management's purposes. Bowen and Lawler (1992)[91] argue that the use of empowerment or traditional methods of management should be according to the specific needs of the organization rather than a black and white approach—'managers should make sure there is a good fit between their organizational needs and their approach to management' (p.31).

Activity

What do you think about the problems which can occur with both systems? Are their some situations more suitable for empowerment and others for managerial hierarchy? Some people criticize Jaques as being against democratic forms of organization. What do you think about these ideas in relation to the concepts of democracy?

Diversity — the Organization's Greatest Asset

Before we start managing people and what we call *Human Resources (HR)*, we have to remember that being an effective manager begins with ourselves. Take a few minutes and jot down any ideas that come to you by answering the following question:

Activity

What qualities do you think a good human resource manager can be expected to have? Where do you see your own weaknesses? If something goes wrong, what do you think the is right course of action:

1. *Find out who was to blame and if necessary take disciplinary action?*

2. *See what was the cause of the problem and try to luke steps to prevent it happening in the future?*

3. Call somebody in higher authority to deal with the problem?

4. A completely different solution – what?

A manager of human resources is expected to be reflective in his approach to problems. Also, he can reasonably be required to exercise impartiality and to avoid all kinds of discrimination. This may require a closer scrutiny of our own attitudes and behavior as we are required to be an example to others and have high ethical standards.

Later in this course, you will come across many aspects of the skills and knowledge required of an HR practitioner. You are invited to seek ways of practicing some of these attributes in your relationships with fellow-students and friends. There is nothing magic about being a good manager of people, you just need to be a good manager of yourself. Previously we have mentioned Charles Handy's three management precepts of love, forgiveness and curiosity.

Activity

You have, no doubt, come up with these concepts and a few others like honesty, caring, fairness and so-on. What do you think about these ideas in relation to the kind of situation mentioned above?

People as a resource

We could talk about an organization (including a not-for-profit organization) and the role of people in the meeting of its objectives thus:

Human Resources + capital equipment + other inputs = meets organization's objectives

People are an essential part of the choice managers have to make.

Activity

Make a short list of the people working in your organization.

What resources do they need to complete their tasks efficiently?

What problems are involved in talking of people as a 'resource'?

Do you see any ethical issues in referring to people as 'resources'?

Managing people is a very complex matter, as you will no doubt agree. It has been likened to the 'herding of cats' to quote the title of a book by Warren Bennis (1997)[92]. One of the key issues in dealing with this is motivation, which we will discuss later. Unlike machines or equipment, human beings are social in nature and have needs to be fulfilled in this area as well as socialization being an important motor for creativity. Some people do not seem to get on with each other and this social aspect can be a source of tension.

People are more important than ever

Thurow (1995)[93] Argues that changes to the type of demand will make managing people more important. Here is a list of the 12 largest US companies on 1st January 1900:

American Cotton Oil Company

American Steel Company

Continental tobacco

Federal Steel

General Electric

National Lead

Pacific Mail

People's Gas

Tennessee Coal & Iron

US Leather

US Rubber

How many have much strategic importance today?

Micro-electronics, biotechnology, new materials, telecommunications, civil aviation manufacturing, machine tools, robotics, computers and software are amongst the fastest-growing and most significant industries today. While the companies of 1900 were mainly natural resource companies, today the important companies are knowledge companies reliant on the input of human intellect.

Gallie and White (1993)[94] researched into skills change and the nature of work. Their survey found that there is likely to be a considerable increase in the skills people will need to do their jobs in the future.

Acero (1990)[95], in an ILO document discusses the effect of micro-electronics on the skills which people need to acquire, both in developing and developed countries. The author gives the example of machine tools, which are automated using micro-electronics (CNC, robotics etc.) and the fact that the skills required are surprisingly acquired faster by previously skilled workers than by those with higher academic qualifications. He also calls for the respective considerations to be made for the needs in management. People working in hitherto traditional production processes increasingly require knowledge of software and programming, for example. They need a different style of management than perhaps the so-called blue collar workers of the past. In the building next to my company, there is a sheet metal working factory. Thirty years ago, it was a rather greasy hall filled with extremely loud presses, each manned by an equally greasy man or woman, who undoubtedly became deaf in the course of their lives. There was a foreman who made sure they kept at the job and checked if there were any problems with the machines.

Now, if you go there, you will be first taken to an upper floor atrium where some casually dressed persons are sitting in front of large monitors. These people are highly skilled in CAD and programming and at understanding the practical aspects of their work. Somewhere below them a machine is using laser to cut stainless steel with high precision and without human hand. These are knowledge workers with indispensable skills. A manager who lets one of these people walk out of the door is likely to face a dilemma! Germany is one of the most highly automated production countries in the world and learnt early on the importance of worker participation. It should be pointed out that Lawler and Mohrman (1985)[96] were very early in drawing attention to the fact that any participation scheme is likely to fail if the employer is not fully committed to it.

In the meantime, we talk of the 'Knowledge Society' and as more and more sophisticated computers and software take over routine work and new possibilities in communication and the access to information require a more holistic approach to our organizations, we talk of the need for Wisdom. This is certainly a quality (however we define it) that human resource managers will increasingly need!

Another factor is the shrinkage of people of working age and the aging population in western countries. In Germany, the proportion of people living from earned income has dropped considerably to around only 41% in the last 10 years. This is partly a result of the lower birth rate following the post war baby boom but also because of a tendency towards smaller families. In some countries, such as Japan, the cost of bringing up children is so prohibitive that many couples cannot afford it and keep up a reasonable standard of living. Even the children's allowances in Germany, France and Great Britain are not able to compensate to the extent of encouraging an increased childbirth rate.

Increased life expectancy only exacerbates the problem and in the next decade we will have to examine our attitudes to the employment of older people and age discrimination. Some countries are already preparing anti-discriminatory legislation.

Paul Johnson (1996) says that the aging and shrinking population is 'historically unprecedented'.

People are different

Managing people is an ongoing process and, as we said above,
more complex than managing machines. To re-cap, it involves:

> *Motivation*

> *Sociability*

> *There is a moral and cultural dimension*

> *People are not consumed – they can be transformed by the
> process of work itself*

> *Development and training is possible*

With more consciousness of the issues involved with discrimination, legislation has come into being which provides certain
codes of conduct. These laws often were made for ethical reasons – racialism or sexual discrimination are in themselves
morally abhorrent. The passing of anti-discriminatory laws
led organizations to consider the possible advantages of diversity. Brazzel (1991)[97] states that diversity can be understood in
terms of human differences that play an important role in the
culture and operation of organizations.

This situation has of course been exacerbated by the rapid
movement of people from one country or continent to the
next, sometimes forced by political or natural disasters. It was
thus that the so-called 'boat people' Vietnam came to settle in
various parts of the world. With them they brought their eat-

ing habits, often opening 'Chinese' restaurants. Many were well educated and found positions in IT and engineering.

Nevertheless, there are also sound business reasons for avoiding discrimination. Diversity can lead to more creativity and new approaches to problem-solving. It can also be important, for example, in an export business to have people in the front office who share culture and language with clients. Organizations which have a clear understanding of a wide range of customers are more likely to survive in a global society.

In the meantime there is even a discipline called *Diversity Management* and we talk about the *business case for diversity*. Yet, ironically, anti-discriminatory laws can make selection for the intention of achieving diversity illegal. Most state laws in the USA, for example, prohibit taking race or ethnicity into account when hiring new employees.

Race and gender are nevertheless not the only sources of diversity. There are other less obvious reasons for diversity such as:

> *Age*
>
> *Education*
>
> *Race or Ethnicity*
>
> *Family status (married, single, children, etc.)*
>
> *Gender*
>
> *Income*
>
> *Work experience*
>
> *Nationality or region*

Wealth

Ability

Sexual orientation

Social class

Beliefs

Although progress in this area has certainly been made, we can define the prejudice which still exists into two main areas:

1. Concealed prejudice — people cease to express their views. Bias, stereotyping about groups of people. Even if they are not necessarily negative views, can affect a manager's objectivity.

2. Institutional barriers — e.g. Women working late, physically disabled where workplaces are not suitable, etc.

Activity

Think about the above three types of prejudice. Can you think of any examples you have experienced yourself? Are there areas for improvement where you have worked or in the college where you are studying? What suggestions can you make.

Do you have any examples of advantages of diversity in your organization or the world around you?

Tensions

Moving to a historical view of the subject of the management of people, we can detect distinct paradigms:

The Taylorist paradigm

F.W. Taylor (1911)[98] stated: 'Workmen want high wages, employers want low cost of labor'. This is the concept of scientific management and includes concepts of the division of labor as the overriding methodology towards greater industrial efficiency. The metaphor of the organization is the 'well-oiled machine'. Taylor believed that it was better to apply scientific approaches and measurement to streamline work processes rather than heuristics. Splitting manufacturing processes into component parts, it uses an extreme form of the division of labor to achieve what seems to be more production efficiency.

There is of course a big difference between the industrial society of the early 20th century and the knowledge society of today, as discussed above. Even in the manufacturing industries, the methods of production using robotics and electronically controlled machines often makes the idea of division of process components less efficient in fact. The desire for improved quality has led some automobile manufacturers to employ work teams to assemble a whole vehicle rather than conveyor belts. In Taylor's time it was a seller's market—if you could produce enough at the right price you could attempt to meet demand. Since the Second World War we have been increasingly faced with saturated markets and a buyer's market where issues like quality or innovation play a bigger role often than price. It is as much about being effective and it is about being efficient.

Taylor is by no means dead and buried and the prevalence of this kind of thinking amongst managers demonstrates the gap between espoused theory and real practice. Where it still survives today, there is often a link to the firm belief in the effectiveness of money as a motivating factor. These ideas are often supposed to have had their greatest realization in Henry Ford's production line and the consequent approach towards industrial rationalization.

However, Sorensen and Williamson (1956)[99] dispute the influence of Taylor on Ford, revealed by Sorensen's vehement statement:

One of the hardest-to-down myths about the evolution of mass production at Ford is one which credits much of the accomplishment to 'scientific management.' No one at Ford — not Mr. Ford, Couzens, Flanders, Wills, Pete Martin, nor I — was acquainted with the theories of the 'father of scientific management,' Frederick W. Taylor. Years later I ran across a quotation from a two-volume book about Taylor by Frank Barkley Copley, who reports a visit Taylor made to Detroit late in 1914, nearly a year after the moving assembly line had been installed at our Highland Park plant. Taylor expressed surprise to find that Detroit industrialists 'had undertaken to install the principles of scientific management without the aid of experts.' To my mind this unconscious admission by an expert is expert testimony on the futility of too great reliance on experts and should forever dispose of the legend. that Taylor's ideas had any influence at Ford.

Undoubtedly, despite the critics of Taylor and Ford, we have to admit that Scientific Management was probably largely responsible for us being able to acquire complex products like automobiles at an affordable price. It can also be said that for the first time in history, it made world wars a terrible possibility. The dissatisfaction caused amongst workers by Taylor's methods were certainly instrumental in the strengthening of union power.

The Human Relations Paradigm

Elton Mayo (1933)[100], one of the first scientists to state the importance of groups in the workplace, stated that people's performance owed more to social interaction than to rationally designed amendments to their tasks and that workers are motivated by a 'logic of sentiment' whereas managers by a 'logic of cost and efficiency'. If this gap is not bridged it is bound to lead to conflict. He concluded that workers were more likely to be motivated by belonging to a group than by material rewards. The resulting thinking means more emphasis on the human face of work and assumes that people value what they do and seek respect and recognition for their achievements. These factors are strong motivators.

The resulting managerial consequences should be greater respect for employees, a participative style of management and such concepts as self-control and empowerment. It has resulted in many efforts towards the humanization of the workplace and in such ideas as flexible working hours conceived in the Black Forest area by Wilhelm Haller (1990)[101] in the 1970's as a backlash against a strongly Taylorist environment.

The movement has gained impetus due to changes in the business environment, the evolving of mature markets with strong competition and saturated customers, the need for more creativity, better quality and for int/entrepreneurial skills to maintain competitive advantage.It assumes that people want to contribute to obtaining the goals which they participate in setting and are willing to take responsibility.

In a Human Resource Management (HRM) environment, managers' aims are the development of the workforce. It finds its expression in ideas like the Learning Organization, Servant Leadership, Team-working and Empowerment and Management by Objectives (MbO). Total Quality Management (TQM) and ideas of lean management depend on the flat organization structures which normally come in its wake.

HRM should not be confused with personnel management, which tends to come out of the Taylorist paradigm and is very much a top-down approach and suits hierarchical structures better. With HRM, the responsibility for people is not the prerogative of a dedicated department (which will probably still be retained for the administrative tasks) but is seen as the responsibility of team managers. Thus, there is a requirement for general managers to have a good knowledge and skills in human resources management.

In reality, any organization is a mixture of both approaches and many firms are in a transitional state. This is well illustrated by the managerial grid from Blake & Mouton (1964)[102]. Concern for people and concern for production. Any manager's approach shows more or less of these constituents.

This model orients very much on the role of leadership style which is defined by the following behavioral attributes:

Blake & Mouton Managerial Grid

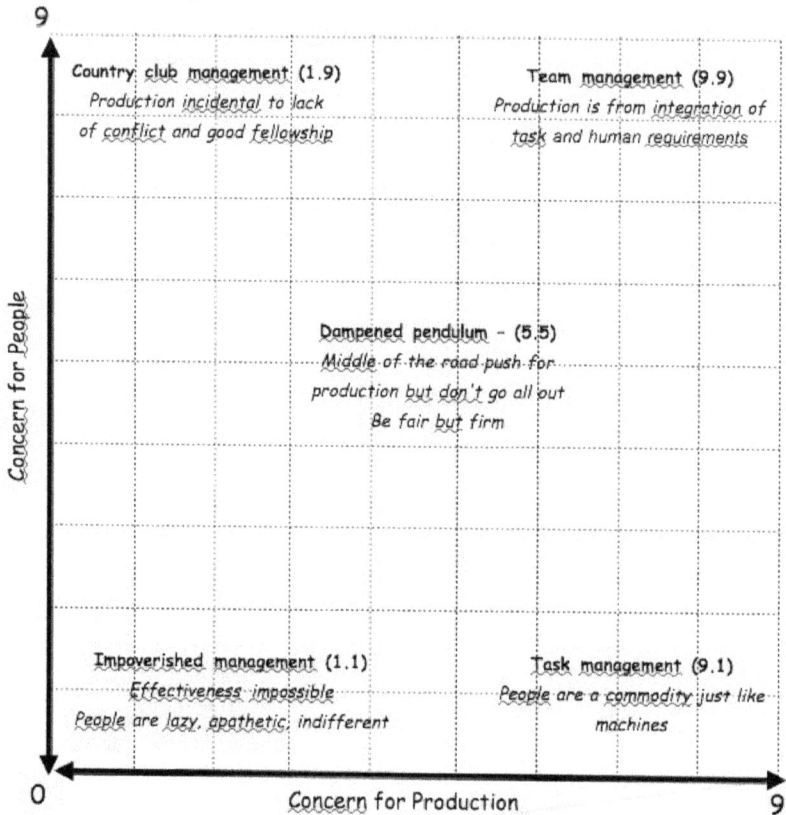

Fig. 22: The Blake & Mouton Managerial Grid

Element	Description
Initiative	Taking action, driving and supporting
Inquiry	Questioning, researching and verifying understanding
Advocacy	Expressing convictions and championing ideas
Decision making	Evaluating resources, choices and consequences
Conflict resolution	Confronting and resolving disagreements
Resilience	Dealing with problems, set-backs and failures
Critique	Delivering objective, candid feedback

Activity

Plot any organizations you know on the diagram. What would you be like as a manager? Where would you place yourself on the grid? Use different symbols to denote yourself and as many organizations which you can think of.

How would you compare Mayo's thinking to Maslow's needs hierarchy discussed earlier in this book?

Flexible Working Hours

The idea of flexible working hours can be traced back to Christel Kämmerer (Haller, 1990, p.10)[103]. Kämmerer solved the problem of female part-time workers working fixed hours by instead setting an average number of hours to be worked. By the late 1960's, this idea had been extended to full time employees and Messrs Bülkow in Ottobrunn in Germany solved the problem of traffic congestion on the roads leading to their works by introducing a system whereby employees could vary the time they came and left work (ibid. p.11) and from there the idea spread across the world.

In the case of the Ottobrun idea, instead of fixed starting and finishing times and breaks, the day was split into time zones of 'must' and 'can' working times as well as break times. Both starting and finishing times were extended by an additional period to allow for flexible working. It was possible for over-time necessary in busy times to be compensated by taking time off when things were slack.

Haller was instrumental in making flexible working hours a practicability by the invention of time counter systems which recorded the actual time worked rather than the time clocks which had previously been employed to control employee attendance.

By the 1980's the idea had become a multi-million industry and today the time recording industry employees thousands of people just making the equipment for time measurement. The idea has been extended with such concepts as annual work hours, the combination with production time controlling and so on. That the idea became well accepted amongst trade unions and employers alike is much due to Haller's hard work and persuasive charisma.

Activity

The idea of flexible working hours is no longer new but is it practiced in your organization? How do you think it could be employed to increase motivation?

Rewarding Performance

One of the main issues in any organization has to do with fair rewards for work done. Many managers believe that people respond best to financial rewards which are linked to measured performance. One obvious example of this is in sales organizations where sales people receive a commission based on their sales turnover or if they exceed a sales budget. This is a very individualistic reward, of course, with the intention of trying to get people to work harder. Referred to as 'Performance Related Pay' or 'PRP', such rewards may be introduced in order to encourage people to support change programs or to align them with the vision of the organization. Unfortunately, this does not seem to work so well in practice as in theory and there have been some extensive studies carried out on the subject. The Institute of Manpower Studies (1993)[104] states that: 'The benefits most often claimed for PRP are not met in practice' and Kohn (1993)[105] states: 'As for productivity, at least two dozen studies over the last three decades have conclusively shown that people who expect to receive a reward for completing a task or for doing that task successfully simply do not perform as well as those who expect no reward at all. Deci and Ryan (1985)[106] say that: 'research has consistently shown that any contingent payment system tends to undermine intrinsic motivation'.

It would seem from the above that the advantages of PRP are at best doubtful yet many managers believe it to be effective.

Activity

What do you think motivates people to perform well? Make a list of things which you think could be used to increase performance.

360 Degree Appraisal

The following information is based on an article from the Chartered Management Institute (CMI) (2000)[107].

360 degree (sometimes referred to as multi-source) appraisals are when not only directly related employees assess their managers but all the people around them as well as themselves. The idea behind it is to get more participation but it will not work where there is not a climate open to free speech or where people only feel free to say what they are supposed to. It fits well into horizontal organizations where there is a lot of knowledge not just about the direct manager.

The main components are:

> *Self appraisal*
>
> *Superior's appraisal*
>
> *Subordinate's appraisal*
>
> *Peer appraisal.*

Ideally, the process will result in training and hopefully personal development. CMI state a number of important key features in 360 degree appraisal schemes:

> *It is usually based on a questionnaire, either paper-based, or web-based, facilitated by email.*
>
> *Individuals can choose their own appraisers.*

Feedback is usually anonymous, perhaps through a facilitator who can have a key role in helping the individual interpret results and feedback.

Appraisal is normally followed up with actions for the individual's development.

Of course it is not without its problems, and the system has become somewhat of a business fad, often with lip service paid to it rather than serious implementation.

It does require a fair bit of administrative work and it can damage moral, especially when questionnaires are not completed objectively. Properly managed, it can lead to more openness and be a motivating factor to those who lack confidence in themselves.

Critics of 360 degree feedback such as Pfau & Kay (2002)[108] are skeptical as to whether it really improves performance and may even be detrimental to shareholder value.

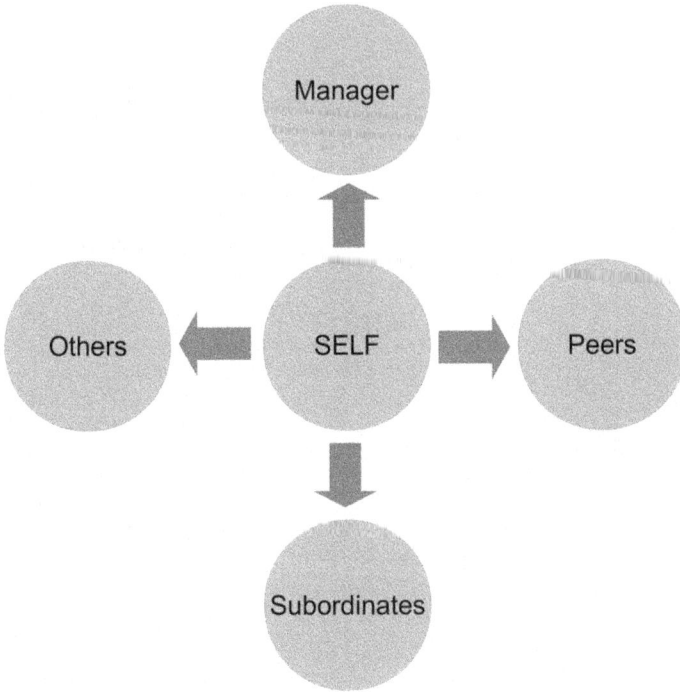

Fig. 23: 360 Degree Appraisals

Activity

Do you think 360 degree appraisal could work in your organization?

Do you think management would be keen to implement it? Design a questionaire which you think could work for you and your colleagues.

Motivation

Extrinsic and intrinsic motivators

Such things which work from then outside to motivate people are referred to by psychologists as extrinsic motivators. Behaviorist science has demonstrated through experiments that animals will modify their performance or comply in order to gain rewards. PRP protagonists assumed that humans behaved similarly. The problem is that humans seem to respond differently. Such extrinsic rewards only have a temporary effect on performance without affecting long-term motivation.

Therefore, there may be situations where PRP will work and where only a temporary result is required (e.g. the vacuum cleaner salesman). Kohn (1993)[109] lists six reasons why PRP is domed to failure:

1. Pay is not a motivator — if people receive too little they will be de-motivated but the opposite is not necessarily true.

2. Rewards are a covert form of punishment — not receiving a reward may be seen as a punishment. If a drop in performance is 'rewarded' with less pay, this will tend to de-motivate and perhaps lead to a further reduction in performance.

3. Rewards disrupt teamwork — the concept of individual gain is contrary to the team spirit. It may hinder co-opera-

tion and cause envy and jealousies. A sense of resentment may arise if rewards are not seen to be fair.

4. Other things affect performance—lack of performance could be due to lack of resources or persons could be over-loaded with work.

5. PRP discourages risk-taking—people will concentrate on gaining short-term rewards rather than proposing new ideas.

6. Rewards undermine interest—intrinsic motivation (coming from within the person) is reduced because it may be felt that the extrinsic reward is being used to force them to do something against their will. Deci (1971)[110], amongst others, has demonstrated that the larger the incentive the more the negative the perception of the task.

One of the major problems with PRP is that it is a self-perpetuating belief. Because a low level of pay is known to de-motivate, this generates the belief that paying more will increase motivation. At first, there are some changes in behavior which seems to confirm the effectiveness on PRP which in turn leads to an increased reliance on it. When performance drops off, it is assumed that this is due to insufficient PRP. Finally, teamwork suffers, intrinsic motivation drops, risk taking is reduced more attention is paid to PRP and so on.

To summarize, PRP is a simplistic solution and is not compatible with a holistic view of the organization, its needs nor of the needs of the individuals or teams within the organization. Finally, it can be said, that a society that relies solely on material rewards in order to get results is doomed to stagnate. The great advances in science would not have happened and the great leaders of history would not have appeared if material rewards had been the main driver. Nevertheless, there may be moments when we see a temporary application and it should not be completely excluded from our thinking.

More ideas on motivation

Motivation is a word we often use without thinking deeply about what it means. Sometimes we talk about being motivated to do something, as if it were something intrinsic and at other times, with respect to others, we talk of it as an extrinsic value — the ability to motivate others. Mullins (1993)[111] has described the relationship in terms of the effect it has on the individual in the following formula:

$$\text{Performance} = \text{Ability} \times \text{Motivation}$$

Activity

Take a moment to think about 'motivation'. What kinds of things motivate you? Is everybody the same? Are some people more 'self-motivated' than others and do some people require more of a shove? Do you have experience with children or do you remember your own childhood? Did you always feel like doing your homework? What devices were and are used by others to encourage you to do your work? Write down some ideas on motivation and try and define the word. Take the opportunity to discuss with someone else.

What is motivation?

Mullins (1993)[112] states that motivation is a 'driving force' through which people strive to achieve their goals, fulfill a need and uphold values.

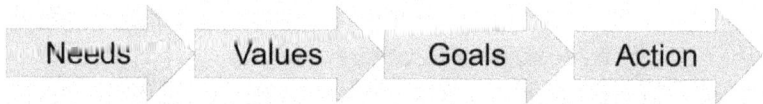

Needs ▷ Values ▷ Goals ▷ Action ▷

Fig. 24: Goal Setting Theory: Locke and Henne (1986)

Maslow's needs hierarchy

Most of you will probably have come across Maslow's (1987)[113] needs hierarchy as an explanation of motivational forces.:

Beyond vision we could re-open the pyramid to
incorporate enlightenment as the ultimate aim of Man

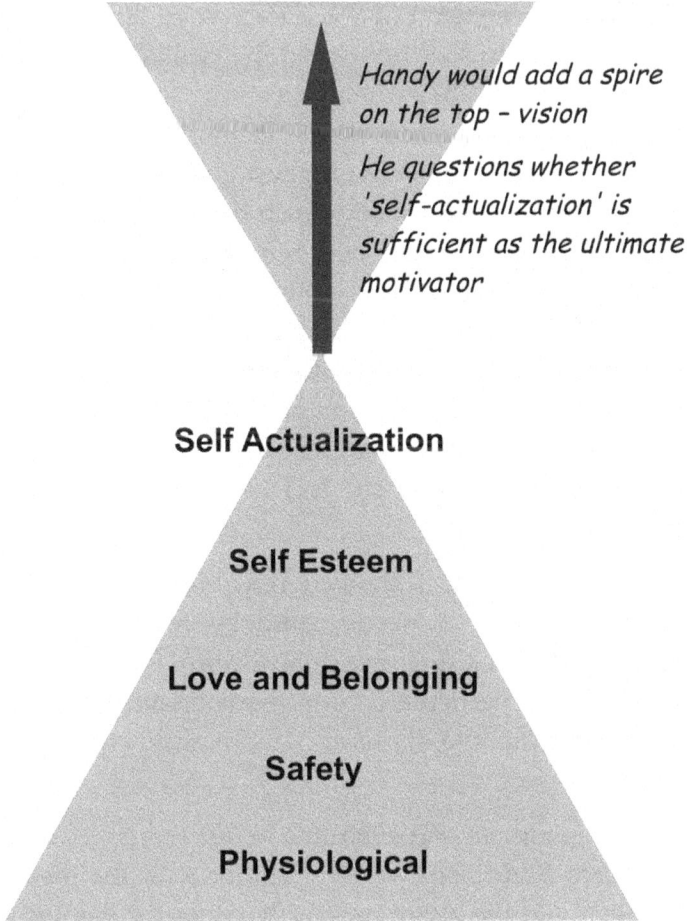

Handy would add a spire
on the top – vision

He questions whether
'self-actualization' is
sufficient as the ultimate
motivator

Self Actualization

Self Esteem

Love and Belonging

Safety

Physiological

Fig. 25: Maslow's Needs Hierarchy from a different perspective

Applying holistic theory to Maslow and using ideas borrowed from Handy (1994)[114] and elsewhere, we have extended Maslow's concept to include vision and mission, which are seen as being essential motivational drivers by Handy. If people do not have a vision of what they want and can achieve they are unlikely to stay motivated, particularly when the going is tough, even if they do have a strong feeling of self-actualization. Also, there is an ethical element, as Handy points out. If self-actualization is the highest goal, then we are liable to end with an egoistic society which has no aims beyond personal development. This would belie the great achievements of innovators and discoverers of the past who have often battled on in the obsession of a dream. Also, a strong sense of mission can be a powerful motivational force. This is often demonstrated by religious or political movements whose members will often suffer the greatest of hardships in order to carry their message to others. In fact we use the word 'missionary' in just this way.

In my previous book, I showed how these ideas based on Maslow's hierarchy of needs could be combined with the holistic model of IGOS (Individual, Group, Organization and Society). This is particularly important because, as we shall see as we continue the discussion, motivation is an extremely complex issue.

But we are going beyond even this in our search for an explanation. From Buddhism we are familiar with the idea of enlightenment and the attainment of Nirvana for the individual seeker. This may seem to the reader as having no application in the tough world of business but we can learn from the gurus! Driven by the desire to be the 'perfect manager' we can place ourselves in the role of the seeker after truth and wisdom. For the reflective manager, this can be an extremely powerful motivator and we are familiar with the image of the researching scientist always looking to discovering a better and more effective way of doing things. Robert K. Greenleaf (2002)[115], in his concept of Servant Leadership, sees the need for a leader to be servant first. Most of you will have read Hermann Hesse's book Siddhartha already mentioned elsewhere and perhaps remember the passage where he shows the 'Taylorist' merchant that there are better ways to run a business if only you can 'fast' (do without something for a while until you get clarity), 'think' (spend time reflecting on a problem before making a decision) and 'wait' (sometimes it is better to wait for a more opportune moment). Siddhartha manages to 'motivate' his suppliers to give him priority on future deliveries just by applying these principles and the principles of caring, love and service.

Activity

What do you think of these rather esoteric and idealistic ideas in regard to motivation? Does it compare with any of your own life experiences? Is it possible to apply it in practice or is it too other-worldly to be of any earthly use?

Developing the concepts of motivation, we can take a glimpse from a different perspective. Sometimes, our comparison with the efforts and rewards of others in a social or work situation have a considerable effect on our behavior. J.S. Adams developed a concept referred to as 'Equity Theory' in an attempt to explain this:

Equity theory

People hold different ideas about the relationship of their inputs (qualifications, ability, level of effort and so on) to the outcomes (e.g. Pay, benefits, status, etc.) from the work they do. According to this theory, people weigh this in their minds and make comparisons and when the ratios of inputs and outputs are equivalent they consider this to be equitable and continue to contribute accordingly. Thus, equity exists when:

- Effort exerted is related to the rewards received.

- People hold beliefs about inputs and outcomes of their jobs and their perception of this is seen as equivalent to others.

- They compare their ratio of input to outcomes to that of other people. Based on their own perception. There is a difference between perception, beliefs and reality. If they are equal, equity exists.

- Equity exists if any of the three following are met:

    1. *Inputs compared = outcomes compared*

    2. *The person receives more outcomes for extra input*

    3. *The person receives less outcomes for less input*

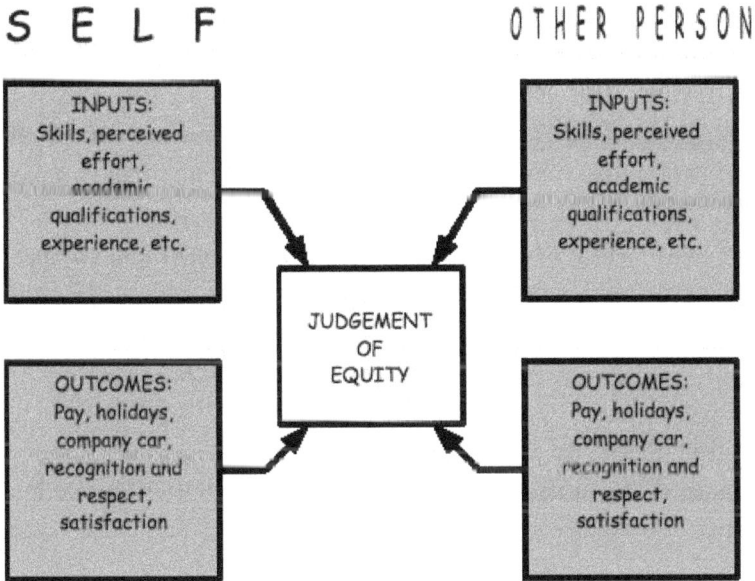

Fig. 26 Equity Theory

If these are not in equilibrium we have a state of inequity which usually results in changes to behavior, such as:

Inputs may be changed

Outcomes may be changed

Views on inputs and outputs may become distorted

The person may quit his job

Reference individuals may be influenced to change their inputs/outcomes. People start making comparisons.

Activity

> *Think about this idea. Being absolutely honest with yourself, if your partner does much less work at his studies than you, seems no cleverer than yourself, but always seems to get better marks, how do you feel? If you find out that he or she cheats at exams and gets away with it, what will you think? How will it affect the effort you put in and the value you place on your studies? If you are working in a group with group assessment and one person never takes any active part but shares the same mark, how will you feel? What motivational forces could help you fight against a negative reaction to a feeling of inequity?*

Another theory of motivation which tries to explain what we value and the effort required to obtain it is called 'Expectancy Theory'.

Expectancy theory

According to expectancy theory, there are three main factors which determine our performance:

1. **Expectancy:** to what extent does our perceived effort lead to better performance?

2. **Instrumentality:** how much does improved job performance lead to desired outcomes?

3. **Valence:** attractiveness of the outcomes obtained from effort—more pay, security, etc.

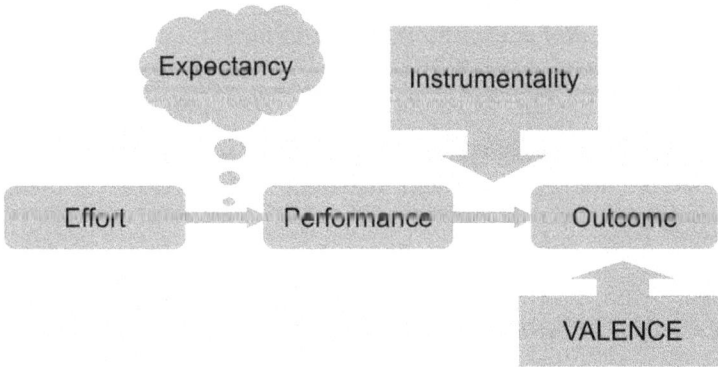

Fig. 27: Expectancy Theory

Motivation is highest when all three are high.

Rewards must matter and be likely to be obtained by effort.

Rewards that come anyway are not likely to motivate.

The three areas are described as:

1. **EXPECTANCY:** to what extent does out perceived effort lead to better performance.

   Person must be capable of the required performance

   Clear and measurable objectives

   Resources available

   Allocate work far in advance and specify deadlines.

2. **INSTRUMENTALITY:** Degree to which improved job performance is perceived to lead to desired outcomes.

People need to believe that there is a clear link between performance and reward.

Praise and performance are important.

3. **VALENCE:** The attractiveness of the outcomes to be obtained from increased job performance. E.g. increased pay, less chance of the sack, intrinsic satisfaction of doing a good job.

Types of outcomes available

It is essential to match rewards to an individual needs. E.g. increased pay will only be valued if people can spend it and enjoy it. Sometimes, people can even be demotivated by a pay rise when they receive their check and find that the taxman has taken most of their reward. This means that human resource managers need to know their colleagues well in order to match the reward to the person. We are often childlike in our habits and which child, looking forward to a particular present for his birthday and spending the last two weeks being especially well-behaved, will break out in spontaneous joy if he receives a present which does not suit his or her interests?

The final motivational theory we wish to examine in this section is goal-setting theory whose proponents are particularly Edwin Locke (1996)[116] and Mullins (1993)[117].

Another look at goal setting theory

The results of research show that people's goals play a large role in motivation and :

People's goals or intentions affect their behavior. People set goals and try to achieve them

According to their needs and values.

Notice the consequence of their behavior. Goals can be modified or behavior changed to achieve the goal which has been set.

Effort improves when goals are demanding but not impossible.

Effort increases when one is committed to a goal.

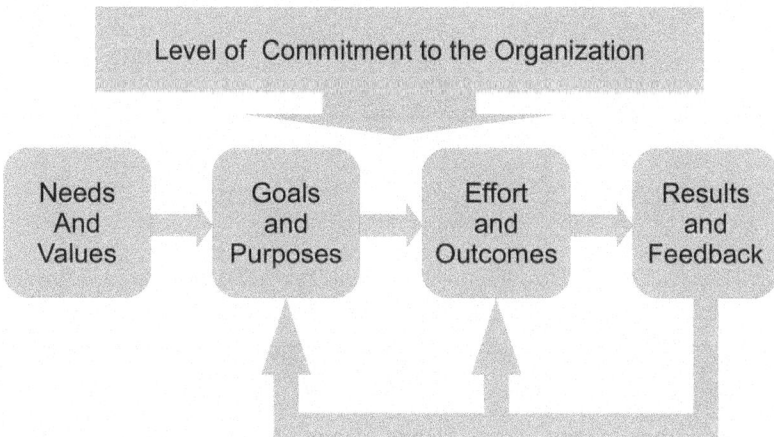

Fig. 28: Goal Setting Revisited

Activity

In the light of the above discussion, think about how you would apply these motivational theories to

1. Increase the sales performance of a car salesman who likes the thrill of selling a car and of earning a lot of cash and,

2. A nurse in a hospital whom you require to work overtime for the tenth night in a row.

Job design and psychological health

The purpose of job design is to arrange work in such a manner that it reduces fatigue and frustration. It attempts to reduce feelings of dissatisfaction which occurs when people have to carry out repetitive tasks or ones which require little mental input. It aims at raising productivity and does away with the need for extrinsic rewards by providing a greater sense of satisfaction through increased challenge and responsibility.

People need to enjoy what they do and derive pleasure from doing their work. Work should lead to a great sense of self-esteem (Maslow, ibid.). Less anxiety and depression result if jobs are designed with these points in mind.

So job design is closely linked with our previous discussion on motivation. One of the increasing issues is that people may tend to work long hours and this can lead to tiredness and be linked to expectancy theory. Sometimes people are their own slave drivers and it may be necessary for a manager to ensure that employees are given the necessary support to keep working hours within reasonable limits.

To sum up the main points:

> *Job satisfaction – people enjoy and derive pleasure from their jobs.*

Self-esteem is an important factor which can be enhanced through correct job design

Absence of anxiety and depression is important for the feeling of well-being.

Job design is closely linked to motivation but people can suffer if they work too hard or extremely long hours (work-life balance and the individual's private agenda are issues worth noting here.

Karasek and Theorell (1990)[118] claim that job strain is influenced by the interaction of three job characteristics: job demands, supports and constraints. Karasek's (1979)[119] matrix below visualizes this:

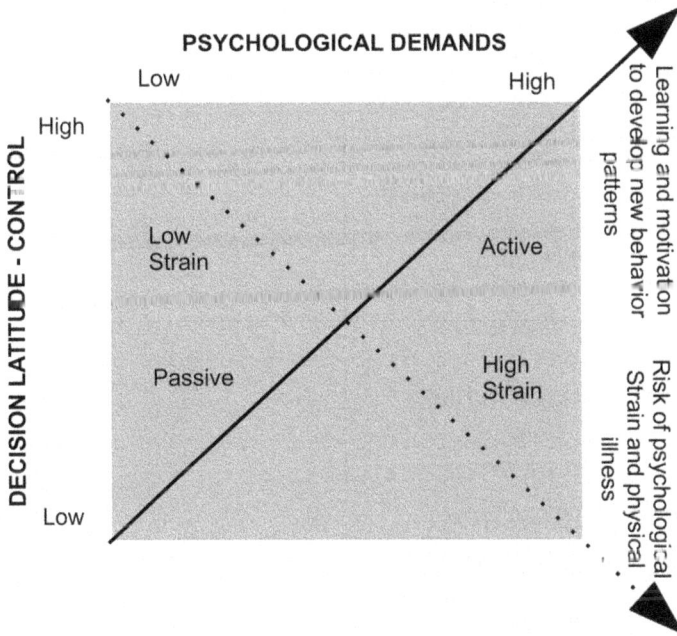

Fig. 29: Job Demands and Control — adapted from Karasek (1979)

Benefits of well-designed jobs

The benefits of well-designed jobs are fairly obvious and it is a win-win situation both for employees and management:

For employees

> *More interesting work*
>
> *Scope for development*
>
> *More autonomy*
>
> *Companionship and team pride*
>
> *Share in benefits (higher pay)*

For management

> *Better quality*
>
> *Reduced absence*
>
> *Lower turnover of staff*
>
> *More flexibility*
>
> *Higher productivity*
>
> *Improved performance*

To the organization

> *High level of commitment*
>
> *Improved industrial relations*
>
> *Organizational growth*

Nine principle job features which affect mental health

This was termed the 'Vitamin Model' (Peter Warr, 1987[120]) because the effect of these features on mental health of employees was considered to be analogous to the effect of vitamins on physical health.

1. Opportunity for control — Individual must be able to control activities and events

When individuals feel they do not have control over the processes necessary to do their job well this leads to frustrations and eventually can lead to an 'if they don't care, why should I' attitude and the inner resignation. The have quit the job although they are still there and being paid!

2. Opportunity for skill use

Often there are untapped skills in our organizations. We often don't even bother to find out what people can do, especially the things that may not have been necessary for them to get the job in the first place. An obvious example is language capability. I have known many an organization which has paid an outside organization to do a pretty second rate translation job when they had people in the organization with mother tongue ability of which they were not aware. It is not just about saving money for the organization but imagine what a sense of self-actualization this can bring an individual employee if it is felt that those skills can be valued and used. That is why one should always carry out a skills and knowledge inventory of the organization and preferably keep a data bank of this knowledge.

3. Goals and task demands

There are intrinsic job demands which may not be immediately obvious. One of these is sensory deprivation. A low workload can in fact demotivate and low demands which are demonstrated by few opportunities to control one's work or use one's skills can be highly demotivating and cause stress.

On the other hand, high work loads can lead to overload and exhaustion and reduce job satisfaction. It has been demonstrated that Coronary heart disease is more prevalent amongst high work load employees. (*Karasek et al., 1981*[121]). The feeling of high work load can be exacerbated by issues relating to the task identity and feelings that it is Pleasant to be 'pulled along' by an activity (Baldamus, 1961[122]). Time demands and conflicts between private and work life balance or shift working are all sources of work overload sensibility.

Yet, Cain (2012)[123] states that 'Despite interest in the topic for the past 40 years, there is no clearly defined, universally accepted definition of workload'.

4. Variety

The Industrial Fatigue Research Board (1920)[124] — Repetitiveness leads to low satisfaction.

5. Environmental clarity

Task feedback is important.

Information about the results of behavior needs to be clear.

Information about the future to deal with uncertainty.

Being able to forecast what will happen — e.g. future career development. There is a need for clarity and future perspectives.

Information about required behavior — what will be rewarded and what will be punished. Kahn (1964) states that 'Role ambiguity' which refers to a lack of clear information associated with a particular role, can be associated with lower mental health.

6. Availability of money

Employees have an expected standard of living. Very low incomes affect psychological health. This is more important at lower levels of the organization.

7. Physical security

Injuries from work can lead to poorer mental health and such conditions as post traumatic stress disorder (PTSD), or depression or it can make a previous mental health condition much worse [125].

8. Opportunity for social contact

Friendship opportunities, privacy, personal territory are all issues which relate to job design and mental health. The workplace layout is an important factor and yet whilst social contact is necessary, problems can occurwith open plan offices – Oldham and Brass (1979)[126]. Employees react differently to open plan offices, despite the apparent advantages to employers as has been reported by Maher and von Hippel (2005)[127].

9. Valued social position

As previously mentioned, the esteem attached to the job plays a considerable role. Perceived social value has been shown to have a significant relationship to job satisfaction – Hackman and Oldham (1975)[128].

Activity

Make a table of these nine principle job features and enter how they might apply to your organization

---

Redesigning jobs

Job rotation has increasingly been applied in the re-designing of jobs. Originally used with trainees to give them a broader perspective of the organization and to acquire multifarious skills, it can be used as a device to help employees gain better understanding of colleagues' tasks. It can also be used as a means of alleviating the stress which occurs when a person has to do the same job year after year – especially when the work is limited in scope and routine. The down side of job rotation is that it cannot work where a high degree of specialization is called for and it may also meet with resistance from unions. Employees may feel threatened that their knowledge power could be weakened.

The following table from Garg & Rastogi (2006)[129] is a summary of the Effects of Job Design Applications on Employees' Performance from a variety of authors:

Researcher	Date of Research	Findings
Heckman et al.	1975	Job enrichment increases motivation and job satisfaction.
Loher et al.	1985	There is a relationship between job design and job satisfaction, which becomes more important at times when a need for development is more strongly felt.

Researcher	Date of Research	Findings
Fried & Ferris	1987	Studies carried out using the job characteristics model developed by Fried and Ferris reached the conclusion that generally job design studies were effective in increasing motivation, job performance and levels of productivity.
Griffin	1989	Job design activities create significant changes in employees and increases employees' sensitivity to change.
Adler	1991	Arrangements which provide job autonomy and skill variety increase job satisfaction and motivation.
Renn & Vandenberg	1995	Job design implementation has a positive effect on both directly and indirectly at a personal level and on the output of the work.

Researcher	Date of Research	Findings
Sokoya	2000	Rotation has a place among known factors of job satisfaction.
Bassey	2002	Skill acquisition, job clarity, job autonomy, feedback, job security and reward system are all factors which increase employee motivation.
Morrison et al.	2005	Job designs obtaining greater autonomy provide the opportunity for development and is a way for skill utilization.
Love & Edwards	2005	With the help of job design, more control on job related issues increase productivity.

Fig. 30: The Effects of Job Design Applications on Employees'
Performance: The Related Researchs and Findings – Garg and Rastogi
(2006).

Job Enlargement

Job enlargement is about amalgamating several tasks into one job. By doing so it increases the range of activities and duties as well as responsibility of the employee. It is the antithesis of the division of labor discussed above and Taylor's or Ford's principles. It seems to be a complete turnabout in fact, due to the experience with mental health and job design which has tended to demonstrate that monotonous repetitive jobs increase boredom. One method is the use of modular or cell manufacturing where actual tasks may be rotated in a team. Long term effects can be negated where all the tasks involved are equally boring. It can also increase work overload in the long term and even be seen as a form of exploitation by those affected. It is sometimes referred to as 'horizontal loading'.

Job Enrichment

This is where the concept of job enrichment appears, conceived and developed by Friedrich Herzberg (1959)[130]. This can be described as 'vertical loading' where the attempt is made to break the disadvantages of job enlargement by providing a variety of tasks of varying difficulties. Employees are also given a complete task in itself which is accompanied by training, feedback and encouragement.

Increasing the level of responsibility

Giving employees more responsibility and more control of decision making can positively affect motivation because it can lead to an increase in self esteem, recognition and a feeling of achievement—especially if this is linked with requisite training.

Critics of Job Enrichment

WIlhelm Haller (1973)[131] in an article made the following observations:

Under the headline "job enrichment" all sorts of programs and plans are being worked out and tried, all designed to make the employee happier and more satisfied with what he is doing. Some no doubt "will be doomed and some will succeed but the basic attitude with which employee and management approach the problem will most probably make all the difference.

Wherever the employee is still looked upon as a living piece of equipment usable and disposable as the situation requires, a job enrichment program obviously is nothing more than better fodder and a more beautiful cage for the beast. But the beast no doubt, will take little time to realize this. The worker realizing he is still being used, still manipulated, still nothing more than a cost factor-like materials and equipment, will soon resume being bored, frustrated and rebellious.

Unless management realizes that the total work force is a community of human beings and not a number of employees who accept a job for a certain price which is primarily determined by the weight (the power) they can bring to bear at the bargaining table – any program to solve the problems will only scratch the surface.

Two Factor Theory

Herzberg is best know for his so-called two factor theory where he attempts to identify and clarify the basis of motivation.

He founded his theory on interviews amongst accountants and engineers as their professions seemed to display growing importance at the time. He described the analysis in this way (Herzberg, 1964, pp. 3-7)[132]:

Briefly, we asked our respondents to describe periods in their lives when they were exceedingly happy and unhappy with their jobs. Each respondent gave as many "sequences of events" as he could that met certain criteria – including a marked change in feeling, a beginning and an end, and contained some substantive description other than feelings and interpretations...

The proposed hypothesis appears verified. The factors on the right that led to satisfaction (achievement, intrinsic interest in the work, responsibility, and advancement) are mostly unipolar; that is, they contribute very little to job dissatisfaction. Conversely, the dis-satis-fiers (company policy and administrative practices, supervision, interpersonal relationships, working conditions, and salary) contrib-ute very little to job satisfaction.

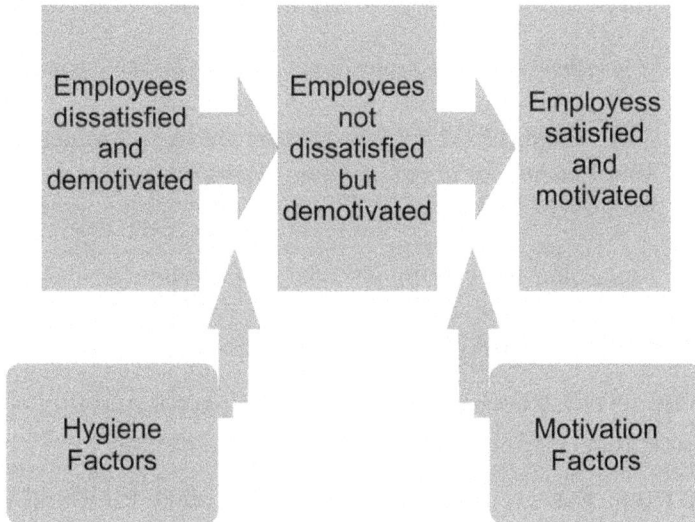

Fig. 31: Herzberg's Two Factor Theory

This can be summed up as in this table[133]:

Satisfiers	Dissatisfiers
Achievement Recognition Work itself Responsibility Advancement Growth	Company policy and administration Supervision Working conditions Interpersonal relations (with peers, subordinates and superiors) Status Job security Salary Personal Life

Fig. 32: Satisfiers and Dissatisfiers According to Herzberg

There are critics of Herzberg's theory which can be summarized as follows:

> *There may not really be a link between satisfaction and productivity and yet productivity was not part of the research.*

> *It is subjective on the part of people making the assessments*

> *May be subject to bias as employees are likely to blame external factors for dissatisfaction. They automatically credit themselves for satisfaction.*

> *Blue-collar workers are not taken into account..*

Seven Possible Principles:

1. Remove some controls while retaining accountability — outcome: responsibility and personal achievement

2. Increase the accountability of individuals for their own work — outcome: responsibility and recognition

3. Give each person a natural unit of work — outcome: responsibility, achievement and recognition

4. Job freedom—outcome: responsibility, achievement and recognition

5. Make reports available directly to worker—outcome: Internal recognition

6. Introduce new and more difficult tasks—outcome: Growth and learning

7. Assign individuals specific tasks to make experts—outcome: Responsibility, growth and learning

Quality circles and self-managing work teams:

Quality circles developed during the 1980's and involved people from different areas of the business to solve quality and efficiency problems. Pearson (1992)[134] states that they were not always given the full responsibility to make necessary changes and that later self-managing teams evolved focusing on innovation and which were multi-skilled. Participation and goal-setting with individual feedback kept teams focused on goals (ibid.).

To summarize, self-managing work teams can be defined where:

Membership is voluntary.

Group selects the problems to solve and decides how it is to be done.

Members are trained in communication, quality assurance and group dynamics.

The group recommends solutions to management.

The group is empowered to make decisions within its brief.

Organizational Entry

Various Approaches

Person-job fit (Traditional approach)

The idea with person-job fit is that one tries to find the right person for a particular task. This approach can be criticized for a number of reasons:

> *The pace of change means jobs can change.*

> *Organizations are more interested in outcomes than in performance.*

Social negotiation Peter Herriot (1993)[135]

In this case there is a process of negotiation between employer and employee. The reasoning behind this is:

> *People are constantly changing*

> *Self perception is important*

> *Jobs are constantly changing*

> *Both parties select each other*

> *Information is exchanged*

> *Negotiation takes place*

Establish or test feasibility of a psychological contract

Arriving at a so-called psychological contract should be the outcome of this approach.

The Social Negotiation model is based on the assumption that external factors have an effect on the individual's behavior, whereas the person-job fit model assumes that the factors come from within the individual.

Walter Mischel (1968)[136] states that behavior is not driven by people's own personality characteristics but is specific to the situation. Nevertheless there is a certain degree of stability and predictability.

Because organizations are constantly changing, ther terms of the psychological contract are also changing. As Noon and Blyton (1997)[137] have noted, there is a degree of change weariness amongst employees. This can mean changes in skills requirements but also behavioral and social changes.

Person-organization fit

An "Interactionalist" perspective which takes the standpoint that human behavior stems from the interaction of person and situation. It is an important concept because:

> *It analyzes a person's fit to organization in order to predict behavior and performance*
>
> *Creates a suitable environment – the job should be satisfying and motivating*
>
> *Interaction with situational factors – the person may perform differently in different jobs. There is a need to explore*

reasons why so that it is known how he/she will behave in a new job.

Influences the future of the organization – organizations are affected by people and people by organizations.

The following table provides some ideas of when to use what:

Approach to organizational entry	Person-job fit	Person-organization fit	Social Negotiation
Behavioral assumptions	Individual traits in relation to job	Relationship of individual to sort of work, others in the team, organization goals and values	Psychological contract which develops between person and organization's in the course of the entry procedure
Based on psycho-logical theory	Trait theory	Interactional Theory	Situationalism or Interactional Theory
Most appropriate circumstances	Stable work roles Individuals work on their own in a buyer's market	Rapid change situations Retention of staff important Team working important in smaller organizations	When the senior executive is being head-hunted Seller's market When the job can be adjusted to fit the person

Fig. 33: Fitting Theory to Suit Needs

Employment agencies – Are good if you can identify skills needed. It is a quick fix and the process is speedy. The use of temporary workers can cause problems of inconsistency of work quality and feelings of non-equal treatment can arise (equity theory). There has been an increasing tendency to use temporary workers because it allows for a flexible response to demand fluctuations, especially in production. There has been a call in Germany for legislation or union agreements to ensure that temporary workers receive the same pay as permanent employees.

It can be a useful way to find people and to check their team working capabilities as well as suitability for the task. However, there can be high costs involved.

It helps the risks involved in employment such as redundancy yet the employer has less control over the persons employed. Labor laws may extend employees rights to the disadvantage of the indirect employer of which he might not be aware. For example, an employee working for an employment agency could have the same right to representation in the works council of the employer and in that of the agency.

Executive selection consultants—These advertise on your behalf and screen applicants. When looking for particular skills or experience these consultants can be useful as they may have a data bank of information.

Executive search consultants—So-called 'headhunters'. They tend to be used mainly for senior positions but also for sales staff or technical staff which are in short supply. The process can be slow and of course it puts any prospective employee in a more powerful position and candidates can be more demanding.

Online Services—There are a number of offline services available where employers can enter job details and where candidates can offer their skills. These can be useful but the process can be time consuming. Some services from labor offices are free of charge whilst private portals usually charge employers a fee. These services are being increasingly used by job seekers.

Social Networks — There are a number of professional social networks which can be a useful source for searching for potential staff. Individuals post their CV's and can be searched for. This is a sort of do-it-yourself head hunting. It requires a long term approach building contacts and connections because most persons do not make their personal data generally available.

Selection

Managers who take a person-job fit approach will use techniques including interviewing but there are dangers in this:

> *Interviews can be inaccurate. Hunter and Hunter (1984)[138] noted that interviews have a predictive value of 0.14 on a scale of 0 (chance) to 1 (perfect prediction).*

> *First impressions are made in the first five minutes.*

> *The interviewer looks for reasons to reject rather than accept — the 'least bad' gets the job.*

> *The so-called 'Halo and Horns' effect, where interviewers perception of one good or bad comment influences perception. The halo, and its opposite, the horns or devil effect, is defined as "the influence of a global evaluation on evaluations of individual attributes of a person". (Nisbett & Wilson, 1977)[139]. According to publication by Creighton University[140], this is caused by:*

Membership in a weak team

(Guilt by association) The good player on a weak team usually ends up with lower ratings than he or she would have if on a winning team.

The self-comparison effect

The person who doesn't do the job as we remember we did it when we held that job will suffer more than those who do work unfamiliar to us.

The boss as perfectionist

Because the manager's expectation level is so high, he or she is somewhat disappointed and rates people lower than they deserve.

The effect of the person's past record

The person who has done good work in the distant past is assumed to be okay in the recent past.

The impressions of past good work

Carries over into later periods.

The effect of recentness. The person who does an outstanding job the previous week or the day before the evaluation discussion can offset mediocre performance over the previous months."

Also it can be noted that:

> *Appearances affect judgment*

> *It is difficult to assess skills and abilities in an interview*

Structured interviews are an attempt to remedy this. McDaniel, et al (1994)[141] contradicts the view that interviews are inaccurate, mentioned above. They found that interviews were actually better than their reputation.

Other tools which can be used are:

Application forms – it is important that the application form contains the relevant questions and that the applicant has the opportunity to express themselves.

References – sometimes these are of doubtful use and there are considerable restrictions on the content of them. It is unlikely that there will be any clear statements of detriment to the candidate. Informal calls to previous employers must only be made with the specific permission of the candidate. Even then, a previous employer may be reluctant to say much due to date protection laws. In my experience as an employer, I have often found the best employees were those who had be recommended to me. Unfortunately, like head hunting, that process can take a long time. I am afraid you won't know what you have got until they have been working for you beyond the trial period! As a leader, it is up to you to get as much out of the people you have got rather than making the eternal search for the perfect employee.

Cv's. These may be 'tuned' to suit the job description so they give only a basic indication.

Personality tests and self-assessment tests. These can be useful. I have found the use of Belbin's team attribute test very useful in practice because it can give an indication of how well the prospective employee might fit into the team. That can be more of an issue than certain skills or experience which are often easier to acquire than personality traits!

Literacy tests. This depends on the needs of the job and may not always have priority but if you need somebody who is able to write business correspondence, for example, it would be important. It might also be important to know if the candidate has basic arithmetic, and particularly computer skills. The modern business world also may require ability in e-so-

cial skills and of course telephone skills if the person is to be employed in sales for example.

Ability/aptitude tests. These can be useful where particular skills are required.

Assessment centers will give you a chance to take a closer look at personalities but the amount of effort may exceed the possibilities of smaller organizations.

Trial employment, which is more or less normal these days in employment contracts can give you a chance to see somebody's suitability. You can offer a short trial of say a week to test suitability but always remember that employees will be on their best behavior if they are seriously wanting to have the job.

Activity

Do a survey in your organization to see how the above issues are handled. Could you make any recommendations for changes or improvements?

Induction

Anxiety is caused by uncertainty and formal programs try to reduce this. There is a need for briefing about expectations. According to Swanson (2005)[142] anxiety peaks on the first day and Latack (1981)[143] states that this is due to multiple role transitions. Wanous (1992)[144] offers guidelines for designing anxiety reduction programs.

> *Include realistic information*
>
> *Provide general support and reassurance*
>
> *Show how others coped*
>
> *Discuss how others managed*
>
> *Rehearse the procedure*
>
> *Teach self-control of feelings*
>
> *Associate stressors with newcomers*

Conflict and disagreement

Types of conflict and behavior

Conflict can be both overt (openly apparent) or covert (hidden) and is linked closely to the fear of the consequences of action. Because overt action could cause a loss of personal position, jeopardize promotion and open opposition could become obvious, that opposition will go 'underground' and become covert.

Additionally, there are ideas of legitimacy. The conflict remains covert because it is believed that the other side is acting legitimately.

Conflict is often caused due to the exclusion of certain parties from the discussion or from information – e.g. people being made redundant yet finding out afterwards that decisions have been made. This demonstrates one of the advantages to employers of works councils (even though many employers actually fear them) as it puts a long term process into place which can avoid conflict before it escalates. Openness and the provision of information is a key concept in running an organization which is proposing to be holistic in nature. Taking the principle of 'none are enemies' discussed in the first volume in this series, we can reconsider our stance towards people in our organization. At the moment you would announce redundancies to employees without intensive prior discussion and sound reasoning, you will undoubtedly have built up an 'them and us' situation and provoked the employees affected into a conflict situation where you are seen as the enemy. Just as employees can be affected by covert conflict, it is possible for them also to suspect hidden agendas on the employer side once trust has been lost.

Taken-for-granted assumptions often cause conflict and can be unfounded. This applies to employers and employees alike. The golden rule is here never to make any assumptions about others. It is rather like the old splinter and beam adage. First take the beam out of your own eye before you take it out of the other person's.

Conflict potential can also occur because neither side is actually aware of a conflict. There is also conflict which is actually constructive as well as that which is destructive.

Often conflicts are approached in win-lose terms. It is possible for both sides to be losers. But many conflicts are potentially win-win, e.g. pay negotiations. Seeing conflicts as win-lose instead of win-win makes them difficult to resolve. Win-win is only possible if the conflict is overt and there is a mechanism for open discussion. The challenge to you as a leader is to make sure your dealings are always open and honest. In this way you can build trust. You can also encourage participation (even without a works council) by sharing issues and laying cards on the table. Even in a crisis situation you are more likely to come up with solutions in the interests of all those concerned. If your organization has built a reputation for hire fire and you wish to change this culture, then you will have a hefty challenge building trust of course.

Assertion and co-operation in conflicts

Responses fall into five categories reflecting different degrees of co-operativeness and assertiveness (Ruble and Thomas, 1976)[145]:

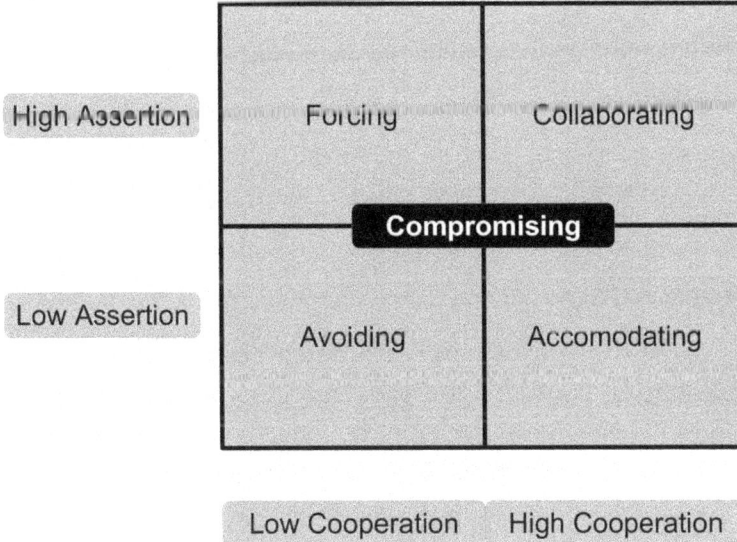

	Low Cooperation	High Cooperation
High Assertion	Forcing	Collaborating
	Compromising	
Low Assertion	Avoiding	Accomodating

Fig. 34: Conflict Solving

Forcing

The need to satisfy one's own need at the expense of others, e.g. formal authority, physical threats, majority rule, etc.. This results in resentment and hostility.

Accommodating

This is about satisfying other's needs at ones own expense. "How to win friends and influence people", (Dale Carnegie, 2009[146]). People can take advantage and a manager can lose self-esteem and others' respect ending in a win-lose situation.

Avoiding conflict

This is common when a manager lacks self-confidence and ends in a lose-lose situation because the issues are never resolved. It is frustrating but it can nevertheless be used on certain occasions for example, when time is short.

Compromising

This can be useful with complex situations or issues but it does require sufficient time to implement it.

Collaborating

This is the only true win-win strategy. Its effectiveness depends on the conflict. One should focus on the problem not the people. The manager must be assertive and yet co-operative. It is not always possible when there is a sense of urgency.

Ideal solutions to conflict would end in a consensus where every party feels re-united in purpose. Unfortunately this is not always possible because the will to collaborate and reach consensus and clearly see the other party's needs is not always available or time may be pressing a short term solution.

Layers of conflict

Conflict can be quite comples and there may be misunderstandings with people 'getting hold of the wrong end of the stick'. This must be recognized but it can be so deep that it is difficult to bring it to the surface.

People also have differences in their values and beliefs. Each individual brings his or her own experiences and beliefs into the work situation. Some occur even during the organizational experience. Sometimes it has to do with structural divisions, age, culture, etc. and this needs to be recognized. Knowing your colleagues and the workforce is extremely important here. Also accepting differences as something positive, as previously discussed is essential.

There are bound to be differences in interest. Position, status and resources are all scarce commodities so people naturally form alliances to get or defend them.

One also needs to be aware of interpersonal differences. Some people have difficulty "getting on" with others and there can be personality clashes. These can be more difficult to resolve and may often have to do with issues like self esteem.

People have strong feelings and emotions and one is not always aware of the reasons and we may find ourselves denying how strongly one feels.

Ways of managing conflict

Non-intervention. One tries to ignore the problem because of the difficulty in dealing with the conflict. Constructive conflict may be acceptable but the avoidance of dealing with destructive conflict will be seen as avoiding managerial responsibility.

One should try to prevent conflict happening in the first place and encourage a climate in which people seek win-win solutions.

One way to avoid conflict even brewing is to establish common goals. Often we find ourselves on a different wavelength because we have not yet arrived at a common purpose.

We can try restructuring the issue so as to get down to the root causes and find a common way ahead.

Improving the levels and processes of communication can also help the flow of information and help avoid conflict happening.

When the conflict is serious and damaging one may need to intervene by:

> *Facilitating (Giving individuals support, letting people explain their feelings and trying to put things into perspective.*

> *Imposing. Forcing or threatening into stopping conflicting behavior. This may make people feel more angry or resentful. Be careful not to blame the wrong party. This is the scapegoat syndrome and may not really solve the problem. Blame is a bad philosophy in an organization so you should check if your organization does not display the symptoms of a culture of blame.*

> *Negotiating — either yourself or encouraging others to do so.*

Activity

Think of a recent conflict, either at home or in your work or place of study have recently occurred. How would you analyze the situation and how would you tackle it based on the above ideas?

Non-Violent Communication

Marshall Rosenberg (2009)[147] approaches the subject of communication and conflict from a different point of view. According to Rosenberg, conflict and violence occur from the assumption that other people are responsible for one's problems and that they therefore deserve some form of punishment.

Rosenberg tells of an experience with a man in prison for murdering his friend during a fight. He taught the prisoner about the different ways anger occurs and erupts into violence, about being responsible for one's emotions, and about nonviolent communication. After having absorbed the points of Rosenberg's lessons, this prisoner stated that if he had understood how to manage his anger before, he would have never killed his friend. Rosenberg suggests various causes of violence, one of which is that people in western societies usually learn to be judgemental of everything at an early age. This judging creates not only anger that can lead to conflict and violence, but Rosenberg believes, is violence itself. People also tend to be critical due to actions that their parents, society, or even they themselves deem to be wrong or bad. Gandhi agrees with Rosenberg. He is of the opinion that judging everything as right or wrong leads to violence because people tend to fight against what they perceive as being "wrong."[148] We cover this subject in more detail in our book, Creating a Nonviolent Culture in a Modern Organization, Baermann and Engelking (2013).

Activity

Thinking about such a situation as in the last activity, what underlying needs can you identify in the conflicting parties?

The Question of Power

Power and Conflict

Power is itself is considered by some authors to be in itself a form of violence. Wilhelm Haller[149] discussed the issue of power in the works of Martin Buber, whom we mentioned in the first volume:

The Principle of Dialog

The problem of the power issue can perhaps best be represented in the dialogical principle of Martin Buber. Broadly, this principle states that the human being is coordinated to towards the 'Thou' which is necessary for the dialog to become human. The encounter with the 'Thou' happens when I discover the other person in his otherness and I accept and realize him as a subject of equal value. However, when I accept the other in his otherness and resist the temptation to 'convince him of my conviction by any means possible', when I take the path with Rabbi Nachman, allowing the other, in the path of service to go his own way in freedom as God gives us the freedom to go our own way, then the different points of view often result in tensions which are felt as pain and suffering. Our avoidance of pain misleads us then to break up the dialog (or rather perhaps to avoid it altogether) and to force the other person to my point of view with any means necessary — in the political world, even to the point of physical destruction.

We attempt to keep the upper hand. To keep the majority and power in order to push through our ideas without the troublesome and drawn out painful process of dialog.

However, this leads to the situation where the one who thinks differently loses his status as 'Thou' and becomes an 'It', a mere object who, when I get the upper hand, will be doomed to becoming heteronomous rather than autonomous.

Seen from a collective point of view, this how oligarchies, parties and factions come to be.

The dialog is then restricted to the faction or group of like-minded within which no tension can develop.

Between the factions (or parties) only monologues take place. Only show case speeches are held and dialog goes missing whilst the process of becoming human (incarnation) is blocked.

However, as humans are made for dialog, missing it will be felt as a fault, even if only subconsciously. Then the attempt will be made to compensate for this fault (this is the addiction characteristic of which Burkhardt talks) and thus the number of people within the faction with whom dialog is exchanged and accepted becomes smaller and smaller. In an extreme case — it is best demonstrated by Stalin — it will end up in complete isolation and loneliness with a persecution complex to top it all.

Activity

In such a conflict we were thinking about in the previous activities, did you notice anybody trying to achieve majorities or could you see factions forming? Could you observe people trying to push through their ideas and avoiding dialog? Applying Buber's ideas, could you identify a I-It rather than an I-thou approach on the part of the parties?

Power and Involvement

Coming back to Etzioni (1971)[150], he argues that a particular kind of power and involvement usually go together. Most common are 1, 5 and 9:

Kinds of Involvement		
Alienative	**Calculative**	**Moral**
1	2	3
4	5	6
7	8	9

Fig. 35: Etzioni's Types of Power

Coercive power produces alienative involvement. Remunerative produces calculative involvement while normative power produces moral involvement and vice-versa.

Types of power

Etzioni (ibid.) defines four kinds of power into which organizations can be classified:

1. Coercive power entailing the possible application of physical force. Examples are prisons, a concentration camp, etc.

2. Remunerative or utilitarian power which is exercised by the manipulation of material resources. Example of this are rewards based on wages, salaries or bonuses.

3. Normative or identitive power which is exercised through the manipulation and allocation of symbols. Typical examples are love, affection and prestige. This method can be employed to extract compliance from others.

4 Persuasive or suggestive power. This is found in religious organizations, universities and charities.

Activity

Think of various situations where you experience or observe the above types of power.

Types of involvement

Each of these types of power is contrasted by Etzioni through the three kinds of involvement of the individual as shown in fig. 13:

Alienative involvement. This is intensely negative because it means a dissociation of the member from the organization. This happens for example with convicts and prisoners of war.

Calculative involvement. There is little intensity and is positive or negative in a mild way. This is typical of many business relationships.

Moral involvement. This achieves a favorable view of the organization and is very intense. Examples are the loyal party or church member.

Power and Influence

The traditional boss and subordinate role is changing. Now knowledge workers may have more power because organizations increasingly rely on knowledge within the organization for competitive advantage. Additionally, people's sensitivity towards democratic decision making is putting pressure on leadership to include ideas from employees in the process. Despite the fact that conservative governments in some countries (the UK for example) have been increasingly attempting to reduce workers' rights since the beginning of the millennium, employees in many countries still have the right to consultation and 'Mitbestimmung' (joint decision making).

Influence occurs when a person affects what another does or thinks whereas power is the potential to influence others and authority is formal power bestowed because of position.

Continuing Etzioni's thinking in our discussion, it is worth noting that he was enrolled in a special academy set up by the philosopher Martin Buber, whose thinking has also influenced this work. Incidentally, it might be worth mentioning that he also questioned whether the right to personal privacy was not sometimes detrimental to society (Etzioni, 1999)[151]. It could be argued that the demand for privacy can also sometimes be used as a form of power and may be classified under 'invisible power' as discussed below.

Activity

Do you think I have thrown in a red herring here where I talk about privacy and power? Can you think of examples of the exercise of such power?

Four forms of visible power

1. Position power. This is the most obvious form and stems from a person's formal position. It is the authority to make decisions and reward people. This can also be compared to French and Raven's (1959) 'legitimate power'[152].

2. Expert power. This power comes from the need for experts with particular knowledge or skills and can often delay decisions. Often people are given the power to make decisions for others because of their assumed specialist knowledge. A good example of this is the surgeon who has the power of life and death in certain situations.

3. Dependence power — e.g. striking or withdrawing co-operation. Emerson et al. (e.g. 1983)[153] carried out extensive research into power dependence demonstrating that mutual dependence brings people together. If people are mutually dependent they are more likely to form relationships which derive influence from 'tit for tat'. If there are differences in dependency a power imbalance can occur leading to conflict.

4. Personal power. Subtle persuasion such as personal charm, charisma, tact or guile. Bass, Wurster and Alcock (1961)[154] discovered that followers often make their leaders and that the real power comes rather from below than from the top down. Admiration and thinking the world of someone bestows power and authority upon them. Maybe we should be thinking of the idea of *followship* as well as leadership!

Activity

Thinking of the people 'in power' who have some influence on your life, make a table categorizing them according to these forms of visible power.

Invisible power

1. Often having contacts and connections can be more important than skills. It is a case rather of who you know than what you know. Vitamin 'C' then stands for 'connections'.

2. Dominant norms and cultures. This is a power based on widely accepted society norms such as racialism. 'The way we do things around here'.

3. Informal networks. These can also exclude people. Not being a member of the 'in-crowd' can create a barrier to advancement.

4. Control of information. People who control information are often called 'gate-keepers'.

The Power of Tyranny

Gary Hammel (2011)[155] talks of the cost to organizations of the type of power prevalent in hierarchical organizations in no uncertain terms:

> *Finally, there's the cost of tyranny. The problem isn't the occasional control freak; it's the hierarchical structure that systematically disempowers lower-level employees. For example, as a consumer you have the freedom to spend $20,000 or more*

on a new car, but as an employee you probably don't have the authority to requisition a $500 office chair. Narrow an individual's scope of authority, and you shrink the incentive to dream, imagine, and contribute.

Negotiating and bargaining

Formal and informal

Positional bargaining. In this event, each party has a demand which it seeks to advance. It is a Win-Lose situation.

Hard. In this case negotiations are a contest of wills, threats, distrust, deceptions.

Soft. Both parties seeking agreement. Give and take. Maybe it is not always the best. Friendliness maybe not the main issue.

Joint problem solving. This is the real alternative to positional bargaining and respects each others concerns.

Collaboration – know everyone needs to find an agreement. The outcome of negotiations are more likely to be satisfactory.

Approaches to negotiation

Separate the people from the problem

Focus on interests not positions

Invent options for mutual gain

Insist on objective criteria

Behaviors avoided by skilled negotiators:

Irritators

Defend/attack spirals

Too many arguments

Counter proposals

Behaviors to be embraced by negotiators

Flagging – "I would like to suggest."

Testing, understanding summarizing

Ask lots of questions

Motives commentary

Telling people why you are suggesting something.

Assess your own performance

Difficult situations

Fisher and Ury (1981)[156] state that there are three pervasive worries for negotiators

1.   What if the other party is more powerful?

2.   What if the other party will not play?

3.   What if the other party use dirty tricks?

In this event you should work out your 'BATNA' (ibid.) – the Best Alternative To A Negotiated Agreement.

Management Teams

When a small group of people come to work together for a specific purpose, we talk of a team. In management this takes on a special meaning and has become in itself a way of managing. Linking on to our previous discussion on empowerment, we can imagine a group of people who manage a task amongst themselves without the requirement of being directed.

However, the question arises as to how to choose the right members of a team. Just on the basis of skills could end up with a bunch of people who really cannot get on or do not really complement each other.

Meredith Belbin (1981)[157] has come up with a concept which has gained popularity. Intensive research initially amongst employees of IBM led him to identify a set of team roles which, when properly balanced, have a considerable knock-on effect. His famous formula is 2+2=5.

Based on nine different team roles, an analysis is made via psychometric testing of the potential team members. The roles are as follows:

Plant

This is used to describe the sort of person who is creative and think out of the box. They are useful for bring in new ideas or innovative concepts. Unfortunately, being free-thinkers they tend to be less interested in details. Sometimes they are compared to the 'absent-minded professor'. If you have too many in a team it can cause things never to be brought to fruition. Plenty if ideas but nothing happens.

Resource Investigator

A resource investigator is very good for getting contacts and finding where to get things done. Their interests might be more outside of the team and usually know what is going on around the world. They do not mind borrowing ideas and might be better at this than with coming up with new ideas. Might be more interested in networking than seeing a project through.

Co-ordinator

This is the typical person for taking over the role of chairperson in the team. They are good at mediating and seeing the strength in others. They should be good at delegating tasks and making sure things get done. They prefer to do this than get their own hands dirty which can cause resentment.

Shaper

This kind of person is very much about getting the job done. Essential in a team because he or she can often drive the team when despondency sets in. They would like the team to do its best and will try to encourage others to do this. Sometimes being pushy can cause resentments in the team and they may be impartient with those who do not comply with their aims.

Monitor Evaluator

They play an observing role and are more detached in their viewpoint. Often bring clear thinking into the team. Sometimes they are too critical which can suffocate enthusiasm from others or squash new ideas. They are not usually inspiring leaders.

Team worker

You certainly can use team workers in your team. Without them you will probably make little headway. Often they are not even noticed because they work in the background and are not seeking glory for themselves. They may not be so good at making decisions themselves.

Implementer

This person puts things into reality which others have discussed. Usually they are efficient and loyal to the team. Sometimes they are the type that do work which nobody else will do. They do tend to be rather inflexible and are not too keen on new ideas which are only half baked. They prefer to stick with the tried and tested.

This is the traditional perfectionist who prefers to first move forward when everything is one hundred percent. He or she will take a lot of trouble to check that everything is perfect. Accuracy is important which can take time and frustrate others who want to get on with the job.

Specialist

They love to learn more in their area of specialization and will often know a lot about their subject area. If they do not know something they will investigate this for the sake of knowledge. They are good at concentrating at a task but may not help with things which they do not consider important.

This role was later added because original research was not required in the early exercises for simulating the roles.

Activity

Take a close look at the team roles above. Where would you see your tendencies? Give yourself marks out of 10 for each of these roles in terms of how you think they fit your traits. Ask a colleague or a member of your family to do the same. What does this tell you about working together?

Virtual Teams

We speak of virtual teams when the members of a group working together are geographically dispersed. They are often temporary in nature and use mainly electronic means for communication.

Also it needs to be noted that teams are not restricted to members within the organization and one can expect a considerable amount of boundary crossing where teams are composed of a combination of members for example from an outsourcing supplier, marketing, end customer and so on.

Kimball (1997)[158] points out that teams have changed:

From	To
Fixed team membership	Shifting team membership
All team members drawn from within the organization	Team members can include people from outside the organization (clients, collaborators)
Team members are dedicated 100% to the team	Most people are members of multiple teams
Team members are co-located organizationally and geographically	Team members are distributed organizationally and geographically
Teams have a fixed starting and ending point	Teams form and reform continuously
Teams are managed by a single manager	Teams have multiple reporting relationships with different parts of the organization at different times

---

Activity

*What might be the advantages for motivation of individual em-
ployees by using virtual teams? What difficulties might you encounter if you were operating flexible working hours as described
above together with team working in some form?*

Criticisms of teams

Some research[159] seems to show that teams do not perform as
well as one would expect. Whilst they tend to get extra resources, poor coordination and motivation get in the way of
them performing in an optimal way. Sometimes teams compete against each other which is not necessarily the best way
of getting the job done.

Willis (2007)[160] states:

> *Going off on digressions and Other Tangentsdiverts from the
> common objective of teamwork. It is possible for members of a
> team to ignore what had brought them together and start dis-
> cussing other topics which are not meaningful to the com-
> pany. In a manufacturing company like this, the most impor-
> tant thing in jump starting the profitability is to ensure total
> commitment of all the employees in the company. This can be
> easily achieved via an individual coaching and performance
> monitoring by the company. However, in a teamwork situa-
> tion, the monitoring and analysis of such levels is difficult be-
> cause some lazy guys will be hiding behind hardworking indi-
> viduals.*

Groupthink

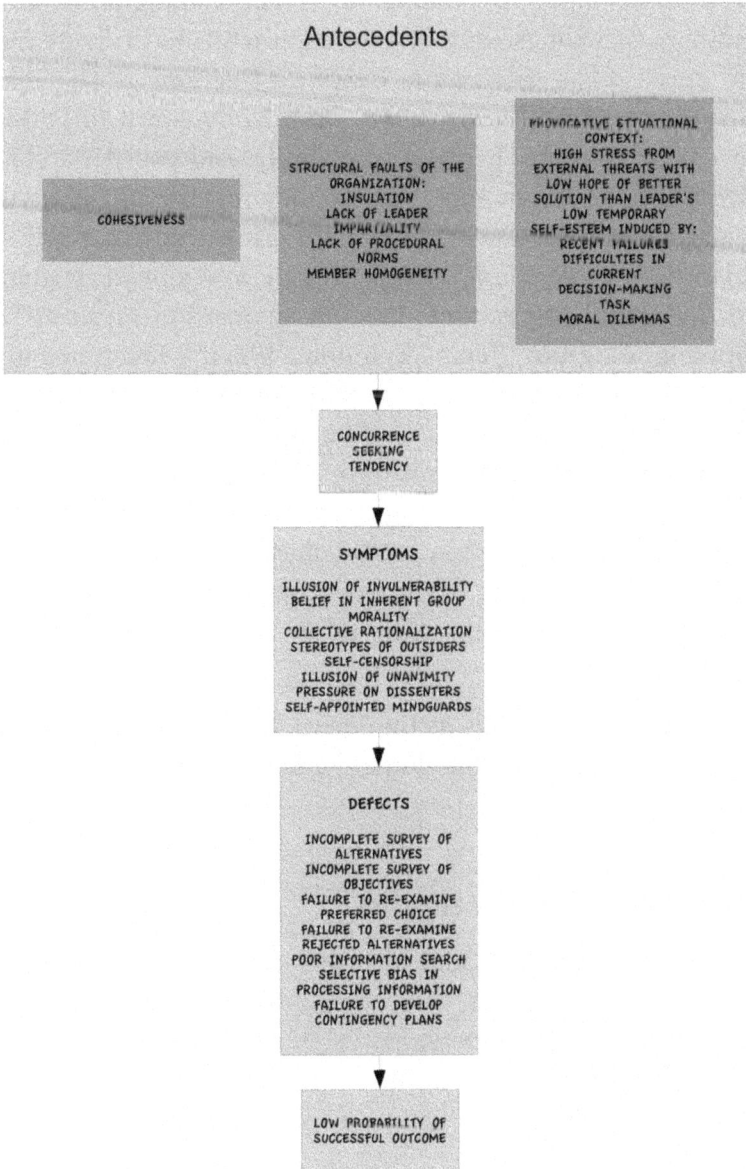

Fig. 36: Groupthink model (adapted from Janis & Mann, 1977)

Groupthink is defined (Janis, 1971)[161] as 'the mode of thinking that persons engage in when concurrence-seeking becomes so dominant in a cohesive in-group that it tends to override realistic appraisal of alternative courses of action ... The main principle of groupthink, which I offer in the spirit of Parkinson's Law, is this: The more amiability and esprit de corps there is among the members of a policy-making in-group, the greater the danger that independent critical thinking will be replaced by groupthink, which is likely to result in irrational and dehumanizing actions directed against out-groups'. The following diagram (Janis & Mann, 1977)[162] illustrates this process:In the voluntary sector or in private life, teams are often composed of the people we like or we find share our opinions. Just this can lead to groupthink. The best way to avoid this is to use a team building model based on psychometric testing such as the Belbin model mentioned before. That is more likely to be objective and chooses team members based on their complementing each other rather than being the same.

Also, using such models as the Johari Window mentioned below can increase the consciousness of the dangers of groupthink.

The Johari Window model

The Johari window model is a tool for understanding and training self-awareness, personal development, improving communications, interpersonal relationships, group dynamics, team development and inter-group relationships and can help when working with teams to solve some of the problems mentioned above.

It was developed by American psychologists Joseph Luft and Harry Ingham (1955)[163], calling it 'Johari' after combining their first names, Joe and Harry and emphasises on and influences co-operation, inter-group development and interpersonal development.

It operates between the individual and the group by identifying four areas of perspective or 'windows':

1. The open area which is about that which is known by the person about him/herself and is also known by others.

2. The Blind area or 'blindspot' which is that which is unknown by the person about him/herself but which others know.

3. The Hidden area of the hidden self, avoided self or 'façade' which is that which the person knows about him/herself that others do not know.

4. The Unknown area or unknown self being that which is unknown by the person about him or herself and is also unknown by others.

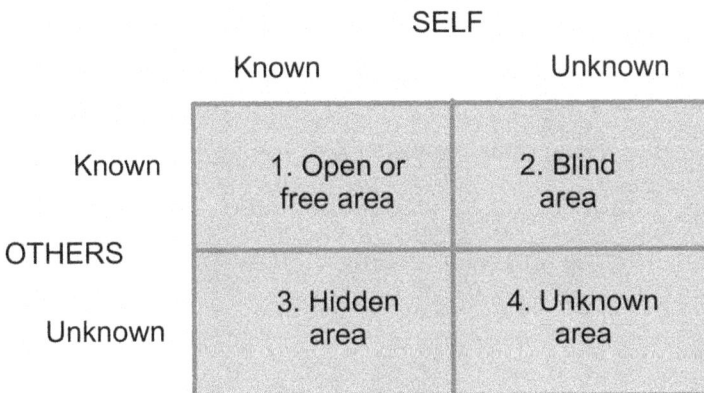

| | SELF | |
	Known	Unknown
Known	1. Open or free area	2. Blind area
OTHERS		
Unknown	3. Hidden area	4. Unknown area

Fig. 37: Johari Window

The areas can be changed in size to reflect each team members situation. The model can be used as a discussion point and items entered into the square.

Servant Leadership and teams

In our first book in this series, we discussed various types of leadership. One of these was Robert Greenleaf's concept of servant leadership.

Research carried out by Irving and Longbottom (2007)[164] came to the conclusion that "servant leadership themes are recommended for those leading in the team-based context:

a) Providing accountability,

b) Supporting and resourcing,

c) Engaging in honest self-evaluation,

d) Fostering collaboration,

e) Communicating with clarity, and

f) Valuing and appreciating".

Conclusions

We have discussed a number of ideas which can influence working together in groups. As you will no doubt have realized, this is a vast and endless subject which could only be covered sketchily in so few pages. I would suggest to the reader that he or she picks up the themes and investigate further.

It would seem that the working world is moving to a less hierarchical and more group oriented way of working which also requires a new kind of leadership, as discussed elsewhere. It is necessary for us to make changes in two directions: from the individual towards the group (requiring less individualism and more collectivism) and from the organization to the group (requiring a reduction of coercive power and an increased willingness to respect the ideas from those one used to call 'subordinates').

This makes the acquisition of management and leadership skills no longer a luxury but a necessity for all in a position of management.

As Lanny Goodman (2008, p. viii)[165] has stated so well:

Americans invented "modern scientific management", the foundation on which all contemporary management has been built. It gave us huge growth in productivity. It was ultimately responsible for our ability to win World War II. But now we are its prisoners.

Modern management was designed at a time when capital was scarce and expensive and talent was plentiful and cheap. Today we find our world turned upside down from the days of Frederick Winslow Taylor and others who pioneered the art. From a design perspective alone we should realize that with the economic conditions spun 180°, the assumptions, principles, and practices of what is now "traditional" management must fail.

There are obvious dangers in any changes but we will either rise to the challenge or join the league of those organizations and nations who have neglected to do so.

Part Three

The Organization, Entrepreneurship and Change

Organizational Analysis

Organizations are relatively new. Before 1800 very few people worked in what we call 'organizations'.

The concept is now taken for granted but, 'organizations are necessary and important because they enable people to accomplish what cannot be efficiently accomplished by individuals acting on their own. The maintenance of complex industrial societies is inconceivable without the existence of large-scale organizations, together with a great number of very small organizations'. (Aldrich, 1979, p.3[166]).

Activity

Describe what you think an organization is. Is it a good thing? What are the advantages and disadvantages? Is there a danger of organizations getting out of control – of becoming more powerful than governments?

The agency theory of organizations says that they are rational, unitary, goal-seeking entities. But sometimes, organizations are hard to identify.

The Changing Nature of Organizations

Recent decades have seen a change in the way organizations operate. External factors like the spread of the use of information technologies and communication are opening the way for more flexibility in the way we run our businesses. We are thus seeing the emergence of so-called virtual organizations.

Pang (2001)[167] defines virtual organizations as:

> *A flexible network of independent entities linked by information technology to share skills, knowledge and access to others' expertise in nontraditional ways.*
>
> *A form of cooperation involving companies, institutions and/or individuals delivering a product or service on the basis of a common business understanding. The units participate in the collaboration and present themselves as a unified organization.*
>
> *Virtual organizations do not need to have all of the people, or sometimes any of the people, in one place to deliver their service. The organization exists but you cannot see it. It is a network, not an office.*

One well cited example of a virtual organization is given by the firm Benetton.

Luciano Benetton with his three siblings founded the business near Treviso, Italy in 1965, a small undertaking named "Fratelli Benetton". From its beginning, color was its main them.

Now Benetton is a European or global clothing company. In the first 25 years its turnover was $1 billion worldwide. Based in Italy, it finds itself in a very labor intensive industry. It has to compete in the fast-moving fashion-oriented industry. The company is involved in design, manufacture and distribution. and has adopted a special organizational form which involves subcontracting most operations.

Styling and design is done by outsiders by freelance designers whilst the responsibility for style remains in house. In 1988 over 80% of manufacturing was done outside by 350 contractors who employ about 10,000 people. Only dyeing is done in-house. Even logistics and distribution is done by outsiders. The company has one large warehouse for finished goods yet it has 80 agents to manage the retail system and 4000 shops on a franchise basis.

The company has often received negative press due to advertising practices which have been considered by some to be offensive or even unethical. Their treatment of retail franchisees has also often been the subject of criticism. However, this bad press may in fact one of the factors which has led to the fame and success of the organization, bringing it considerable publicity. The slogan and brand "United Colors of Benetton" which it has used since 1985, in the meantime has become a household word.

The ideology of the organization is very much driven by Luciano Benetton who is also politically active in Italy. His philosophy is very much oriented on free market thinking and principle driven business. The claim is that the company's purpose is around social justice rather than the bottom line[168].

Activity

Where are the boundaries of the Benetton organization? Make a diagram of the organization based on the above description. Which parts are the legal entity and which are not? Should we talk of an operation rather than an organization?

The next question is whether organizations have goals apart from the people within them.

Reminding ourselves of the underlying concept of the *Beans and the Dreams*, we would have to analyze how far such an organization goes in meeting the criteria for a holistic organization. We would have to ask if it meets all the criteria for taking into account the real interests of all of its stakeholders in a balanced manner. In the first part of our investigations, we talked much of principled leadership and cited principles such as the ilbs[169] principles:

> *No-one is an Enemy*
>
> *No-one is a Foreigner*
>
> *Service to All*
>
> *Complete Impartiality*
>
> *Work for Peace*
>
> *True Democracy*
>
> *Equity and Justice*

Activity

How would you assess Benetton with regard to the above principles? What could the managers of the organization do to make it more conform to these ideas? What kind of leadership style does the organization have ? (You may need to do some of your own research to be able to answer these questions). Considering your own organization, how would you answer these same questions?

Many of the ideas describing the organization are based on machine or biological metaphors. Morgan (1986)[170] states, 'It is easy to see how this kind of thinking has relevance for understanding organization and management. For organizations are complex and paradoxical phenomena that can be understood in different ways. Many of our taken for granted ideas about organization are metaphorical, even though we may not recognize them as such.'

If we say that organizations are machines, this would seem to suggest that we think that they operate reliably and efficiently. We might easily loose the human face. In the knowledge society, we might prefer to think of a machine as a brain.

Activity

Choose a company you know of and research it in Internet. Draw a diagram showing how the organization is structured and discuss. Present your findings by summarizing them on a piece of paper. Search for a metaphor for the organization. Does it already have an apparent one or can you invent one?

Terms

Now let us take a look at some of the terms used in organizational analysis.

Differentiation and Integration

Differentiation means breaking down an individual task of the organization into small achievable units.

Integration is the job of putting the different pieces together so that the task can be accomplished effectively.

Transaction costs

These are the costs incurred in the handling of goods and services, negotiating prices and finding and comparing technical
data. If the costs of the time involved are higher than the potential saving, you may not end up 'saving' anything at all.
This may be less important in the private sphere where shop
ping may be seen by some as a leisure activity in itself but in
an organization, we have to pay for these processes and they
are part of the costs incurred.

It is often assumed that an organization can arrange these
transactions within its own boundaries at a lower cost than
elsewhere. This would always make it cheaper to produce in-
house than to buy in the market place. The consequence
would be to have just one big global manufacturer for everything. Unfortunately, organizations become less efficient as
they grow.

According to Powell (1990)[171] frequently recurring transactions which involve uncertainty about their outcomes and can
thus less easily be transferred are more likely to be carried out
within hierarchically organized firms. Simple operations
which are non-repetitive are most likely to be out-sourced.

Activity

*In the case of Benetton, how do you see these rules applying?
What about the organization you chose, are there signs to confirm Powell's theory? Would you see potential for changing this?
Imagine you wish to build a house. Make a list of the criteria you
would set for deciding which work you would out-source and
that which you would do yourself. What reasons are there for*

---

these choices. How much time would you expect to spend compared to buying an existing house or buying a house from a building company?

Bounded rationality

Bounded rationality is the term given to the way we try to tackle solving simple problems. However, managers tend to try to use bounded rationality where it is not appropriate. An example of this is contracts. The delusion makes it difficult for managers to write perfect contracts because in fact it is not known how the other party would react under certain circumstances.

Opportunism

Managers are in looking for their own advantage including 'guile or deceit' (Powell, 1990)[172]. This is rather a cynical way of looking at the issue but it is not unusual for managers to be looking to building their own empires and other less extreme forms of opportunism.

There is also a tendency particularly amongst organizations in the public sector, which in themselves are conceived as not-for-profit organizations to have a self-service culture. What I mean by this is, that certain monopoly situations are created, sometimes by government decree to create such organizations, and then they build hierarchies. At the top of these hierarchies there will often be a president or managing director who is being paid an astronomical salary. The managing members are kept quiet by paying them above average salaries. Typical organizations of this kind are universities, organizations like (in Germany) GEMA[173] (for collecting artist's fees), IHK[174] (Chamber of Commerce) with compulsory membership, GEZ[175] (for collecting telecommunication license fees) and so on. The list is continually growing and finds its counterparts all over the planet. Often the positions held in the organization may be the result of political connections. If you find yourself working in such an organization, you may find it difficult to change things.

Yet the same thing happens in a different way In the private sector. It is not seldom that not the good manager but the one with the right connections who is the one who manages to climb the ladder. Make no mistake, advocating change can harm your career!

This demonstrates the importance of creating a strong identity and shared sense of mission in the organization as a means to limiting the effects of opportunism. Sometimes, external organizations will misuse perceived weaknesses in an organization and they may not identify with the firm's mission. There is also a strong case for more transparency.

Activity

Thinking of your own organization, make a list of the operations which you at present carry out in-house and which are outsourced. What changes would you make and what transaction costs would be involved? What would be your reasons for making these changes and what advantages, costs and disadvantages can you identify? Can you detect any areas of opportunism in your present organization?

Co-operation

Ouchi (1980)[176] sees a possible way of reducing transaction costs through the encouragement of more co-operation and the seeking of advantages for both parties in attempting to create win-win situations.

Traditionally, the equity of transactions is arrived at through the market mechanism or through bureaucracy. Ouchi suggests, in his study of Japanese firms *(Theory Z (1981))*[177], that the conditions for reciprocity and equity can be attained through the socialization of members. In fact, Japanese companies often take on inexperienced workers and train them, keeping them in the womb of the company for their lives and compensating for length of service and number of dependents. Ouchi refers to this as the 'clan' form and makes for very efficient transactions between individuals. Others have suggested that such organizations have very strong cultures.

This idea is elaborated to include the possibility of building such relationships with external suppliers. Powell (1990) discovered, in fact, that many small firms actually grew because of the relationships and contacts they had and these networks often allowed them to build up sizable businesses in a short time.

This would seem to argue for collaboration as a more realistic means of regulating the process of exchange rather than contract.

Activity

Can you identify any relation to the ideas we discussed on leadership in the previous section. Are there concepts here that may

help us find a way of behaving in business which will allow us to
replicate the kind of ideas which Ouchi and Powell advocate and
which might work well in a Japanese culture?

Handy (1988) talks of society moving towards 'Shamrock' organizations and sees three types of people working in organizations. These concepts can be represented as a matrix:

	Explicit (contractual)	Implicit (relational)
External	Market	Network
Internal	Structure (Bureaucracy)	Culture (Clan)

Fig. 38: Organizational Transaction

1. **The Professional core** — managers, supervisors, professors
   etc. They provide the framework of the organization and
   possess the key knowledge resources. They are expensive
   and therefore have to buy in work on a contractual basis.
   This is provided by the:

2. The Contractual fringe

3. **The flexible labor force** — who do not work for a career but usually for money or socialization.

Each of these groups has special needs which need to be catered for.

Activity

Try applying the above ideas to the company you are researching. Draw a matrix and place the functions in the respective areas. Comment on how applicable Handy's idea is. Do you see signs of these developments? What are the advantages and disadvantages for all parties in these different models?

Towards the virtual organization

The opportunities provided by ICT (Information and Communications Technology) means that it is now possible for organizations to work globally and around the clock. An example of this is software companies who use a virtual contractual fringe for programming. Book publishers may also have printing carried out in India, while the typesetting is produced elsewhere. Car manufacturers can have a range of globally dispersed suppliers. Call centers are often located elsewhere (although there are sometimes language problems with this). No doubt there will be further developments of this in the future. Additionally, more and more people are working from home, reaching currently a level of some 25% of employed persons in the UK for example. This does not always work as efficiently as one would wish and there are also transactional costs which need to be considered. Customers may not like being handled by foreign sales persons who do not intimately understand their culture and this can incur losses for the organization. The issues surrounding these kind of decisions are very complex and should not be entertained unless everything has been carefully considered. It is important to involve all the stakeholders involved before actually making a final decision. This is particularly important when it may involve human resource issues, loss of jobs or relocation.

One of the reasons that has led to an increased application of homeworking is the difficulties of traveling to work in urbanized and centralized cultures such as the UK. Countries such as Germany, which has a highly decentralized economy and industry has less need for home working as many people live and work locally. Whilst some 15 million people in the USA work from home and only relatively few in Germany, even here it is increasing considerably. A recent survey in Germany related that 82% of those asked would prefer to work from home[178].

Activity

What scope might there be for virtual working in your organization? How much is practiced at present? What advantages and disadvantages are associated with this?

Organizational structure and culture

Deal and Kennedy (1982)[179] define organizational culture as 'the way we things get done around here'. This definition could be confused with structure. The main difference is that culture is more the intangible things, shared values, ways of doing things, relationships, etc., whereas structure can more easily be expressed by charts and a description of the routines. Deal and Kennedy (1982)[180] also describe culture in terms of **risk** and speed of **feedback** in an organization.

Risk = the degree of uncertainty of success in the work it carries out

Feedback = how quickly people receive knowledge of the effect of their actions.

Deal and Kennedy describe these categories as follows:

Tough guy, macho culture

A world of individualists who regularly take high risks and get quick feedback on whether their actions were right or wrong.

Work hard / play hard culture

Fun and action are the rule here, and employees take few risks, all with quick feedback; to succeed, the culture encourages them to maintain a high level of relatively low-risk activity.

Bet your company culture

Cultures with big-stakes decisions, where years pass before employees know whether decisions have paid off. A high-risk, slow feedback environment.

Process culture

A world of little or no feedback where employees find it hard to measure what they do; instead they concentrate on how it's done. We have another name for this culture when the process gets out of control — bureaucracy![181]

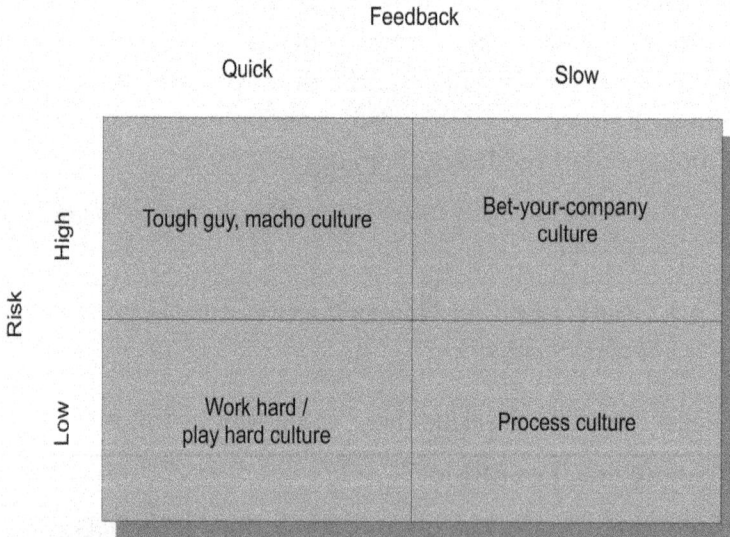

Feedback

Quick   Slow

		High	Tough guy, macho culture	Bet-your-company culture

Risk

		Low	Work hard / play hard culture	Process culture

Fig. 39: Deal and Kennedy – Organizational Culture

The meaning for management studies has been developed from anthropology, where it refers to the shared life of a community. It includes symbols, myths, legends etc. This model becomes difficult to apply, however, as organizations become more fluid.

In the meantime, it is recognized that an organization needs to have a strong culture because everybody is then aware of how things operate and thus reduces the necessity for rigid rules and structures. Thus, if a culture is weak, it requires a more rigid structure if it is going to survive.

Activity

What do you think the word 'culture' means when applied to an organization? Do you think it makes sense to talk of organizations having a culture? Do you think there are real differences in culture between organizations?

It has been argued that successful management must be carried out by managing meaning rather than structures. Such an organization is able to respond faster and more flexibly.

Ouchi (1981)[182] saw the secret of success of Japanese companies as being closely linked to their strong cultures in contrast to large American companies which relied on rigid structures. Japanese companies paid more attention to human relationships and those American companies which were successful shared some of the characteristics of Japanese firms.

Peters & Waterman (1982)[183] pointed to the danger of just adopting Japanese ideas instead suggesting the idea of **'loose and tight coupling'** which means that firms with strong identification to core values need to pay less attention to formal structures and require less detailed instructions. Deal & Kennedy (1982)[184] point out that the Japanese culture, with its emphasis on conformity, is in itself strong and is a factor for the country's success. Accordingly, people expect conformity to cultural ideals.

Japan's success is also due to other factors such as the availability of low cost financing and the population is more homogeneous. This is often not true in European and American countries and it may not be possible to implant Japanese cultural concepts on the western mind.

Therefore this is a very complex issue and has to be tackled differently according to the type of organization and the area of activity. Running a hospital is going to be different from running a car factory.

Activity

Try to describe the culture of your own organization or of an organization you know. Make a list under the following headings:

Basic values

Beliefs

Things taken for granted

Stories and myths

Rituals

Language and slang

Décor of offices and buildings

How people dress

How do they address each other

Parties, meetings – how they are held

What kind of people work there

What is the boss's attitude

Now draw the above matrix and mark the area which is nearest to the company you chose above. Also draw in any organizations you know of. Talk about these cultures and ask yourself what type of culture suits you as a person best. If we can talk of organizations having culture, what about people? Where would you place our society on this matrix. Draw in some other national cultures you know about.

Handy's Models

Power Culture

Handy (1985)[185] also defines four types of culture. You may be familiar with the type of culture often found in small companies which Handy refers to as the **Power Culture** which is centered on central control but with few rules. Decision-making tends to happen more by coincidence than design. Such organizations are responsive but rely very much on individuals for their success who are judged accordingly. Often the atmosphere can become very competitive and people may become frustrated and leave when they see little progress or are heavily criticized. Handy symbolizes the power culture in the following diagram:

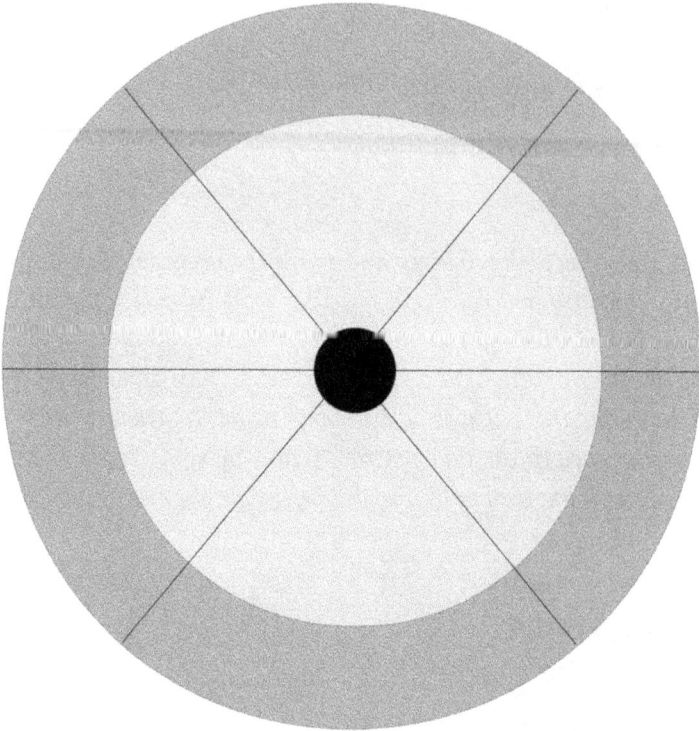

Fig. 40: Handy (1985) Power Culture

Role Culture

This is often referred to as a bureaucracy and has a highly structured and formalized organization. It is usually hierarchical and work is governed by a strict set of rules and procedures. Individuals and their personal power are relatively unimportant. They have the advantage of offering employees high security and are used particularly where work has to carried out to (often publicly) accountable standards. Government bodies and local authorities are obvious examples but some large companies are also run on these lines. Handy pictures this kind of organization as a temple:

Fig. 41: Handy (1985) Role Culture

Task Culture

This type of culture is oriented more on the project or the job. The strands of the net vary in thickness and signify the strength of their influence. The knots signify the points of power. This type of culture is prevalent amongst task cultures. The main thing is to get the job done. There are often task-oriented groups or teams who produce the work. The advantage for the individual is that he or she is often left to work on their own. Ability is the main source of respect. Control from senior managers is more general in nature and people are left to their own devices. It works well when resources abound. If things go bad, however, morale is likely to drop and rules may be introduced changing the culture into a role or power culture.

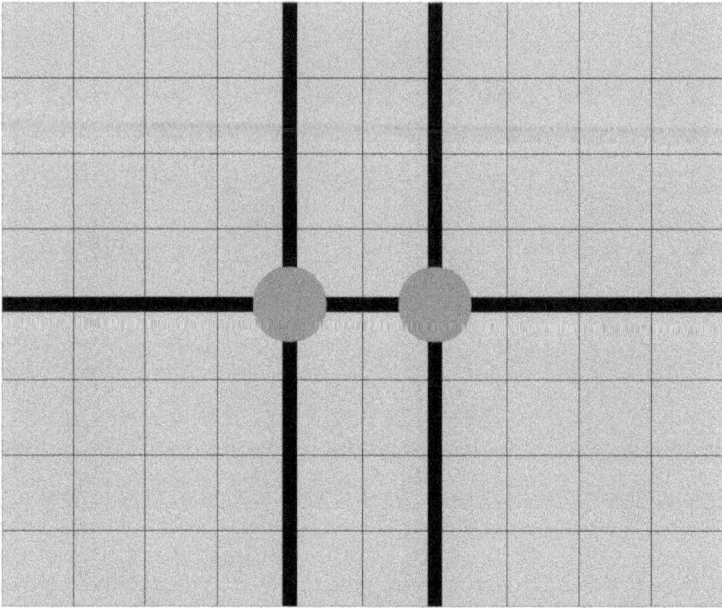

Fig. 42: Handy (1985) Task Culture

Person Culture

This is a more unusual type of culture which is concentrated on the individual. The organization only exists to serve the in-dividual within it. Handy describes it as 'a cluster of stars'. Such organizations as lawyer's practices or consultancies have this type of culture and some colleges of higher education. Some people within organizations of other cultures operate as if this were the case, often following private agendas than feel-ing their allegiance to the organization as a whole. Often these are professionals and because they are not easy to replace be-cause of specialized knowledge, have a lot of person power.

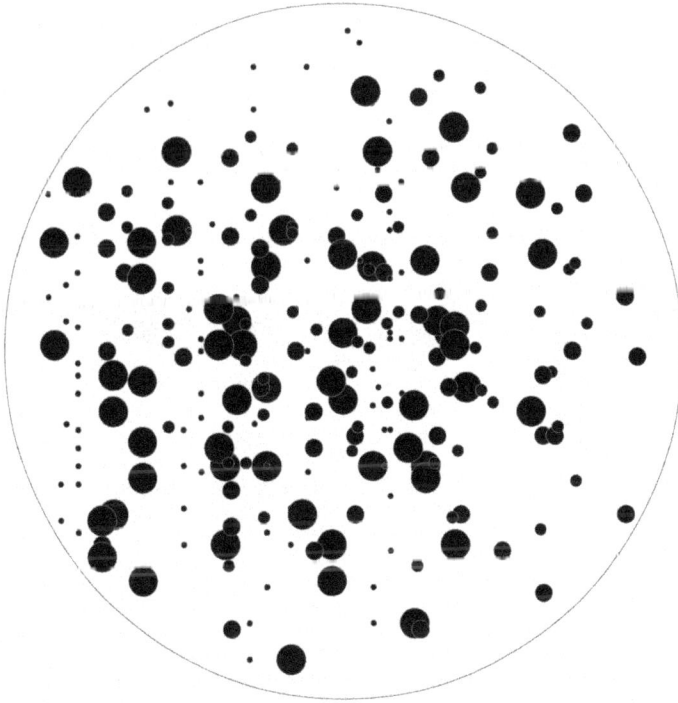

Fig. 43: Handy (1985) Person Culture

Activity

What kind of organization is yours? Modify one of the diagrams above to suit your organization. Why do you describe your organization in this way?

What about yourself? In what kind of organization would you fit best, do you think? Ask a friend or colleague what they think. Why?

What sort of culture would suit a) a software company, b) a me-chanical engineering company, c) a school, d) a logistics organi-zation? Why?

The Six Dimensions of Organizational Culture (Bate, 1984)[186]

Dimension	Description
Unemotionality — 'Avoid showing or sharing feelings or emotions'	In some companies there seems to be a hidden rule that showing feelings or emotions is in some ways bad for the individual and the organiza-tion. This is referred to as the *'civil service mentality'*.
Depersonalization of issues — 'Never point the finger at anyone in particular'	In most organizations people are purposely vague about their problems and things with which they are dissatis-fied. It is considered unkind or even dangerous to con-front people when it is felt that they are to blame. The re-sult is that people often do not accept responsibility when things go wrong. This can be compared with the *'government cabinet'*.
Subordination — 'never chal-lenge those in authority and always wait for them to take the initiative in resolving your problems'	In this case, employees are to-tally reliant on their bosses and wait for them to speak before making a move.

Dimension	Description
Conservatism — 'Better the devil you know'	This is often due to the in-grained belief that nothing is going to change anyway — it could even become worse. You will even hear 'it's all down to 'them' and you won't change that in a hundred years'.
Isolationism — 'Do your own thing and avoid treading on other people's toes'	A very individualistic approach where one has an area of one's own and you do your job and leave others to do theirs. Problem-solving is usually carried out on a one-to-one basis.
Antipathy — 'on most things people will be opponents rather than allies'	'Them and us' feelings between groups. Antipathy is the rule of the day.

Fig. 44: Bate's Six Dimensions of Culture

Any organization can be analyzed on a scale from negative (as above) to positive — the opposite case for each of these dimensions.

Activity

Using the matrix on the next page with a scale of 0-9 for each of Bate's dimensions, rate each dimension on the scale and add your comments for an organization with which you are familiar:

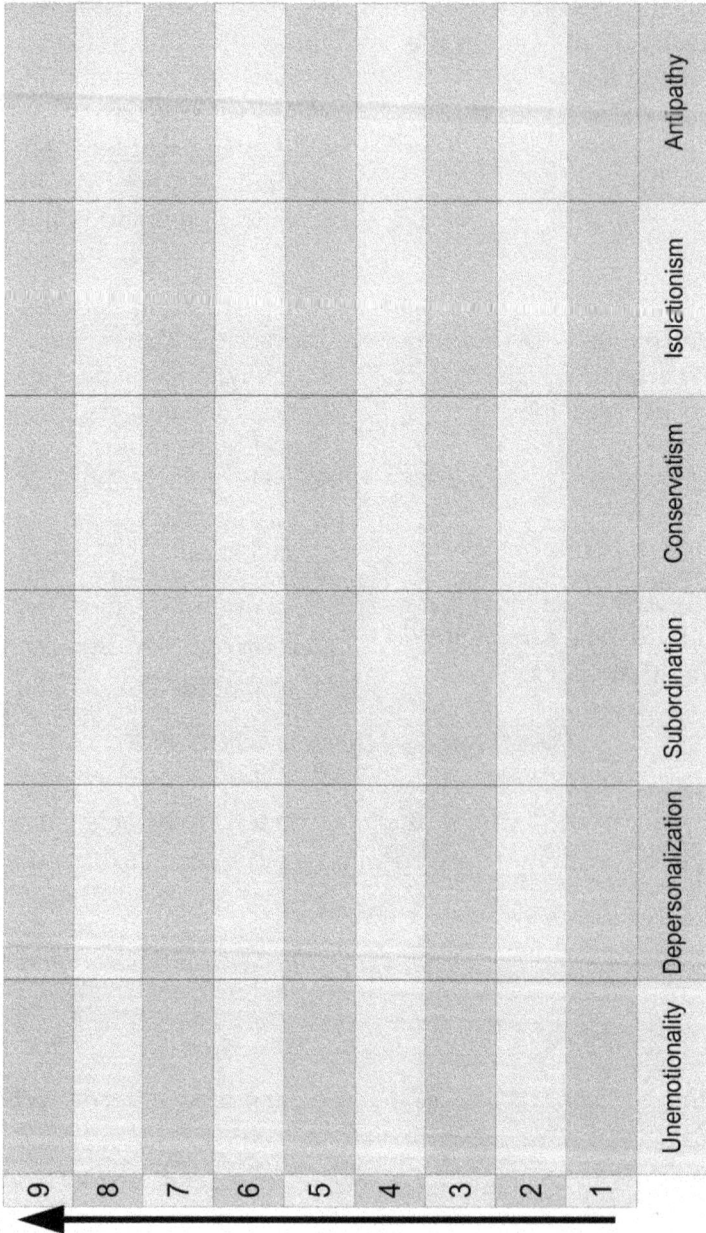

Fig. 45: Bates Dimensions Chart

Now plot on the same graph in another color your own personal profile – how you see yourself. Finally plot in a third color which type of culture you would prefer to work in. Compare and discuss. Compare with your results with Johnson's (1992) diagram below.

The cultural web (Johnson, 1992[187])

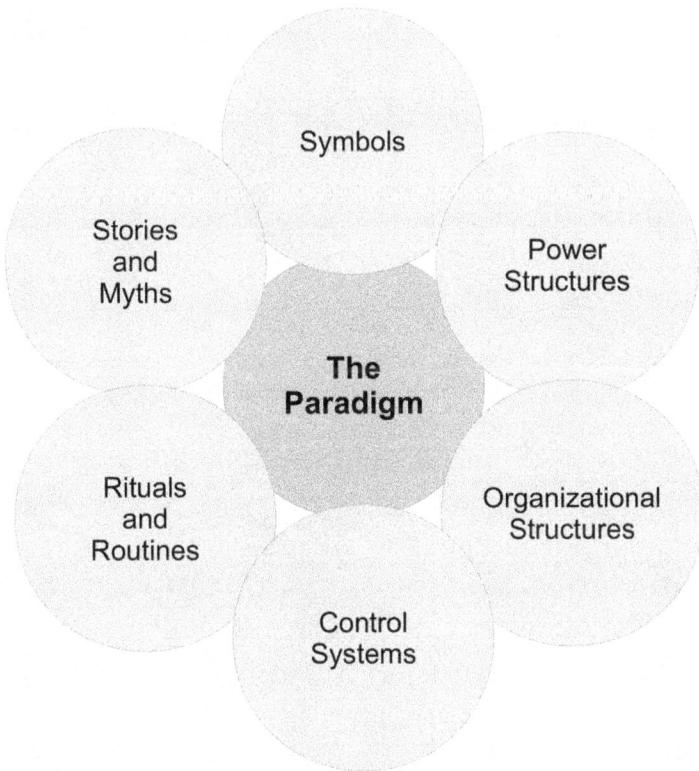

Fig. 46: The Cultural Web, Johnson (1992)

Entrepreneurship

What is Entrepreneurship?[188]

The origin of the word Entrepreneur is to be found in 17th Century France where it was used to describe 'an individual commissioned to undertake a particular commercial project'. It would often be the case that the king would appoint an individual to take responsibility for a special project which needed to be accomplished. It was in this way that it became increasingly linked to the idea of starting and organizing a business venture.

Blaug (1996)[189] states that entrepreneurship as a role goes back to Richard Cantillon, Jean Baptiste Say and Karl Marx and that it is first defined by Johann Heinrich von Thünen. The classical economists did not properly define the actual characteristics of the entrepreneurial function.

The word is expressed in various ways such as:

> **Entrepreneurship** is what the entrepreneur does.
> **Entrepreneurial** is an adjective describing how the entrepreneur does it.
> **Entrepreneurial Process** is the way value is created by the entrepreneur.
> **Entrepreneurial Venture** is the project created.

Peter Kilby (1971)[190] pointed out that in the meantime an entrepreneur can be said to be: 'like a Heffalump: a rather large and important animal. He has been hunted by many individuals using various trapping devices, but no one so far has succeeded in capturing him. All who claim to have caught sight of him report that he is enormous, but disagree on his particulars.' In this way, Kilby wished to point out that the term has become increasingly indefinable.

William Gartner (1990)[191] carried out a survey amongst academics, managers, politicians and was able to collect 90 different attributes.

The notion of risk is not always applicable in terms of financial risk because it can also be investors who accept the financial risk. Thus an entrepreneur does not need to be financially involved. Thus entrepreneurship can be, for example:

> *Founding a new business*

> *It can be turnaround of a running business*

> *The entrepreneur working to reward all stakeholders*

> *Innovation can be a key factor in understanding entrepreneurship.*

Three basic understandings:

1. It can be a manager undertaking an activity

2. An agent of economic change

3. An individual

The entrepreneur can be the owner but this does not necessarily have to be the case. If he does, he performs two roles, the role of investor and the role of manager.

He or she brings together the different elements of an organization:

People

Property

Productive resources

and gives them a separate legal identity (Bygrave & Hofer, 1991)[192]

Alternatively, sometimes an entrepreneur 'buys into' an organization or develops an existing organization.

In terms of the 'Mittelstand' (SME's) the entrepreneur can be observed as one who makes major changes in an organization or creates a completely new idea.

A more holistic view may see the entrepreneurial role as an agent of radical change in society as a whole (compare this with the leadership examples previously discussed). In any case, leadership certainly plays a definitive role in entrepreneurship.

Schumpeter (1928)[193] sees entrepreneurship linked to innovation, believing that entrepreneurs must do something new. Innovation can mean a new way of doing something and does not necessarily have to be product related. It involves bringing something to market so it can be a reinvention of the delivery chain to create new value and service for the customer. With existing well-established areas of business, this can be the only kind of innovation possible. A famous example of this was Amazon, changing the way books were delivered to customers. The advent of the eBook is an example of a change to the delivery chain combined with technical innovation.

Entrepreneurship is also involved with the identification of gaps in the market. A good entrepreneur looks actively for these gaps, constantly looking for new opportunities. Also, they may also have to be experts at allocating scarce resources efficiently because this can be a source of entrepreneurial opportunity.

Another approach may be in saying that entrepreneurship is 'the way we manage'. In this context we could talk of an entrepreneurial approach to management. This would describe a dynamic kind of management which is constantly looking for new ways of doing things and even managing people. This is in strong contrast to the kind of management which is purely concerned with maintaining the status quo.

Altogether, it has to be concluded that entrepreneurs are important because they profoundly affect not only the world economy but change the way we will live in the future.

Activity

Have you come across the word 'Entrepreneur' before? Write a few lines expressing what you think an entrepreneur is in your own words.

The three basic economic factors

Three basic economic factors can be generally identified (which can be linked to the above role of the entrepreneur):

1. Raw materials (from Mother Nature)

2. Labor

3. Capital

Value is created when these resources are combined to meet human (customer) needs. Organizations play this role and entrepreneurs find new combinations. Through their activities of offering better value and thus more dynamic competition, they increase economic and market efficiency. However, the most successful entrepreneurs are often those that actually avoid direct competition.

But entrepreneurial activity is not only to be found in for-profit companies. In fact, not-for-profit organizations can often be very entrepreneurial. This has lead to the concept of *social entrepreneurship* which takes a number of forms from charities to companies run on a social responsibility basis. The Skoll Foundation defines a social entrepreneur as "society's change agent: a pioneer of innovation that benefits humanity." or "Social entrepreneurs are society's change agents, creators of innovations that disrupt the status quo and transform our world for the better."[194]

An example of social entrepreneurship which has proven to be extremely successful is that of the Indian company TATA (the company which owns Tetley Teas and Jaguar). The company, founded by Jamsetji Tata in the 19th century already had introduced pensions for its employees in 1877 and the eight hour working day in 1912. Today it is 66% owned by charities. Jamsetji believed that business is sustainable only when it serves a larger purpose in society, stating that, "In a free enterprise the community is not just another stakeholder to business, but is in fact the very purpose of its existence".[195]

Entrepreneurial personality

Are entrepreneurs born or bred? This is a perpetual discussion and extension of the old nurture/nature debate. No doubt the answer is to be found in a combination of both:

Born (Nature):

Often they are visionary leaders and able to inspire others with their ideas. This view tends to think in terms of an inborn capability (great person mentality)

It has been said that entrepreneurs are actually social misfits — they are unable to fit into the existing frameworks and are thus forced to rebel and create their own world. Studies of the childhood of entrepreneurs shows that they have often suffered privation or hardship and lacked self esteem giving them a feeling of insecurity and the need to control things themselves.

Studies have shown that all types of personalities are to be found amongst entrepreneurs and that they are not necessarily extroverts.

Bred (Nurture):

Another school of thought sees social development — personality as a result of a reaction between personality and social influences. With this way of thinking, behavior is dependent on experiences and the possibilities to act. The following factors are considered to play a role in social development:

1. Innate — intelligence, creativity, personality, motivation, personal ambition

2. Acquired — learning training, organizational experience, mentoring, role models

3. Social — place in family, family experiences, socio-economic group, parents' occupations, society, culture, economic environment.

The concept of trait (a tendency to a type of behavior) is of some help. McClelland (1961)[196] found a 'need for achievement' amongst entrepreneurs. Also the need for autonomy, risk, creativity, independence and loving to lead.

McClelland claimed that needs were generated through life experiences. He classified the needs as achievement, affiliation or power needs. This theory is referred to as the three need theory or learned need theory.

People with a high need for achievement are classified as n_Ach and avoid both high and low risk situations. These kind of people usually prefer to work alone or at least with others of like mind.

People with a need for affiliation are classified as n_Affil and are more interested in harmonious relationships, choosing situations where they can get a lot of personal interaction. They tend to be good in sales positions and dealing with customers, for example.

The other group are the n_Pow — power types who are keen to have personal power over others and in decision-making.

People with a broader portfolio of experiences have been shown to have a "disposition toward entrepreneurship." Qualities that predicted against entrepreneurship included a desire for job or income security, as well as, perhaps surprisingly, having an apprenticeship or internship — since those lead to specialization.[197]

Activity

This is just a brief description of McClellands theory and you should be able to find a lot more about it by doing some research yourself.

Do you think a person has particularly one of these traits? How do you think such traits might affect a person's inclination to being an entrepreneur?

Thus there is no definitive explanation of what causes entrepreneurs to be what they are. Even luck plays a part in the success of entrepreneurs.

Cognitive style

Perception processes (our view of the world)	
Complexity	simplicity
leveling	sharpening
verbalizing	visualizing
Problem solving processes	
scanning	focusing
serialism	holism
adaption	innovation
Task processes	
constricted	flexible
impulsive	reflective
uncertainty	acceptance avoiding

Fig. 47: Cognitive Style

Activity

How do you see yourself in terms of entrepreneur? Would you say that you were born that way or is it due to your life experience? Think of some famous entrepreneur and investigate their life story and write a few lines explaining what made them entrepreneurs.

Types of entrepreneur (Webster, 1977)[198]

Webster delineates three basic types of entrepreneur:

1. Cantillon (classic type) — brings money, people and materials together and creates a completely new organization. Identifies unexploited opportunities.

2. Industry maker — creates a whole industry because of his initiative. Not just new products but whole concepts (e.g. Henry Ford (mass produced automobile), Wilhelm Haller (flexible working hours)

3. Administrative entrepreneur — operates within an established organization in a position of leadership (e.g. Lee Iacocca). This type are often referred to as 'Intrepreneurs'.

Webster also classifies according to the expected payoff from a venture:

1. Large payoff: many investors

2. Small payoff: few investors

3. Large payoff: few investors

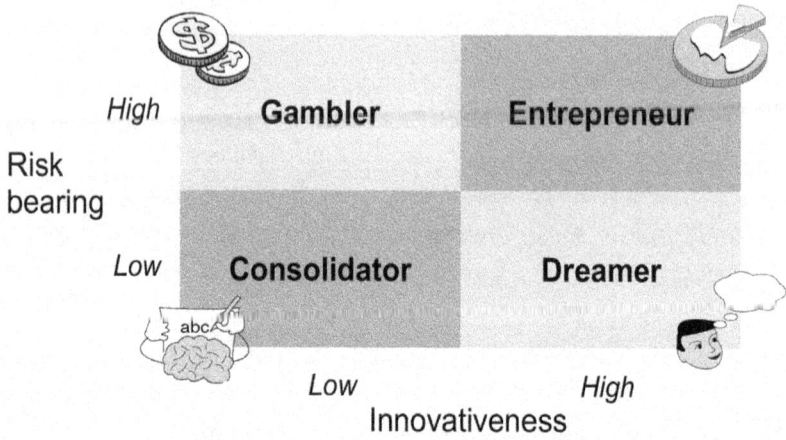

Fig. 48: Landau's (1982) Matrix – Types of Entrepreneur

In Landau's (1982)[199] matrix above, the 'gambler' is the one without an innovative idea who has to win by being able to deliver better value than the existing competition.

Jones-Evans (1995)[200] categorizes technology-based entrepreneurs as follows:

Type of Technical Entrepreneur		Experience
RESEARCH	Pure research	Based on academic research
		Academic with commercial exposure
	Research producer	
PRODUCER		Decision-making in industry or commerce
USER		Knows about usage—e.g. From marketing
OPPORTUNIST		No previous exposure to technology—but keen to develop an understanding of the technology

Fig. 49: Types of Technical Entrepreneur

Serial Entrepreneurs

Move from one success to the next—making money is less important than the desire for autonomy, prestige and sense of achievement. Some authorities such as Gartner (1985)[201] say that true entrepreneurship ends when building stage of a business is completed.

Two types:

sequential (run one business after another – James Dyson)

portfolio (run several at a time)

Wright (1997)[202] classifies **serial** entrepreneurs as follows:

Defensive serial entrepreneurs – new enterprise because of a forced exit from the previous one

Opportunist serial entrepreneurs – *undertake subsequent ventures because of new opportunity*

Group-creating entrepreneurs – *a number of companies is fundamental to their strategy (Branson). This includes* *deal-making serials* *who use acquisition and* *organic se-rials* *who start businesses from scratch.*

Ways of managing — entrepreneurship vs. small business management

1. Innovation (this can be technical, organizational, market-ing, etc.)

2. Potential for growth

3. Strategic objectives:

   Growth targets

   Market development

   Market share

   Market position

Entrepreneurship as a style of management

1. Focus on change

2. Focus on opportunity

3. Organization-wide management

4. Entrepreneurial managers as venturers (risk rather than security)

According to Czarniawska-Joerges and Wolff (1991)[203].

> *MANAGEMENT is the activity of introducing order by co-ordinating flows of things and people towards collective action*

> *LEADERSHIP is symbolic performance, expressing the hope of control over destiny*

> *ENTREPRENEURSHIP is the making of entire new worlds*

The following diagram[204] describes management scope in relationship to entrepreneurship:

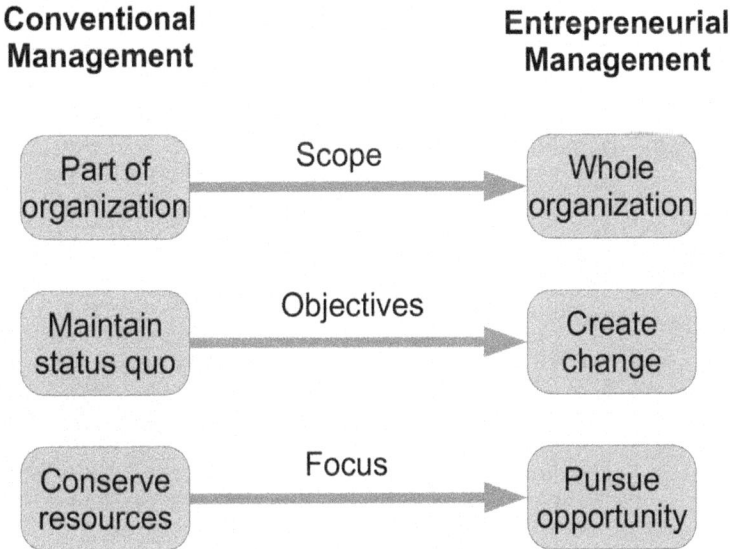

Conventional Management   **Entrepreneurial Management**

Part of organization	Scope	Whole organization
Maintain status quo	Objectives	Create change
Conserve resources	Focus	Pursue opportunity

Fig. 50: Conventional vs. Entrepreneurial Management

New ways of teaching business studies

An ulterior motive in the concept of holistic strategic management is in the search for new and more effective methods of teaching business theory and management science. By breaking mind-sets and opening the minds of prospective and continuing managers to a wider view, it is hoped that those entrepreneurial concepts can be formed which can create, as Luthans (1988)[205] said, 'effective rather than get-ahead managers'.

Entrepreneurship Education — Germany vs. USA

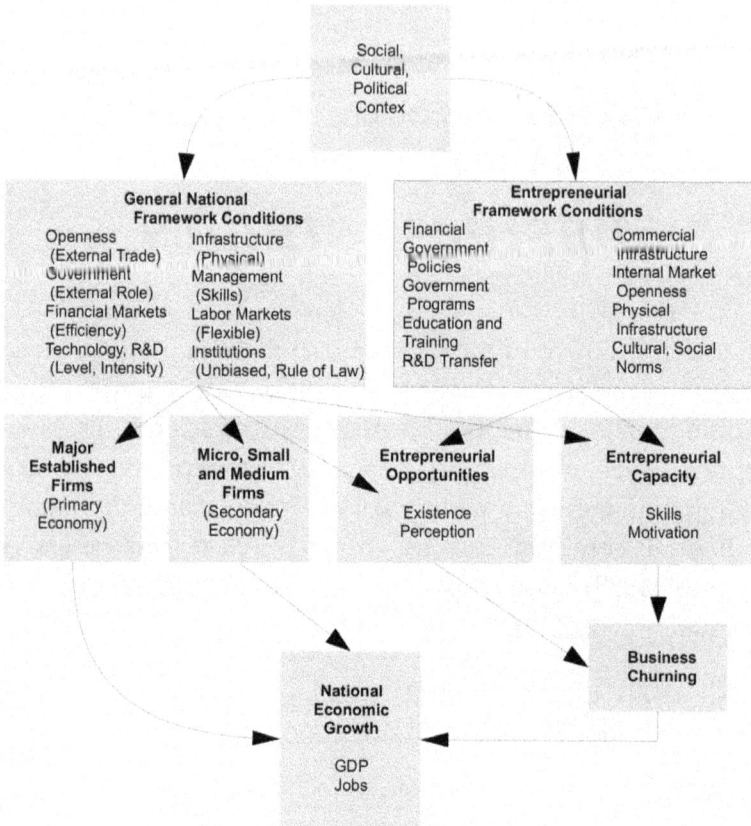

Fig. 51: The 'GEM Model' illustrating the relationship between entrepreneurship and economic growth

As any education system is dependent on considerable funding from state, corporate or private sources, the relationship between entrepreneurship and economic growth has to be clearly established in the minds of prospective stakeholders. This relationship is clearly illustrated by the so-called 'Gem model'[206]:

Entrepreneurial education, within the bounds of our definition, is very much concerned with negotiating and developing the so-called 'soft skills' to provide the intangible resources and capabilities essential to complement the tangible and hopefully existing resources such as capital, finite skills and inherent capabilities. In discussing this, it is interesting to compare Germany and the USA.

The rationale behind comparing the two somewhat different states of the German Federal Republic and the USA is driven by the fact that while the USA is one of the nations with the highest level of start-up rates, Germany only takes a middle position in an international comparison. While cultural, economic and political factors undoubtedly play a large role in producing these differences, they in turn are also affected by education, which has to remain the arena where grass-roots change can take place. Verheul et al. (1999) demonstrate this by pointing to three main ways in which education can influence entrepreneurship[207]:

1. Education provides people with the necessary qualities and mindset, e.g. mentality to start their own businesses.

2. Education may, in part, determine the success of new business ventures as it provides the necessary business skills.

3. Education only stimulates entrepreneurship when it teaches adequate qualities and skills.

Governed by the absolute understanding of the meaning of entrepreneurship as defined above, the higher echelons of education such as universities, polytechnics and management academies, as well as those initiatives dedicated to entrepreneurial development as the providers in Germany, for example, are challenged by this educational need. Despite the emphasis and rigorous teaching of the 'solid facts of business' such as economics and financial accounting at German business educational establishments, this has not proven to meet the needs of the rapidly changing global environment, allowing Germany to slip way behind. While taking a leading place in the provision of technological innovation and manufacturing quality, it has often left the reaping of the benefits from these advantages to the entrepreneurs abroad.

Thus, it would appear that these two countries are governed by differing educational paradigms which are affecting the way they are approaching the subject.

Paradigms

The various approaches to curriculum design and pedagogical methodology have been investigated by Szyperski and Herting (1997/1998)[208]. Their research revealed that students found lecturing very ineffective whereas activity based methods were highly appreciated. The learning process requires continual feedback rather than knowledge transfer. It was thus that Twardy and Esser developed their 'WIS-EX' system[209] which claims to be '..a development concept for sustainable motivation, training and support for self-employed people in universities in North-Rhine-Westfalia....'.

There is also the 'problem of acceptance of entrepreneurship education and the formulation of realistic teaching aims and integration'[210] and the fact that German offers tend to have low integration and emphasize the legal and financial aspects in isolation. The authors find this particularly surprising because Germany has concentrated on the integrative aspects of the founder personality, stating that German empirical research demonstrates clearly that there are three basic characteristics of the self-employed person:

1. Good business and management administration knowledge
2. Particular psychological traits such as risk and performance orientation.
3. Commercial and branch-specific experience[211]

It is felt that the American trend of emphasizing the entrepreneurial process offers a better method and that the following topics should be highlighted:

1. Opportunity identification
2. Opportunity evaluation
3. Exploiting methods
4. Resources
5. Organization
6. Surviving
7. Growing
8. Professionalizing
9. Harvesting

The inductive didactic (going from a real case back into theory) applied by some American institutions such as the Anderson Hall of Entrepreneurs may not be realizable in the opposite framework of the German classical business education. Also, American entrepreneurship education traditionally tends to be addressed to an audience of postgraduate mature students with at least five years professional experience.

Earlier Research on Entrepreneurship Education

Because of the intangible nature of the subject, most research in this area has to restrict itself to qualitative research often taking the form of action research in real projects.

Ripsas (1997)[212] feels that a large German university would not be in a position to promote individual entrepreneurial personality traits. The Cologne CEC project, for example, restricts itself to the following learning aims:

CEC Level	Objects	Resources	Activities
I	Determination of one's own aims	Selection of study contents	Sensitization for economic activity
II	Choice of product to be offered	Selection of resources	Qualification for economic and technical skills
III	Choice of strategy	Selection of personnel resources	Support for self-management and management of others

Fig. 52: CEC Learning Aims

He propagates the idea of setting up management centers where theory can be experienced and data gained on the success and failure of graduates.

They summarize the CEC program under three goals:

1. Sensitization for entrepreneurial activity at the commencement of studies
2. Development of entrepreneurial techniques
3. Evaluation of the founding of new businesses

Günther and Roland Kirchhof.[213] evaluated the project in the Ruhr area of North-Rhine-Westphalia (NRW) under the title of GSR (Gründer Support Ruhr). This project enjoys support from the European Union and the NRW Ministry of the Economy, Technology and Transport and is open to every entrepreneur with an innovative idea. The authors see life-long learning, special training and long term consultation as essential to establishing businesses on a solid footing. While praising classic planned education programs for their high professional standards, it finds that they do not attract the larger proportion of young entrepreneurs. The adult education trainers are often not in touch with the everyday problems of entrepreneurs and often have no business know-how. Using skilled and experienced managers often in retirement or semi-retirement from established businesses means that GSR can adapt to these needs.

While it is not clear as to how directly these projects are related to our definition, Harhoff and Locht (1996)[214] emphasize the role of SME's in German innovative activity identifying that 12% of R&D expenditure came from SME's in (West) Germany. However, they were quick to note that in fact, over 50% of firms with less than 50 employees carry out R&D, whereas this applies to only 15% of firms with over 1000 employees. On the other hand, it is not a prerequisite of innovation to carry out formal R&D. Pfirmann (1994)[215]. The role of SME's may be a cultural parameter which we have to take in account when comparing with the USA.

Nicole Seymour (2001)[216] sees entrepreneurship training in a process of moving from the fringes into the centers of community colleges, universities and business schools in the USA. Drury (1999) estimated that 1500 institutions in the US are offering credit courses in entrepreneurship and small-business management[217]. These apparently contrast considerably with traditional education in that a mixture of classes, clubs, majors, co-majors etc. are offered. Only 100 institutions actually offer formal programs, according to Dunn & Short (2001)[218].

Management Education

Breaking with a didactic approach to business education, we start to look at management education from the 'top' end. We are more concerned with personal and professional development than with setting academic standards. Starting with the aim to make seekers of wisdom, we base our view of what we are thinking from an ethical, esoteric and visionary standpoint, taking account of our actions in terms of their compatibility to newly discovered values and the desire for enlightenment. The manager can now be likened to the guru, the student to the novice. They are both looking for enlightenment. Quoting Robert K. Greenleaf[219], the true leader will be 'servant first and leader second'. Our model for team building will be perhaps the 12 disciples. Often quarreling, often in the dark but clinging to a Messianic vision of a 'Servant Nation to serve Mankind', and as the 'guinea pigs of their own experiment'[220] as Schonfield described their mission.

For this reason, this script has been written the wrong way round! The conclusions are in the introduction because the reader should clearly know what we are aiming at. Here is a mission, the manager is the missionary. So many modern management textbooks are based on presenting standard theory and then presenting ethical and sustainability factors at the end of the chapter as an appendage and moral alibi. The reader will either abandon a further perusal at this stage or will join in the adventure of melting ideas into wholeness. When confronted critically by a hard-headed 'realistic' and successful businessman, Hermann Hesse allows his hero Siddhartha to state, 'I can fast, I can think and I can wait'[221]. The contention here is that this is the route to sustainable personal, business and societal success.

You may remember the diagram in the first volume in this series which is intended to illustrate the scope of holistic strategic thinking. It is no way exhaustive but will serve as the model on which we will base our discussion.

Activity

What opportunities do you have in your organization to use your entrepreneurial talents and skills? Can you think of any opportunities you have outside of your main work which gives or would give you the opportunity to use and develop such skills? The nature of business opportunity

Henry Mintzberg has been quoted as saying that business schools tend to teach what can be taught rather than what needs to be learned. How do you feel about your own business education in this respect? Is it satisfactory? What could be improved and what role could you play in achieving this?

The nature of business opportunity

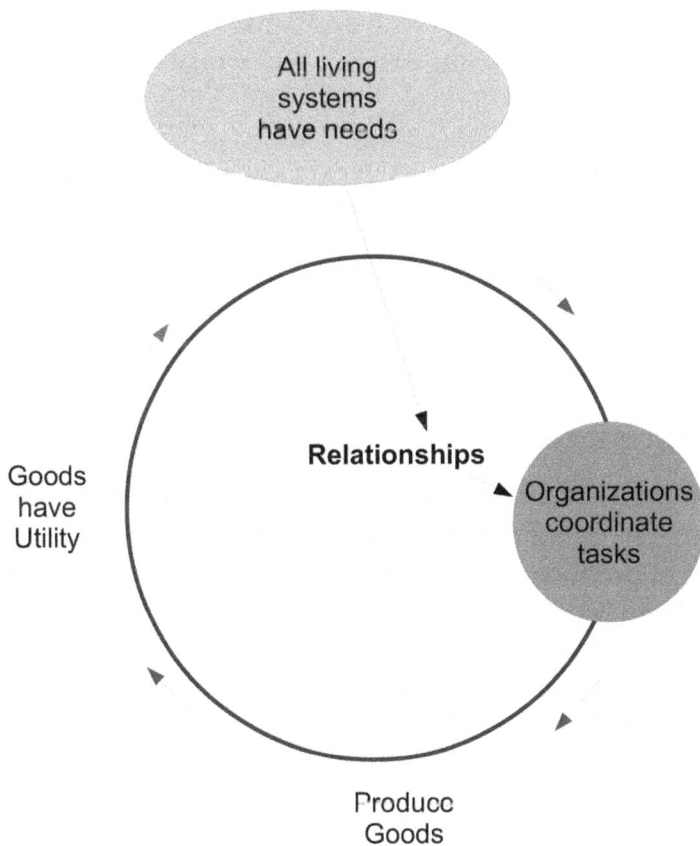

Fig. 53: The Nature of Business Opportunity

Entrepreneurship is about finding better ways of doing things. Therefore, it is about looking for opportunities for doing things *differently and better than before – Innovation.*

New Products

This can mean the further exploitation of existing technology (product innovation) or even the invention of something wholly new. Of increasing importance is the subject of product branding which can be considered part of the product. An example of this would be Richard Branson and his Virgin brand. It is about creating product differentiation.

New Services

By creating new services or new ways of delivering them. Examples are such things as the, now well established Pizza bring services or Fastway's franchising delivery service. Again, branding can play an important part in this.

New Production Techniques

Changing the way something is made can be a form of innovation. The Smart car originally included radically efficient forms of production in its concept. Changing production techniques can lead to efficiencies and therefore lower prices but it can equally well be used in attempt to produce better quality or to meet specific customer needs in the most efficient way (Marbach).

New Operating Practices

Improving the way services or goods are brought to the customer or rationalizing processes through standardization. Wickham (2001)[222] quotes McDonalds in this respect — the standardization of food preparation. Many supermarket chains also attempt this. However, in the area of food, standardization tends to lead to lower aesthetic food quality and possibly health problems. In terms of meeting human needs, such a strategy may not be sustainable.

New Way of Delivering the Product or Service to the Customer

This approach usually focuses on the delivery chain. Toys 'R' Us focuses on a particular market and distributes through its purpose-built stores. Aldi has been successful through its unique store and marketing concept reducing number of lines and delivering these at low cost to customers. Internet business such as Amazon have radically changed the way products are distributed to the customer, completely re-think the delivery chain.

New Means of Informing the Customer about the Product

These are promotional innovations such as is often found in products like beer or washing powders where product differentiation is very difficult. While this proves too expensive usually for the 'Mittelstand', wise use of public relations can provide free publicity and give the organization a positive and unique image. Innovators are generally seen by society as heroes. Sponsoring is also a method to be exploited here. Building a strong corporate vision and relating this with customer aspirations (Body Shop, Greenpeace) can in itself be an innovation especially where this is done in areas where it has not been attempted before.

New Ways of Managing Relationships within the Organization

Improving internal communications or structuring on a different basis to the competition can be an effective way of increasing innovative dynamic. Wickham (2001)[223], in his excellent book on strategic entrepreneurship which has been a great help in compiling this information, does not seem to mention in the possibilities offered by culture in this respect. Exploiting human differences can in itself lead to organizations which in themselves are innovative. Such organizations can also be more innovative in attending to international markets. Building vision in the organization and inspiring employees can be an innovative impulse.

New Ways of Managing Relationships between Organizations

Recent concepts such as customer relationship marketing (CRM) emphasize this aspect. Companies can gain effective advantage by building systems or attitudes which build relationships with customers. Another area here is co-opetition which looks at advantages to be gained in cooperating with competitors. This has already been practiced by airlines. An opportunity may exist in new areas.

Multiple Innovation

Of course, nothing in life is simple and the entrepreneur will often find him or herself combining a number of the above possibilities. This combination in itself can be unique and thus lead to innovative advantage.

High and Low Pioneering Entrepreneurship

Manimala (1999)[224] differentiates between low and high level pioneering innovativeness (PI) based on a study carried out in India as illustrated in the table below:

Strategic characteristics	Low PI entrepreneurship	High PI entrepreneurship
Idea Management	Local contacts, ideas from existing products. Typical *Mittelstand*. Limited strategic vision tend to stick to known ways of doing things or previous successes	Gain ideas from a wider source, willing to use international examples. Ambitious strategic vision. Like new ideas.
Management of Autonomy	Working with close-knit team. Own expertise developed	Appoint from outside organization where knowledge lacking. Learning organization.

Strategic characteristics	Low PI entrepreneurship	High PI entrepreneurship
Management of competition	Avoid competition where experience limited. Good relationships with few known customers	High risk competitive moves. Big efforts to get new customers. Importance of service, quality, product.
Growth Strategy	Want to grow but rely on good market conditions. No risky diversification	Active competition. Diversification not excluded
Human resource management	Rely on own workers. Directions, routines as control	Experts hired as required. Culture and strategic management as control method
Risk management	Limit risks. Tried and tested methods. Look for grants and government support	Risk management — market research, environmental analysis. Will go alone if necessary
Network development	Local, informal and formal	Better at using formal networks, wider scope.

Fig. 54: High and Low Pioneering Entrepreneurship Manimala (1999)

Tips for Entrepreneurs

Entrepreneurs are always on the lookout for new opportunities

Are motivated by opportunity

Be aware of what you want to achieve, why you want to achieve it and know why you will enjoy the process of achieving it

Innovation is secondary to opportunity

Have a clear idea of why customers might buy your product

Be inspired not just by a good idea but with the real possibility to market it

Be knowledgeable about:

  technology

  how it is produced

  customers' needs

  means of distribution

  how skills are used in the industry

  how to promote idea to customers

  competitors

Activity

Considering the ideas above, can you think of any examples of entrepreneurs or entrepreneurial organizations which would fit these descriptions?

Resources

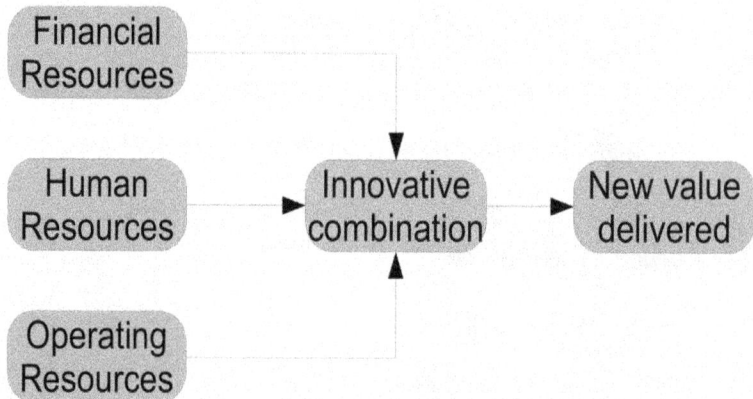

Fig. 55: Resources

The entrepreneur has to be able to bring these resources together and combine them in an innovating way:

Financial Resources

Firstly, it is necessary to make an assessment of the financial resources available. Use the following table as a basis for financial planning:

Source of Finance	Explanation	Examples of sources	€
Cash in hand	Money immediately available	Petty cash	
		Current account	
Overdraft facilities	Short term loan on demand previously agreed with bank	Account 1	
		Account 2	
Loans	With agreed repayments regardless of performance of business	Private from backers	
		Bank	
		State	
Outstanding debtors	Owed to the firm by customers. Depends on payment terms demanded by customer		
Investment capital	Shareholders' assets		
Investment in other businesses	If more than 50% of firm is owned then they are called subsidiaries. Long term commitment — cash not readily available		

Fig. 56: Financial Resources

Operating Resources

In the same way as above, make a list of the operating resources available to the venture:

Premises (this may be a room in your house)

Motor vehicles (perhaps your own car and that of your partners)

Production machinery (this may have to be bought or leased)

Raw materials

Storage facilities (you may have access to low cost storage – the car may have to be parked in the street and the garage used)

Office equipment (you probably already have computers and printers etc. which you can use in the initial stages

The emphasis should be on conserving and utilizing as many resources as possible which are already available. Anything is better than taking up loans, using investors money or taking on huge leasing commitments in the early stages. This can always be done when the venture is proving itself.

Human Resources

Productive labor

Technical expertise

Provision of business services (legal support, bookkeeping)

Functional organizational skills – decision-making, production, marketing, development

Communication skills

Strategic and leadership skills

Human resources also represent a fixed cost for the organization and it will be important to see what human resources are available at lower costs in the initial stages (e.g. Own labor on a part-time basis).

In order to attain the most efficient usage of resources it is possible to apply so-called 'resource leverage'. Hamel and Prahalad (1993)[225] have created a concept where they believe that creating a chasm between resources and vision and bridging this chasm using resource leverage can lever hidden reserves and resources in the organization:

CONVER-GENCE	Create chasm between resources and aspirations. Loyalty to strategic goals.
FOCUS	Identify next competitive advantage. Focus firmly on the task until completed.
EXTRACTION	Apply lessons learnt on the front line. Tapping the best in every employee.
BORROWING	Learning from outsiders. Learning goals for employees working within alliances and joint ventures.
BLENDING	Creating technology generalists. Environment where employees explore new skill combinations.
BALANCING	Excellence across the board. Excellence in one area not imperiled by mediocrity in another.
RECYCLING	Core competencies shared between business units. Ideas mustn't be trapped.
CO-OPTION	Identify industry players dependent on us. Enroll others in the pursuit of our goals.
SHIELDING	Understanding competitors blind spots. Attacking without attracting retaliation. Explore markets through low-cost, low risk incursions.
RECOVERY	Shortening product development, order-processing and launch times. Build global brands and distribution positions.

Fig. 57:Resource Leverage – Hamel and Prahalad

Risk and Return

While it is important to expect a return on investment of resources, in calculating the potential return it is necessary to way the related risk and where there are choices, to chose those possibilities with the best return/risk ratios[226]:

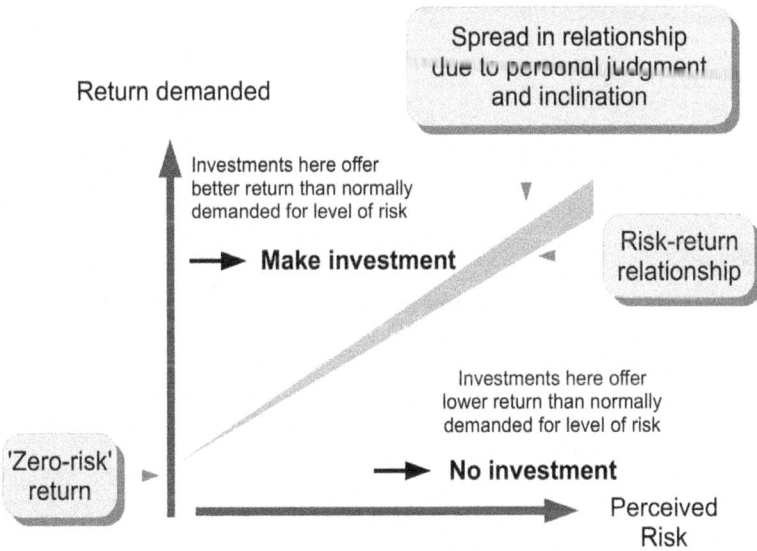

Fig. 58: Risk Return Ratio

Visionary entrepreneurs may be able to use their ability to inspire others with their dreams but if they fail to administer a realistic risk/return scenario, they will soon find themselves without support. If we return to our initial discussions between whether entrepreneurs are born or bred, we may be able to observe that innovators may have to learn some adaption while adapters may have to learn some innovation. Getting the right balance between visionary enthusiasm and hard-headed calculation may be where management science can play a role in giving us the tools with which to be reflective practitioners.

The following diagram from Wickham[227] describes the relationship of resource investment in the entrepreneurial venture:

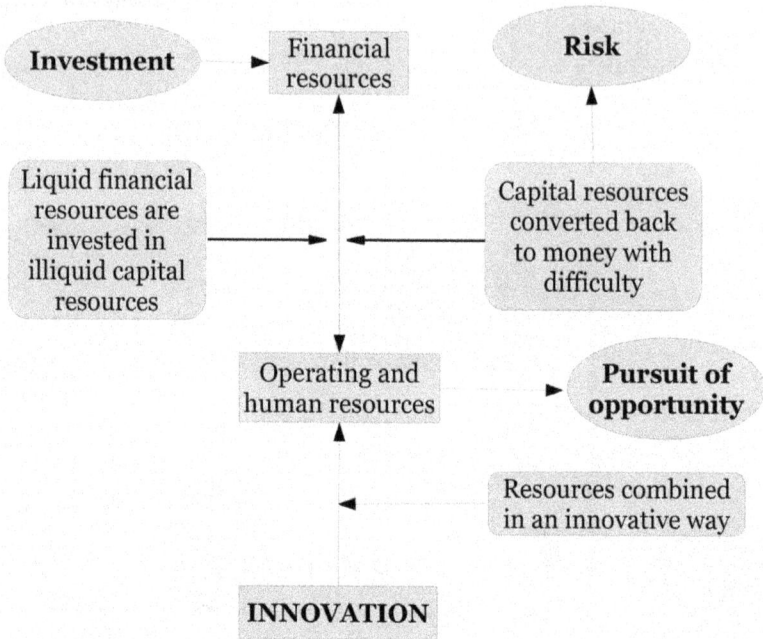

Investment → Financial resources

Risk

Liquid financial resources are invested in illiquid capital resources

Capital resources converted back to money with difficulty

Operating and human resources → Pursuit of opportunity

Resources combined in an innovative way

INNOVATION

Fig. 59: Relation of Resource Investment to Risk

Managing Change

First of all, we need to ask the question, 'Why does large scale change occur?'

We can certainly say that it seems to occur when internal or external environmental pressures give rise to questions that can no longer be ignored. This can be due, for example to costs, profits, new systems, culture, takeovers, mergers, introducing TQM or quality control systems, a revolution, or even just the need to be sustaining success.

Charles Handy's (1995)[228] 'Sigmoid Curve' illustrates that companies tend to go through a life cycle and at the point where stagnation occurs they either have to make radical changes to move ahead or will finally decline:

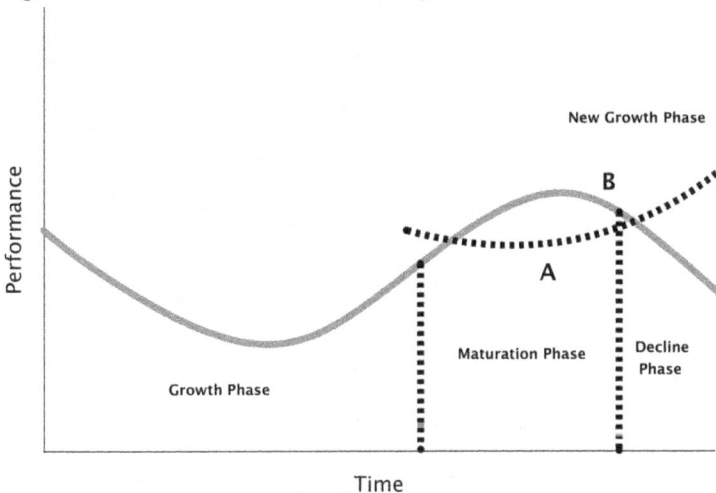

Fig. 60: Sigmoid Curve Handy (1995)

Rumelt (1995)[229] states that 'Transformation is the process of engendering a fundamental change in an organization with the goal of achieving a dramatic improvement in performance'

One approach to large scale organizational change is Senge's 5 disciplines as described in his book 'The Fifth Discipline'[230] which you are strongly recommended to read and which we will discuss later.

The following diagram illustrates the way in which the management of change can be structured:

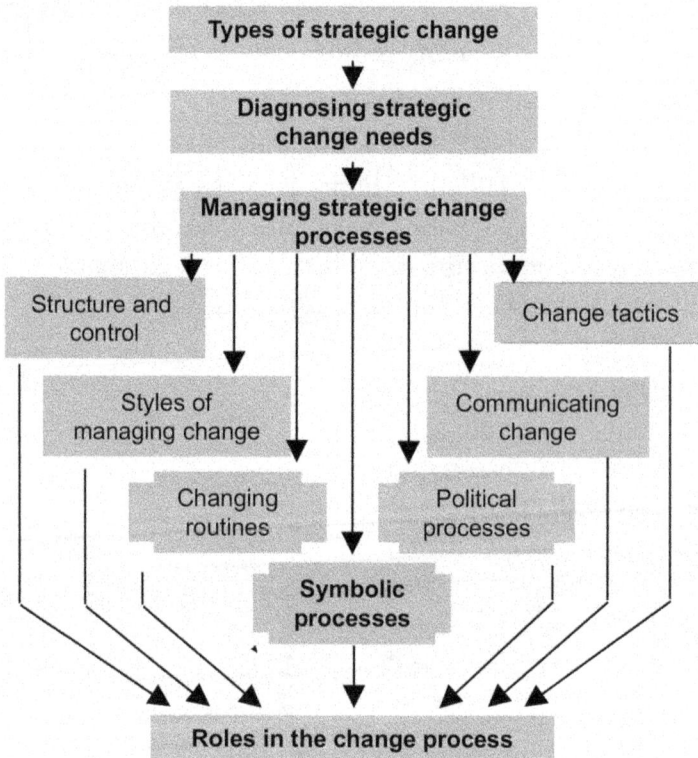

Fig. 61: A Framework for Managing Change

We can also categorize change into proactive — when we take the initiative and into reactive — when change is forced upon us. It is also possible to contemplate change as a step by step incremental process or as a radical transformational change which changes the face of the organization.

	Incremental change	Transformational change
Proactive	Tuning	Planned transformational
Reactive	Adaptation	Forced transformational

Fig. 62 Types of Strategic Change

Activity

Thinking of a change situation either facing you in your private life or your organization, how would you see it in terms of the above brief discussion.

We should note that the tools for examining the topic of change are by no means exhaustive and for our purposes we are going to concentrate on the following models:

1. Forcefield Analysis

2. SIS-Systems Intervention Strategy

3. OD-Organizational development process

4. BPR-Business Process Re-engineering

5. Turnarounds

6. Holistic Change Management

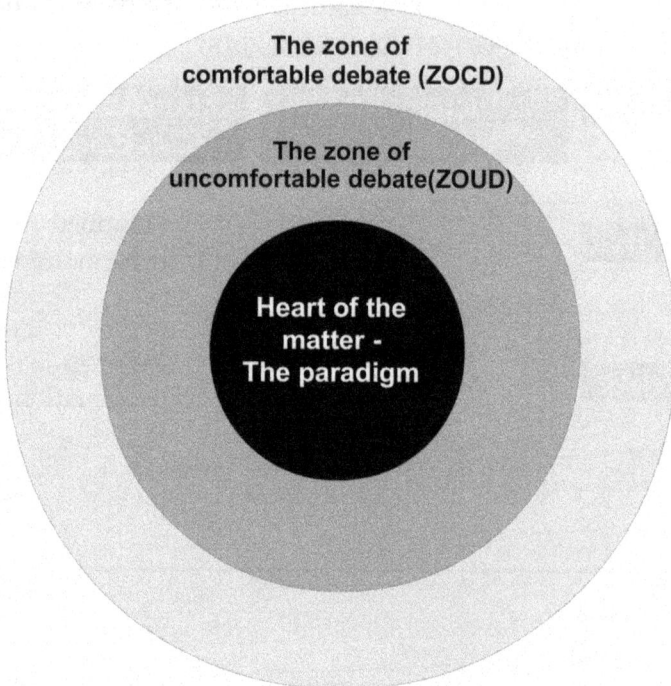

Fig. 63: 'The Zone of Uncomfortable Debate' (Bowman,1995)

The above diagram (Bowman, 1995[231]) shows how the core assumptions of the organization are a result of the zone or area of uncomfortable debate—where people are forced to ask questions and discuss issues which they would prefer to ignore as well as the area where people are comfortable facing the issues.

Kurt Lewin (1943)[232] makes out 3 Distinct phases in change processes:

1. Unfreezing—crucial stage, change equation

2. Changing – design & detail
3. Refreezing – new behaviors become the norm

Below is an example of the use of Lewin's forcefield analysis which is a valuable tool in understanding change and the related processes:

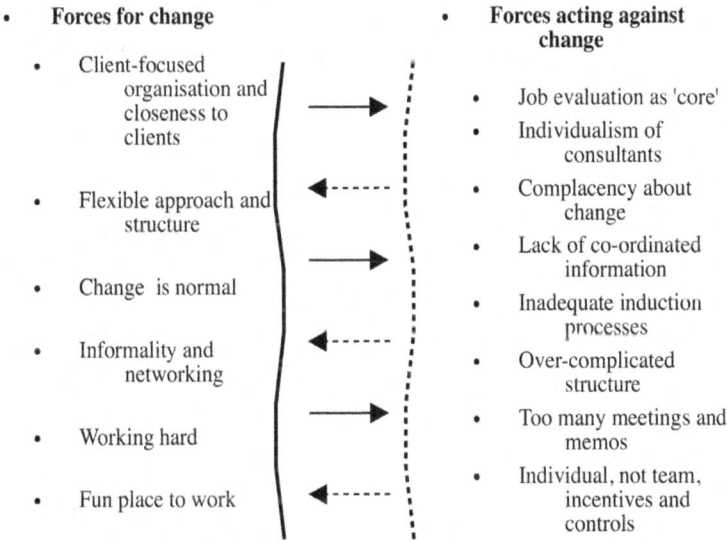

- **Forces for change**
  - Client-focused organisation and closeness to clients
  - Flexible approach and structure
  - Change is normal
  - Informality and networking
  - Working hard
  - Fun place to work

- **Forces acting against change**
  - Job evaluation as 'core'
  - Individualism of consultants
  - Complacency about change
  - Lack of co-ordinated information
  - Inadequate induction processes
  - Over-complicated structure
  - Too many meetings and memos
  - Individual, not team, incentives and controls

Fig. 64: Forcefield Analysis based on Hay's Cultural Web

Up to now we have considered change with regard to a static situation. But change is becoming continuous. We slowly have to ask ourselves if there is a 'stable state' around the corner.

Alexander (1985) states that what is really happening is that:

1. Change takes longer than originally anticipated
2. New problems emerge as you are doing it!
3. Co-ordination of activities are not effective enough
4. Competing crises & activities divert from implementation
5. Capabilities of the people involved are not sufficient

6. Training & Instruction is inadequate
7. Uncontrolled external factors have an adverse effect on implementation

Again, based on Kurt Lewin's force-field analysis we can attempt the first model for managing change, basing it on the processes within the organization which will try and block change and how we use this as a framework of implementing the necessary processes as we combat resistance with specific tactics:

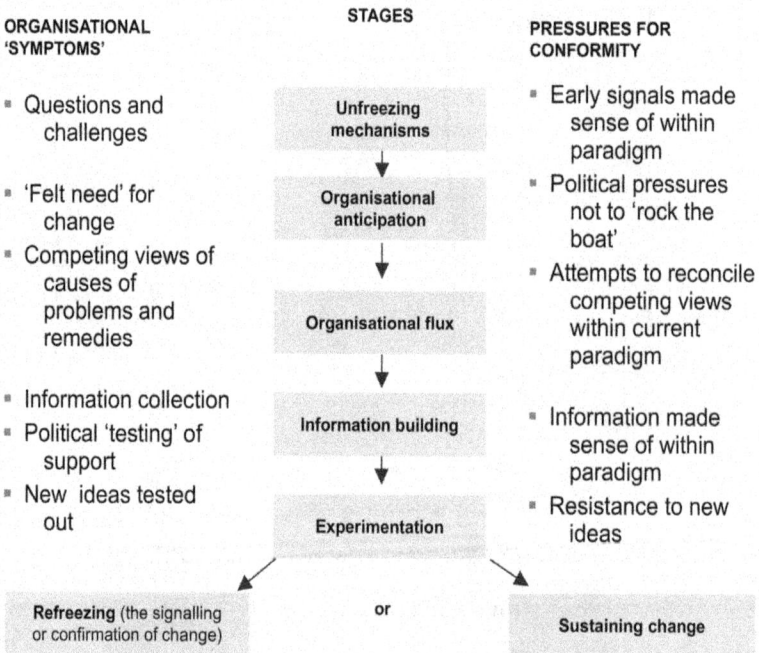

ORGANISATIONAL 'SYMPTOMS'	STAGES	PRESSURES FOR CONFORMITY
▪ Questions and challenges	Unfreezing mechanisms	▪ Early signals made sense of within paradigm
▪ 'Felt need' for change	Organisational anticipation	▪ Political pressures not to 'rock the boat'
▪ Competing views of causes of problems and remedies	Organisational flux	▪ Attempts to reconcile competing views within current paradigm
▪ Information collection ▪ Political 'testing' of support	Information building	▪ Information made sense of within paradigm
▪ New ideas tested out	Experimentation	▪ Resistance to new ideas
Refreezing (the signalling or confirmation of change)	or	**Sustaining change**

Fig. 65: Forcefield Analysis-Kurt Lewin

Activity

In considering the above activity, how would you see the issues of resistance to change and the forces involved? Try using Lewin's models to describe the situation.

Types of problem

When one is intending to make changes in an organization, it is first necessary to gain an understanding of the situation, the needs of the organization and an awareness that the change agent and others will be affected by it. The hardest thing is to get started and to be fairly sure that one is seeing the 'wood for the trees'. It will depend very much on the context and the culture of the organization as to how we go about implementing change.

We can generally define two types of problem. One sort we refer to as 'hard' problems. These are measurable issues and tend to have individual are relatively straightforward solutions. Such a problem might be introduction of new shelving in a warehouse, for example.

Other problems are more tricky and do not have simple straightforward or obvious solutions. These are referred to as 'soft' problems. This could be something like a generation change in an organization, requiring a complete change of leadership style and culture.

Whereas with a hard problem, the outcomes are pretty clear from the start, we might find that we do not know exactly where a soft problem change is going to end up, hoping to discover it on the way. There is a lot of overlap of course and often, seemingly hard issues become soft and complex ones. Generally we can describe them as follows:

Hard Issues	Soft Issues
Solution is clear	No obvious solution
Probably one thing needs to change	Probably many things will need to change
Problem known and clear	Not too sure what is needed
Methodology is clear	Methodology not known
Structured	Unstructured

We can also look at the change issues from the perspective of bounded and unbounded rationality:

Thus a bounded and therefore hard problem or issue (we should really talk about issues rather than problems to ensure a positive attitude) could look like this:

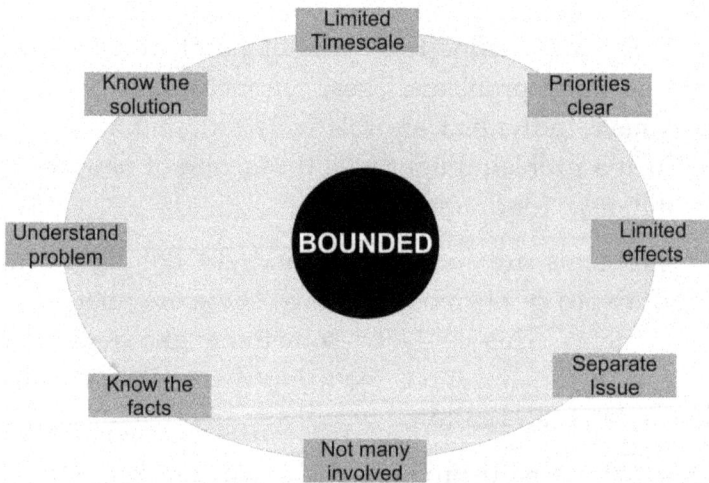

Fig. 66: Hard issues relate to bounded rationality

On the other hand, the more complex problems can be described as in the diagram below and can be classified as unbounded issues:

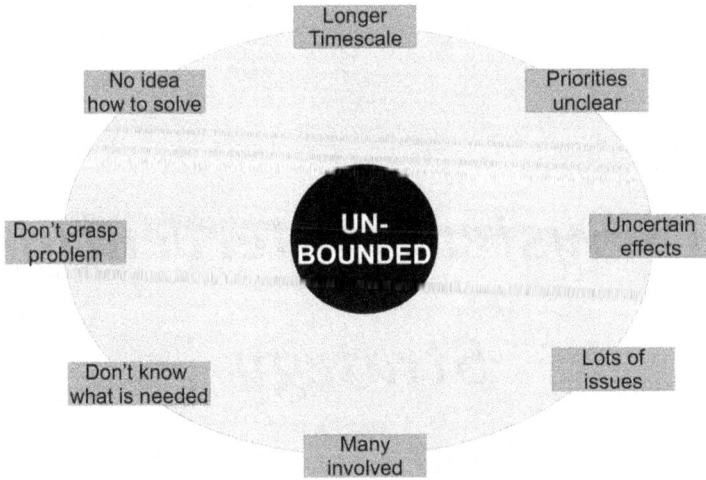

Fig. 67: Soft issues relate to unbounded rationality

In order to define and clarify issues, some preliminary investigation methods should be employed. First, when one is sure of the kind of problem it is, can one move on to deciding on a specific strategy.

Such methods are mind mapping, brainstorming sessions, the use of problem solving techniques, surveys amongst affected staff, flow charts and so on—again, depending on the type of issue involved and of course the organizational culture.

We will now take a look at a number of frameworks for change. Remember that these are just frameworks and this is but a small selection of the methods available. Within the rough outline they provide, you will need to integrate theoretical methods for analysis and implementation as already previously discussed as well as the additional concepts we will describe later.

SIS Systems Intervention Strategy

The main points of this change framework are:

It has engineering Origins and is thus a 'hard' method

SIS is designed to make use of group process & teamwork

It offers a simple explanation

Diagnosis is a get to 'grips' approach and can develop views

Design phase allows for alternative methods and looking at options

Implementation phase is about commitment to a strategy and considers the means as well as the action to be taken.

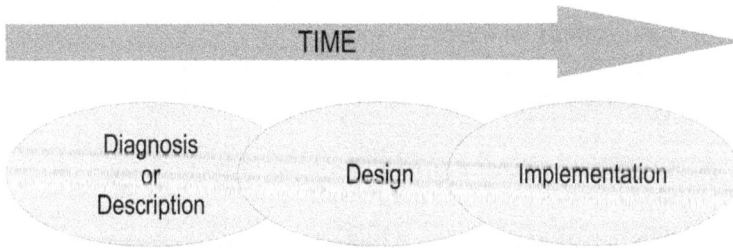

Fig. 68: Systems Intervention Strategy

Steps on the way:

1. Diagnosis phase

   Step 1—Entry & system description—'where are you now?'

   Step 2—Setting objectives & identifying constraints —'where do you want to be?'

   Step 3—Formulating measures—'How will you know when you've got there?'

2. The Design phase

   Step 4—Generating Options—'how can you get there?'

   Step 5—Core of the design phase-modeling of options —'what will it be like?'

There are a range of methods which can be used for the design phase such as:

Physical-mock ups, architectural

Computer simulation-systems

cash flow models

experimental, lab scale plants

Cost benefit analyzes

decision tree analysis

Corporate plans or strategies

3. The Implementation phase

    Step 6 — Evaluation of options — 'will you like it?'

    perhaps use a matrix, allowing comparisons to be made, ranking scales

    weighing up evidence-'politics'

    Step 7 — Planning Implementation — 'how can you carry it through?'

    Big bang?

    Pilot studies

    parallel running

Critical areas for the success of SIS:

Relations within Project Team

Relations with Project Owner-Sponsor-champion

Relationship with those to be affected

In summary it is a rationalist, goal-orientated approach-best suited for challenges 'of how to achieve an agreed end'.

Activity

What do you see as the main advantages and disadvantages of the SIS framework? Can you think of an example where this model could be used to manage a change strategy?

OD Organizational Development

Organizational Development is a more holistic and complex framework and is considered to be a so-called 'soft' method.

It covers a broad spectrum. One could talk rather of an 'Organizational Development Umbrella' and it is more a 'school of thought' than a specific concept.

I can refer to large or small scale changes

Tends to be 'long term'

'OD is an intervention Strategy that uses GROUP processes to focus on the WHOLE culture of an organization in order to bring planned change' Rowlandson (1984)[233]

'a long term program of intervention into the organization's social processes, using the principles & practices of behavioral science, to create attitudinal & behavioral changes, leading to increased organizational effectiveness' (Bowman, Asch 1987)[234]

Essentially a philosophy not a technique

Change strategies that go for Culture

Following distinguishing characteristics

Broad, sustained, medium to long term

Process orientated, not goal-orientated

Involves a facilitator role

It is participative!

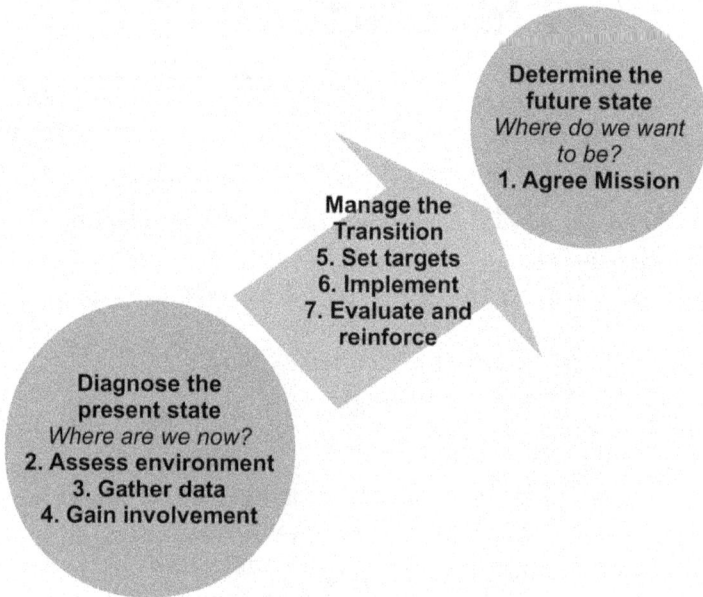

**Determine the
future state**
*Where do we want
to be?*
1. Agree Mission

**Manage the
Transition**
5. Set targets
6. Implement
**7. Evaluate and
reinforce**

**Diagnose the
present state**
Where are we now?
2. Assess environment
3. Gather data
4. Gain involvement

Fig. 69: The OD Process

The 7 separate process stages of OD

1. Agree organizational purpose and mission

2. Assess outer and inner contexts

3. Gather data

4. Gain involvement

5. Set targets for Change

6. Implement change & development activities

7. Evaluate& reinforce change; monitor& communicate success

   OD Values people above tasks — *'unless people are empowered, the organization cannot be fully effective.'Moss Kanter (1999)*

   Main drawback *is that it is a long term process — takes time and usually involve a lot of outsiders!*

   Strength — *culture changes, new units, overcomes resistance by breaking it down!*

BPR Business Process Re-engineering

BPR-Business Process Redesign or Business Process Re-engineering is described by its authors as:

'The fundamental rethinking & radical redesign of business processes to achieve dramatic improvements in critical, contemporary measures of performance, such as cost, quality, service and speed' — Hammer & Champy (1993)[235]

It has its roots in the ideas of F.W. Taylor and it could be said that Taylor was the first to come up with the idea. This was exemplified in the practice of Henry Ford, where manufacturing processes were defined to the last detail and then optimized for maximum efficiency. Some critics of BPR see its fundamental weaknesses in the fact that modern businesses are more concerned with the creation of knowledge and that it therefore cannot be applied. For this reason, the model has been much adapted and there are many versions propagated which adapt the original idea.

'Re-engineering strives to break away from the old rules about how we organize and conduct business — it cannot be planned meticulously & accomplished in small and cautious steps. It's an all or nothing proposition with an uncertain result' Hammer (1990)[236]

Start from Scratch -'obliterate don't automate' – redesign using the latest ICT (Information and Communications Technology) systems

Existing processes are inherently inefficient -so dump them & move on!

Hammer / Champy are the 'gurus' of this thinking

It is fundamental, radical and dramatic. 'Process' is a key word

Seven Principles (Hammer 1990)[237]

1. Organize around **outcomes**, not tasks

2. Have those who use the output of the process perform the process

3. Subsume information processing work into the real work that produces the information

4. Treat geographically dispersed resources as though they were centralized

5. Link Parallel activities instead of integrating results

6. Put the decision point where the work is performed and build control into the process

7. Capture information **once** and at **source**

A five step approach to Business Process Re-engineering[238]

Davenport (1993)[239] prescribes a five-step approach to the Business Process Re-engineering model:

1. **Develop the business vision and process objectives**: The BPR method is driven by a business vision which implies specific business objectives such as cost reduction, time reduction, output quality improvement.

2. **Identify the business processes to be redesigned**: most firms use the 'high-impact' approach which focuses on the most important processes or those that conflict most with the business vision. A lesser number of firms use the 'exhaustive approach' that attempts to identify all the processes within an organization and then prioritize them in order of redesign urgency.

3. **Understand and measure the existing processes**: to avoid the repeating of old mistakes and to provide a baseline for future improvements.

4. **Identify IT levers**: awareness of IT capabilities can and should influence BPR.

5. **Design and build a prototype of the new process**: the actual design should not be viewed as the end of the BPR process. Rather, it should be viewed as a prototype, with successive iterations. The metaphor of prototype aligns the Business Process Reengineering approach with quick delivery of results, and the involvement and satisfaction of customers.

Secrets of Success

BPR projects have been identified as successful[240] when organizations meet the following criteria:

They are strongly supported by the CEO

They break re-engineering into small or medium-sized elements

> *Most have a willingness to tolerate change and to withstand the uncertainties that change can generate*
>
> *Many have systems, processes, or strategies that are worth hiding from competitors.*

The use of IT is a key factor in implementing BPR and this change method is often closely linked to the introduction of new IT systems (e.g. SAP).

Kevin Lam[241] states:

> *The re-engineering profoundly changes all aspects of business and people. Part of the organization is easy to change by reinventing a way to work. However, the other part, people, is very difficult to change. In particular, it requires not only jobs and skills change but also people's styles — the ways in which they think and behave — and their attitudes — what they believe is important about their work. These are indispensable factors to determine whether re-engineering succeeds or not. Leaders must help people to cope with these changes.*

Therefore there is a lot of scope in this model for employing concepts from Human Resource Management, leadership theory, etc.

However, BPR is not always successful:

> *Caron et al. (1994)[242] report a 50 per cent failure rate*
>
> *Murphy (1994)[243] reports a failure rate of 70 per cent.*

Activity

Can you imagine a situation where you might apply the method-ology of BPR? What do you feel about the concept – what are its advantages and disadvantages?

Turnarounds

Turnarounds come into question when:

> *Immediate and speedy action is required*

> *The business is under threat*

> *Surgery is required and the 'big bang' effect.*

There are 4 Phases in a turnaround situation:

1. **Crisis Denial** (management do not even want to acknowledge that there is a crisis. Such statements as 'it must be the economy' are not unusual in such a situation).

2. **Hidden Crisis** (we talk of a covert crisis. Management has slowly become aware that there is a problem but it needs to be kept secret from banks, creditors and employees).

3. The **disintegration** of the organization begins. At this stage, the bank may be withholding payments and creditors could be holding deliveries or suing for payment.

4. **The organization collapses**

What is happening in this situation is as follows:

> *Managerial decision-making deteriorates sharply.*

In such situations, managers become stressed by the fear of failure. Their span of attention is reduced and they become more inflexible. Relevant information is ignored and managers become intolerant of opposing views. They start to operate on a progressively shorter time horizon at the expense of longer term considerations.

Decision making groups become smaller and autocracy increases, there is increased secrecy, less consultation takes place with an aura of 'one of us' vs. dissidents arises where alternative views are discounted

Whilst at the same time, showing optimism in public — 'jam tomorrow' — 'all is well!'

At the fourth stage —

There is a decrease in decision making

Commitment to the organization declines

Individual managers become self orientated

Budget cuts at stage 3 cause power struggles and undermine co-operation with increased centralization

The expectation of failure looms larger, thus reinforcing the mind set of failure

The most able people leave, so the average level of competence falls

Therefore the question arises as to what should be done.

It is a 'Top Down approach' (as BPR)

Speed is essential — days/weeks not months

Eight Key Steps-Prioritized

Some need to be done at same time but in order!

In this situation it is imperative to gain management control. What is vital is:

Cash flow — 'cash is king'. All possible means are used to gain immediate liquidity.

Inventory — excess stocks have to be reduced 'summer sale' approach for items which have not moved for years. If not already in place, a clear categorizing of age of stock becomes imperative and a means of ensuring first in, first out. Items which do not sell fast may not be re-stocked. If appropriate, commission sales could be used in preference to re-selling, especially if suppliers are refusing credit.

Expenditure — culling costs becomes essential. Great care has to be taken not to dispense with important employees at this stage but it will be a heartbreaking time in many cases as long cherished employees have to leave. High costs of employment litigation can lead to new cash flow problems and loss of immediate profitability.

Revenue — getting turnover up is very important because this can help the cash situation, especially if money received is faster than money paid out.

Debtors — making sure to insist on prompt payment. Bonuses for immediate payment and regular chasing of payments are essential tools.

Security — be sure to keep information within the organization and to hang on to what one has.

1. Establish and communicate credibility with stakeholders. Make use of public relations at a time when it is important to know who is who.

2. Assess existing managers and replace as necessary. This is not always easy as there can be emotional ties which make managers reluctant to make consequential changes.

3. Evaluate the business. Time constraints may limit this to a heuristic ('rule of thumb') approach.

4. Action planning which should be kept straightforward and short and simple.

5. Implement organizational change as appropriate, especially those changes that will help cash flow.

6. Motivate management and employees. This may be a time to start reflecting on one's own leadership qualities. Be willing to change oneself and be an encouraging example in this time of crisis.

7. Installation or improvement of budgetary systems.

Activity

Have you ever been in a situation where a turnaround was necessary? Looking at your own organization, do you detect any warning signs as described above? Is any action being taken or can you detect elements of the symptoms described above.

Summary

The question stands to debate whether any systems are better than others This will certainly depend on the situation but one should be able to:

Compare the strategies most appropriate in the organization

Recognize the relevant issues and the contingencies to consider in appraising other approaches to large scale changes that one might encounter

One will need to develop the appropriate leadership style dependent on the needs and contingencies of the situation. The following table suggest some relevant approaches:

Style	Means and Context	Benefits	Problems	Circum-stances of Effective-ness
Educa-tion and commu-nication	Group briefings assume in-ternaliza-tion of strategic logic and trust of top manage-ment	Overcom-ing lack of (or mis-) informa-tion	Time con-suming di-rection or progress may be un-clear	Long term
Collabo-ration and par-ticipation	Involve-ment in setting the strategy agenda and/or re-solving strategic issues by task forces or groups	Increasing ownership of a deci-sion or process may im-prove quality of decisions	Time con-suming so-lutions/ outcome within exist-ing para-digm	Incremental change or long-time horizontal transforma-tional change
Interven-tion	Change agent re-tains co-or-dination/c ontrol and delegates elements of change	Process is guided/co ntrolled but in-volvement takes place	Risk of per-ceived ma-nipulation	Incremental or non-crisis transforma-tional change

Style	Means and Context	Benefits	Problems	Circum-stances of Effective-ness
Direction	Use of au-thority to set direc-tion and means of change	Clarity and speed	Risk of lack of accep-tance and ill-con-ceived strat-egy	Transforma-tional change
Coercion or edict	Explicit use of power through edict	May be successful in crises or state of confusion	Least suc-cessful un-less crisis	Crisis, rapid transforma-tional change or change in established autocratic cultures

Fig. 70 Styles of Managing Strategic Change

Countermoves to change

These are some of the tactics you may notice being practiced during change processes:

Resources get diverted

Inertia is exploited

Goals are kept vague and complex

Encouragement and exploitation of lack of organizational awareness

Statements like: 'Great idea — let's do it properly'

Dissipation of energies

Reduction of the change agent's influence and credibility

Keeping a low profile

Countering countermoves to change

Establish a clear direction and objectives

Establish a simple, phased programming approach

Adopt a fixer — facilitator — negotiator role

Seek and respond to resistance

Rely on face to face communication

Exploit a crisis

Co-opt support early

Create a meaningful steering committee, task force or project team

Fifteen key competences of change agents

Goals	Communication
1. Sensitivity to changes in key personnel, top management perceptions and market conditions	7. Communication skills
	8. Interpersonal skills
	9. Personal enthusiasm
	10. Stimulating motivation and commitment in others
2. Clarity in specifying goals	**Negotiation**
3. Flexibility in responding to changes	11. Selling plans and ideas to others
Roles	
4. Team building abilities	12. Negotiating with key players
5. Networking skills	**Managing up**
6. Tolerance of ambiguity	13. Political awareness
	14. Influencing skills
	15. Helicopter perspectives

Fig. 71: The 15 Key Competencies of Change Agents

Communication

In change situations, it is necessary to choose the right medium and means of communication. This depends very much on the situation and the type of change and we remind of our introductory discussion on the types of issue — bounded or unbounded, simple or complex:

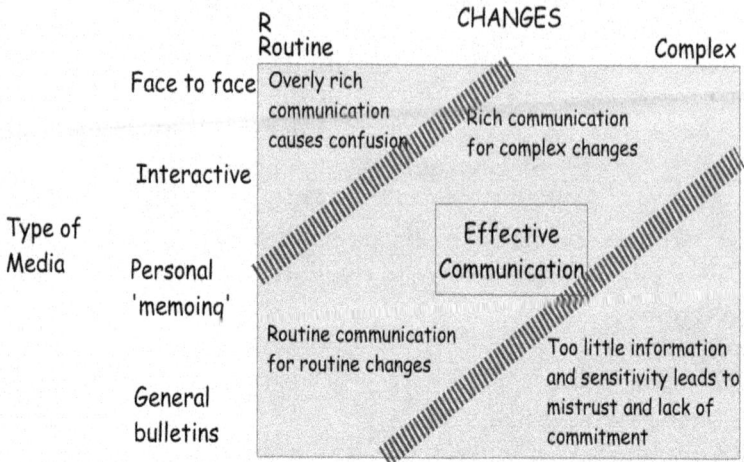

Fig. 72: Effective and ineffective communication of change

Change and the Learning Organization

Before we leave the subject of change management, let us just take a brief look at the idea of the learning organization. We have mentioned these ideas earlier and we will integrate them in the continuation of this series.

To summarize — learning organizations:

Are not hierarchies

Encourage processes which unlock the knowledge of individuals

Encourage sharing of information and knowledge so that each individual:

Become sensitive to changes around them and helps identify opportunities and required changes

Become capable of taking a holistic (strategic) view of their environment rather than a functional or operational view

Avoid power plays and blocking routines

Work on the basis of a shared vision of the future

Support other organizational members

Can cope with ambiguity and contradictions

Senge's (1990)[244] five disciplines for a learning organization	
Personal Mastery	The desire for lifelong learning
The Creative Use of Mental Models	Challenge our assumptions in the organization
Building a Shared Vision	As derived from the leader. Building a future which is positive and innovative. Meet the aspirations of everybody in the organization.
Team Learning	Learning to think and work together. Intelligent individuals are not enough. The organization can only learn when teams learn.
Systems Thinking	Getting a broad view of things, open-mindedness, interdisciplinary, recognize trends and understand complex situations.

Fig. 73: Senge's (1990) Five Disciplines

Activity

Use Senge's five disciplines applied to your organization. Make a table as above but this time add a third column where you add the sort of things which could be done to apply these 5 disciplines. What would you conclude about your organization?

Symbolic Processes in Managing Change

In order to carry out and reinforce change processes the use of symbols plays an important role.

Symbolic activity includes:

> *The use of rituals*
>
> *Changes in organizational systems*
>
> *Changes in physical aspects of work environments*
>
> *The behavior of leaders and change agents*
>
> *Organizational stories*
>
> *Language and terminology*

Change Tactics

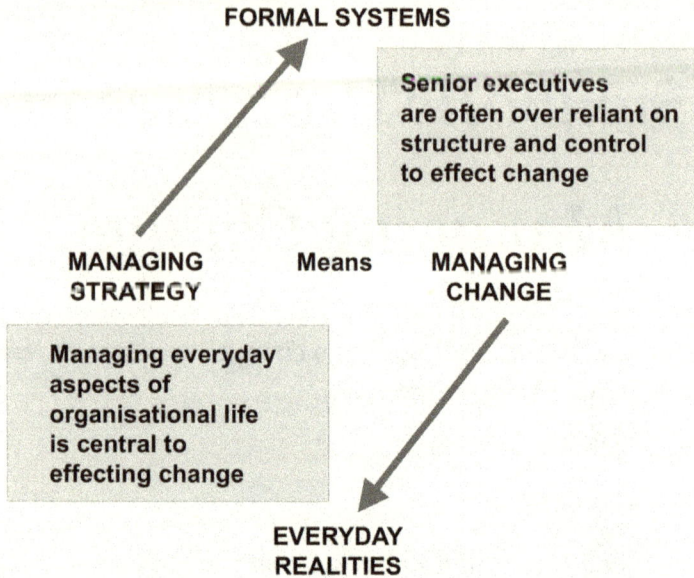

FORMAL SYSTEMS

Senior executives
are often over reliant on
structure and control
to effect change

**MANAGING   Means   MANAGING
STRATEGY   CHANGE**

Managing everyday
aspects of
organisational life
is central to
effecting change

**EVERYDAY
REALITIES**

Fig. 74: Managing everyday aspects of change

Timing

Getting the timing right is another key factor in change management processes. The important moments to watch out for and act are:

Triggers and crises

Windows of opportunity

Signaling time frames

Sequencing change activities

Involvement and partial implementation

Achieving short term wins

The use of outsiders

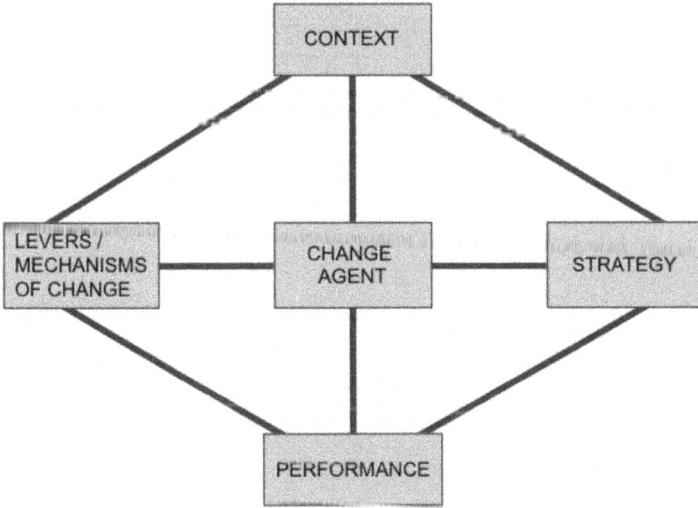

Fig. 75: Change Tactics

Activity

Returning to the above analysis and the other matters previously considered, how would you see your role as a change leader in your organization or environment. How could you act as a change agent? Taking a holistic view, what changes are necessary in order to make a difference in your organization and in society as a whole and how do they affect yourself?

We have now concluded this part of our discussion on the interaction of individuals and groups on the organization and how these can effect change.

In the next volume we will develop the discussion in the search for a holistic model of organizational change which integrates with the needs for society and which attempts to bring together the elements of IGOS (Individual, Group and Society) which was the starting point of our investigation.

Part Four

A New World

Holistic Advocacy (HA)

A Holistic Framework for Managing Change

As the theme of this script is a holistic approach to strategy, it is of necessity that we take a look at ways of managing change in a different way. The framework described below uses the concept of stakeholder advocacy as a means of implementing the change strategy rather than a single change agent. The advocates job is to manage a continuous change process in the organization based on a holistic concept of the organization and a strong sense of vision. Its aim is to leave no stone unturned in the strengthening of the organization to become creative and outward looking. The concept is in its infancy and no doubt will be developed further. It requires dedication from all levels of the organization. It consists of seven steps which are described later in this book.

Plotting and analysis

Before continuing with a detailed discussion of the holistic view, it is necessary to look more closely at what can be attributed to the word itself. It is possible to consider three puns (without reverting to a discussion of the linguistic roots of the word 'holistic'):

1. Whole – istic

2. Holy – istic

3. Hole — istic

It is undoubtedly unnecessary to inform the reader that pun one and pun two have linguistic relevance but pun three carries an implication which needs explanation. This concept has more to do with something which can generically be referred to as 'strategic holes'. These are gaps in strategy and tactics which need to be plugged or repaired and can be sub-divided as follows:

(a) Strategic 'moth holes' — these are gaps which have appeared and need to be dealt with as soon as possible. Some careful 'darning', in the practical sense of the word, will be required otherwise the hole will rapidly spread and become irreparable and can even lead to:

(b) Strategic 'black holes' — these are gaping holes which are now so immense that they are sucking up resources from and destroying effectiveness in other areas.

Thus a hole could be envisaged as a sort of negative whole — the famous 'black hole' which often can suck everything into it. If asked to draw a 'hole', most people will draw an unfilled circle. Given a pair of scissors, they will cut the circle out.

Returning to the two more positive and logical meanings of the word, we could define 'wholeness' as:

The whole is greater than the sum of its parts:

Completeness, perfection, not lacking anything, etc.

'Holiness', a word which is usually associated with religious feelings actually means something very similar to 'wholeness'. It has taken the meaning also of being set apart to do something and thus being a 'whole' person. This correlates perhaps with the idea of dedication. To be efficient in management or in carrying our ones work, it is not sufficient just to do it perfectly (as if this were normally possible!) but it is also necessary to be dedicated to a task. In fact, this dedication can make up for some of the lack of perfection.

At this point, it would be prudent to move over to a more practical approach. Taking the lowest level on the above diagram, we can analyze each strategic level (the so called 'I-G-O-S' — Individual, Group, Organization and Society) using each of these three types of 'holism'. For example, starting with the individual, in what way, in terms of basic needs, i.e. Food, clothing shelter, am I provided for? What about the other persons in my organization, do they have enough of these basic needs? What about people I know, friends, acquaintances, etc.? Society in general? If we are living in an affluent country, this may not be a problem, apart from a few exceptions. However, the provision of basic needs is a rudimentary basis for a healthy motivated organization. Rather than use our own opinion, we could ask people to state their opinions. We would then move onto the group. How are the needs of our management team and the groups of which we are otherwise a part (including those outside our place of work) in terms of communication and meeting together being met?

As far as our organization is concerned, we would be wanting to know if there is sufficient capital available to ensure that the organization has sufficient means to carry on its business. Also, we would ask if sufficient physical resources are available. If we do not have a satisfactory building for the organization to function, for example, this would show a shortfall in basic needs.

In terms of the society in which the company exists, we could analyze whether the population's basic needs are being met. If they are not, this could pose a threat to the organization in its environment as this would be a likely generator of political unrest at worst and reduce potential purchasing power at the best.

These analyses could take the form of individual SWOT (Strengths, Weaknesses, Opportunities and Threats) analyses, looking for strengths and weaknesses. In developing the strategic challenge, we would investigate the opportunities and threats posed and which conversion strategies could be employed.

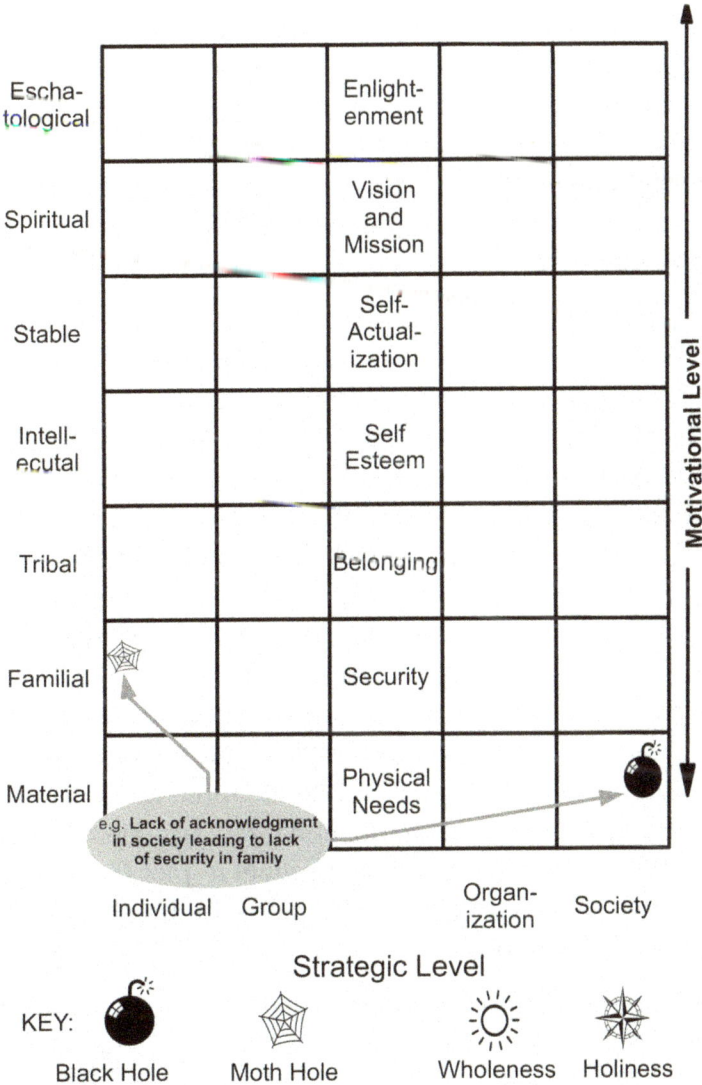

Fig. 76: The Holistic Plotting Matrix

Having made the fundamental analysis, we would continue by plotting these observations diagrammatically on a matrix

based on the Caveman to Angel diagram, using symbols to indicate wholeness, 'holiness' or 'holeness'. We would sub-define the last into moth-holes or black-holes. Against these
symbols, comments relating to the strengths or weakness can
be written within the squares of the matrix. In some cases, one
category may overshadow all the others so it would be justifiable to make this larger — in extreme cases filling the whole of
a square.

So far, the analysis has been illustrated using a horizontal
'IGOS' approach. In many circumstances, it would be worthwhile pursuing this analysis vertically. If, for example, one
would make an introverted analysis of oneself, this could start
with basic needs and move up towards enlightenment. This
may require long periods of reflection and have to be continually modified. The boxes could include plans for action and
improvement, being elaborated in a more extensive strategic
plan under the relevant dimensional headings. The intention
is to construct a complete holistic map of the individual, his or
her group, organization and the societal environment. This
could (and should) be further extended into a detailed elaborate strategic plan, referred to, enhanced and modified as required. Furthermore, it will be essential to plot the interaction
between the different aspects. Problems in the group or organization, for example.

The fundamental purpose of the diagram is to provide a kind
of structured mind map and as a way of gaining an overall
view of the placing and relevance of each strategic level and
the interaction. This initial plot will necessarily develop into
various tactics and strategies for action. In fact, it may be advisable to draw a second matrix showing the situation as it
should be after taking corrective action. A third matrix could
even have squares filled with actions to be taken.

But while the best laid plans of mice and men are doomed to fail so it is necessary to remember that the plans will be subject to continual review.

So far, our discussion has taken an *introspective* view, looking first at the individual, i.e. oneself, and then viewing the group, organization and society from this perspective. However, it is necessary also to take an *extraspective* view. This means looking at all levels from one of the other three standpoints. For example, if our point of interest is the group, we will wish to analyze the individuals within the group and the roles they play, looking for areas of weakness and investigating ways in which individuals can be helped and encouraged to play their parts in the team.

Activity

Make a copy of the matrix above and carefully plot your organization onto it. You might be able to build a team to help you with this exercise.

Applying traditional models

Most educated managers will have an existing library of management and strategic models with which they are familiar and which they find helpful in the decision-making process. In this chapter, various familiar models are discussed and an application to holistic thinking sought.

In general, as mentioned above, we can apply the stakeholder view of the organization. These stakeholders are represented very much by the IGOS levels. The human resources once again become individuals with individual needs, rather than just a 'resource' to be exploited or utilized to meet organizational aims. Cherishing people will be revealed as an organizational purpose as part of the organization's role in society. Maslow's contribution is undoubtedly a key factor in considering what motivates individuals and the holistic strategist will be concerned to go beyond Maslow and investigate individual aims and aspirations and how these strategically fit to organizational aims. There should be a program of monitoring in place which shows genuine concern for the 4 I's as well as developing Senge's (1992)[245] ideas of a learning organization to include responsibility for individual human development. This may mean that our concept of training and educational programs will have to be broadened in scope so that we do not just concentrate on making business specialists but in taking on the responsibility of helping people become whole individuals. This has an admitted advantage to the organization and this private agenda should be publicly confessed. The organization has a justified interest in evoking a creative and innovative culture for its own ends. Also, it is also seeking fulfillment of its mission and vision , wishes to live out its values and to reach a state of enlightened wisdom in order to maintain sustainable leadership in order to fulfill its ultimate purpose of serving society. In this environment, its employees and partners are carried along in its vision, identifying with the servant ideal. Equity theory takes on a new meaning as equity breaks the boundaries of the lower levels of the Maslowian pyramid. Expectancy theory gains a new quality as inputs are consciously felt to be bringing relative rewards and goals achieved.

Grant's (1995)[246] Key Success Factors can be plotted very closely against the motivational dimensions:

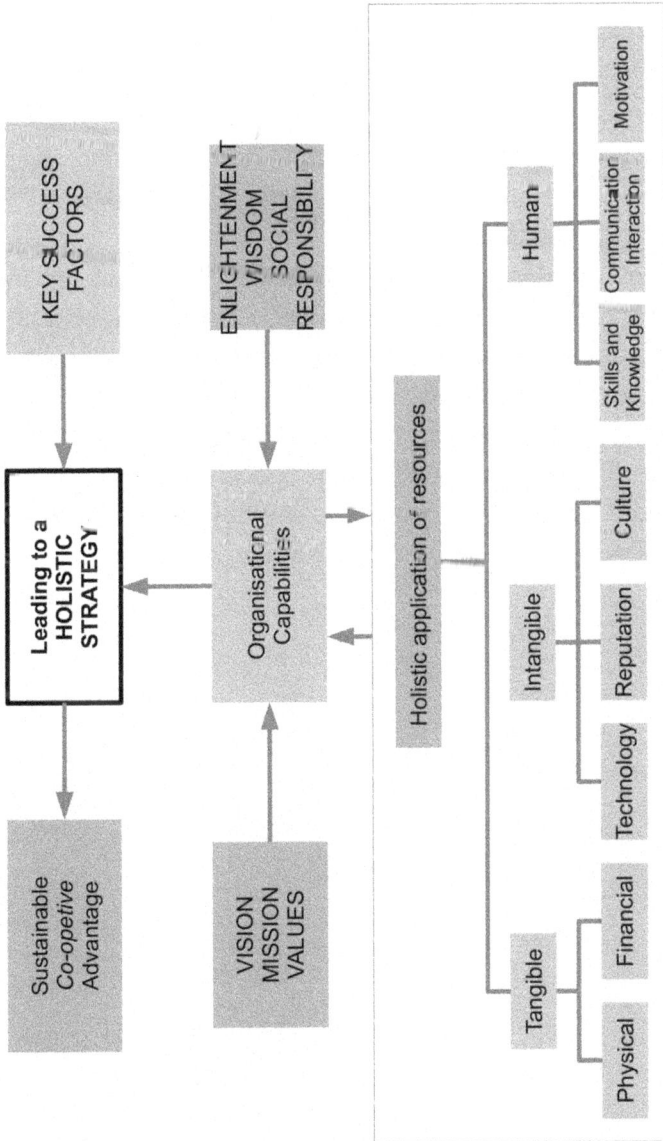

Fig. 77: Application of Holistic Thinking to Grant's (1995) Key Success Factors

---

Activity

---

*See if you can also plot your organization onto this diagram.
What issues arose whilst you were doing this exercise?*

Another, similar model which comes to mind in making
strategic choices is that of Kay (1993)[247]. Kay asserts that competitive advantage and thus corporate success depends on the
possession of distinctive capabilities and strategic assets. In
this event, a holistic approach to strategy is bound to lead to
just this distinctiveness. Kay's model can also be applied to individuals, groups and society as a whole, as demonstrated in
the following adaption of Kay's model:

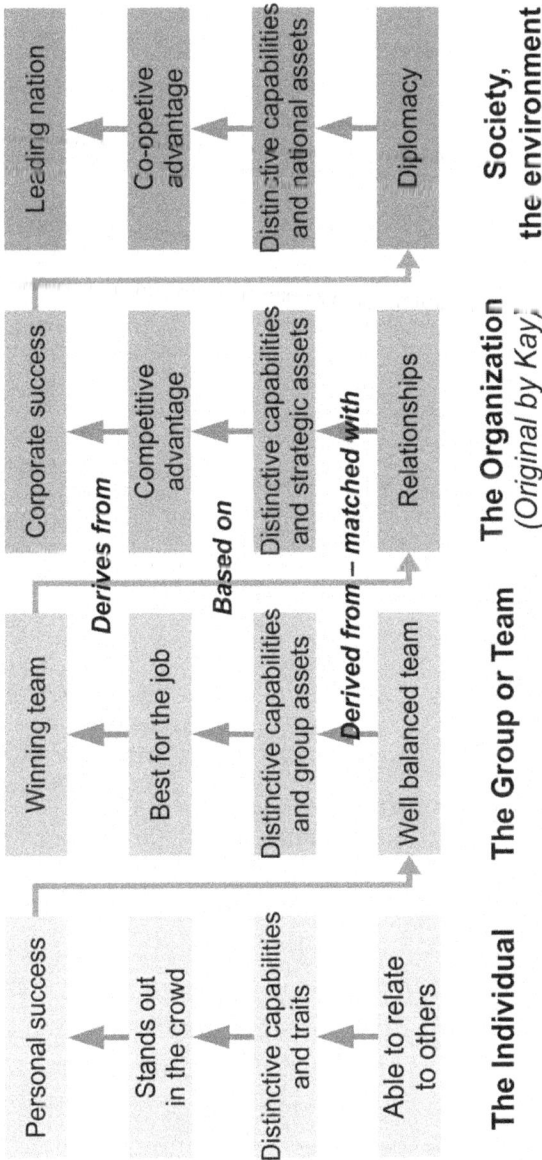

Fig. 78: Kay's (1993) model of corporate success factors applied holistically

Porter (1985)[248] developed a concept of generic strategies which are illustrative for the exploitation of competitive advantage. This idea can also be subjected to holistic application. This would be applicable where the ideas of cost leadership cannot be simply applied to an organization seeking *co-opetive* advantage.

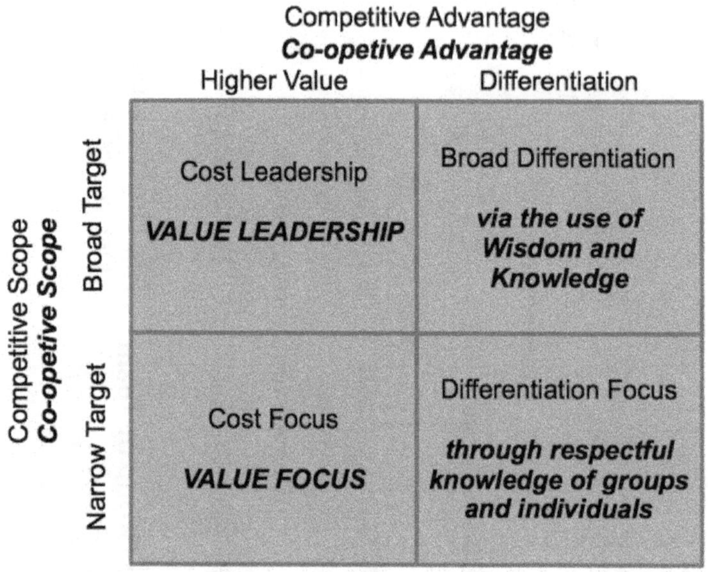

Competitive Advantage
Co-opetive Advantage
Higher Value   Differentiation

	Cost Leadership *VALUE LEADERSHIP*	Broad Differentiation *via the use of Wisdom and Knowledge*
	Cost Focus *VALUE FOCUS*	Differentiation Focus *through respectful knowledge of groups and individuals*

Competitive Scope
Co-opetive Scope

Broad Target

Narrow Target

Fig. 79: Porter's Generic Strategies showing the alternative of value

In this adaptation, cost leadership is replaced by value leadership. Leadership in a co-opetive situation is not achieved by 'killing' the competition through lower pricing but by increasing value (to the customer and other stakeholders) and creating differentiation. This in itself requires a broader scope of thinking and detailed consideration of the 'what is value?' question. Certainly perceived value for money will be included at the lower end of the Maslowian scale but should be extended to include the higher values. This does not mean to say, of course, that the idea of cost leadership is excluded.

This will continue to exist, especially where markets are saturated or near saturation. Value leadership, on the other hand,
can be applied more easily to not-for-profit organizations
where it is clear that the provision of value is more likely to
lead to advantage. However, it should be apparent that in applying holistic thinking, we are considering such aspects as
value to society and the environment. In a co-opetive climate,
attributes like self-esteem play a higher motivating role than
in all-out competition situations because a team spirit and
concepts of fairness and acceptance of 'the best man wins'
should replace feelings of envy. Whereas, in cost leadership,
economies of scale or scope are a prerequisite, with value
leadership superior knowledge and wisdom over broad areas
of an industry are required. If this is not possible, it may be
feasible to concentrate skills in a particular segment where
value is particularly revered. Again, Body Shop would seem
to have been an example of this (although it has recently been
much criticized, particularly after the company was sold to
L'Oreal and many franchisees were disenchanted by the company).

Activity

> *Using the matrix above, in what ways could you fulfill a generic
> strategy which was based on co-opetive advantage and value cre-
> ation? What things would need to be in place to achieve this?*

At this point, the question of reconciling stakeholder interests
will no doubt arise. Again, using a traditional model such as
Kotter and Schlesinger's (1979)[249] seven approaches to developing strategy in a participative manner (which we are as-

suming the holistic strategist will naturally aspire to) we can
provoke the discussion of possible actions thus:

Approach	Application
Involvement	The holistic strategist will use his or her awareness of the full range of Maslowian needs and use these to lever involvement at all strategic levels. Being sensitive to the full range of needs of individuals as well as macro-organisms, wisdom will be exercised in gaining support. The practice of Hesse's *'Fast – Think – Wait'* will be a guiding principle.
Through participation	Allowing stakeholders to participate requires openness and patience. The precepts of forgiveness and purity of motive will play a big role. Taking time out to meditate on such ethical principles will help build the inner strength to cope with this.
Education	As a learning organization continual education of stakeholders is an integral concept as the organization strives to become a knowledgeable servant company.
Through communication	As the means of mediating the mission of the new strategy. Integrating and encouraging knowledge sharing between stakeholders will be important in this environment.
Support	As a servant leader one has learnt to serve first and lead second. This means taking genuine interest in other stakeholder's interests and avoiding the typical stakeholder behavior of pursuing own goals. The precept of absolute unselfishness can be a guide in this process.

Approach	Application
Through facilitation	Not just supporting but actually facilitating the interests of other stakeholders can be a positive approach to 'winning friends and influencing people'.
Negotiation	The wise leader has the patience and foresight to be willing to spend time to negotiate a strategy with which all stakeholders can identify. One will not be satisfied with reaching a compromise but will collaborate to gain real stakeholder support.

Fig. 80: Adapted from: Kotter and Schlesinger's (1979) seven approaches to developing strategy

Again, the motivational dimensions can simply be associated with Mintzberg (1979)[250] ideal structural types of organization:

Structural Type	Motivational Dimension
Simple structure usually found in small or new organizations	Basic **physiological needs**. The organization's survival is likely to be paramount. Unfortunately, the future higher needs are likely to be ignored at this stage and this neglect may be difficult to compensate for later.
Machine bureaucracy usually found where jobs are specialized and where routine processes have become firmly established.	The requirement for **security** for the organization, the individual and the group become highest priority. This can also be observed in societies.
Professional bureaucracy found, for example, where a	A sense of **belonging** may be a strong motivator and hold

Structural Type	Motivational Dimension
group of professionals are working together yet almost independently due to the need for specialized skills on complex projects.	the organization together. Not only the individual members but the organization itself may belong to a professional association which will reinforce the organizations need to belong. A professional practice may behave more like a group belonging to an association of groups.
Divisional form often found in large companies with diversified products.	Each division has almost a life of its own and may compete for resources using its image of success as a lever. Thus **self-esteem** will play an important role both as a group but also as individuals within it. To some extent, the family of nations is divisional within the world as a whole. Gaining recognition and believing it are important for countries and populations.

Structural Type	Motivational Dimension
Adhocracy a very organic structure often found in project-oriented organizations. It is very de-centralized and dynamic.	This is where members usually will seek **self-actualization** in their tasks. The organization is likely to portray this thinking in its products and their delivery. This would be a conceivable societal form which has its aspirants and which has been attempted by some revolutionary movements.
Missionary this denotes a structure with little division of labor and specialization. Standards and beliefs play a big role in holding things together. Members are very much individuals held together by a shared set of values.	Here, of course, **mission and vision** are the key motivators. This will probably be true for the individuals as well as the organization. Some societies, particularly ones based on religious ideals have attempted this.

Structural Type	Motivational Dimension
Anarcho-theocratic this structure has been added to illustrate an eschatological organization which has attributes of an adhocracy and a missionary structure but where the organization has abandoned formal rules and norms and where, assuming that each member has already arrived at a high level of wisdom,'each man does what is right in his own eyes'. it accepts the inherent vulnerability of its lack of formal structure as the price for its search to find the right path. It defends itself through invisibility.	Striving for **wisdom and enlightenment** are the motivators which drive these individuals, organizations and societies. They may partially employ the other structures in order to achieve this. They are taking an essentially long term view and seeking to build regenerative entrepreneurial organizations to last for generations. Their leaders are servants and their fundamental aim is to serve their society and the individuals therein. Such a society could be envisaged in the form of the servant nation

Fig. 81: Organizational Structure from a Holistic Perspective (adapted from Mintzberg, 1979)

Activity

Make use of the above tables to add your reflections on your own organization.

At this point it needs to be emphasized that holistic strategic methodology is not a simple and quickly implemented management fad. It is much more a way of life and a process of continual discovery and learning where the individual manager, groups of colleagues and the organization have the search for wisdom and enlightenment as their acclaimed goal. It is thus a learning process which no doubt will embrace ideas from Peter Senge's learning organization. It will allow contemplated experience and knowledge gained to be reinvented into the strategic decision making processes, taking into account the observed effects on the social and natural environment. It is concerned foremost with long-term sustainable gains rather than short-term profits. The following adaptation of Andrew's (1971)[251] strategic planning model is used here to demonstrate this. No doubt the reader will be able to add further aspects:

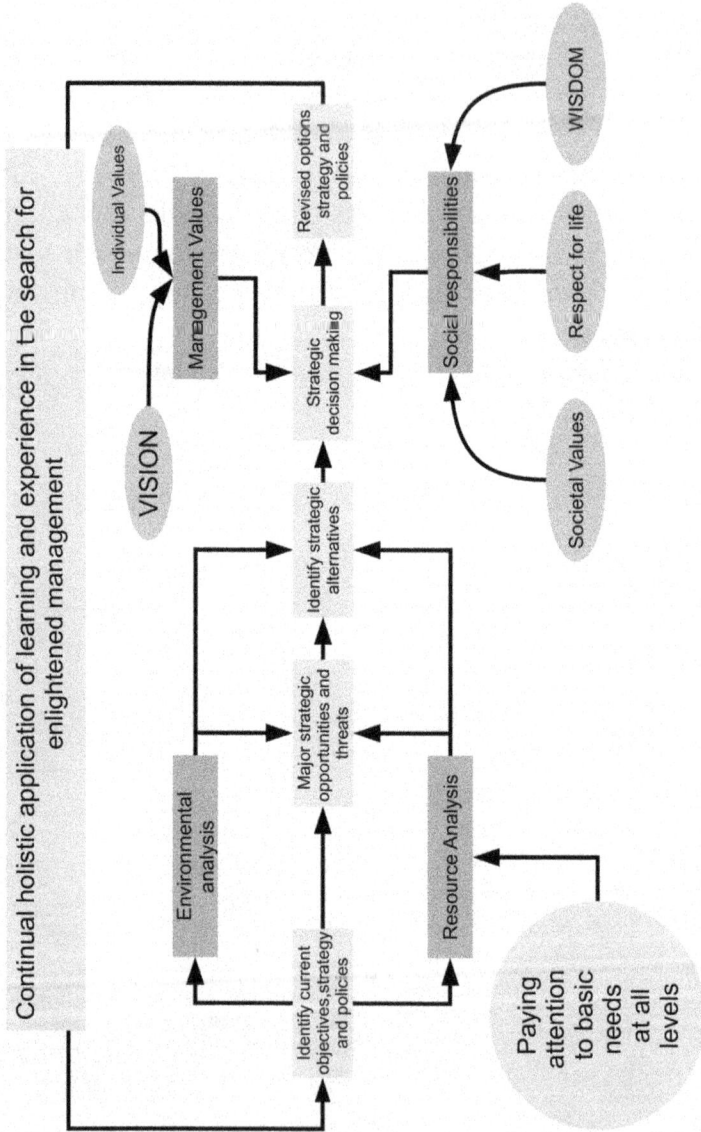

Fig. 82: Recycling of wisdom gained in strategic planning in the search for enlightenment (Adapted from Andrews, 1971)

Managing the Change Process

Under what circumstances can the model be used?

Generation change — particularly suitable because of it can ignore all previous management positions and initiates a radical culture change.

After a turnaround where it is necessary to build a new creative and co-operative culture.

In situations where existing leadership has lost credibility or where there is intensive internal wrangling.

It is pro-active and incremental (like OD — Organizational Development) but nevertheless radical (like BPR — Business Process Re-engineering).

Making Holistic Change Happen

Any concept in management is only as good as its practical application. Therefore it is necessary to consider possible methods of implementation.

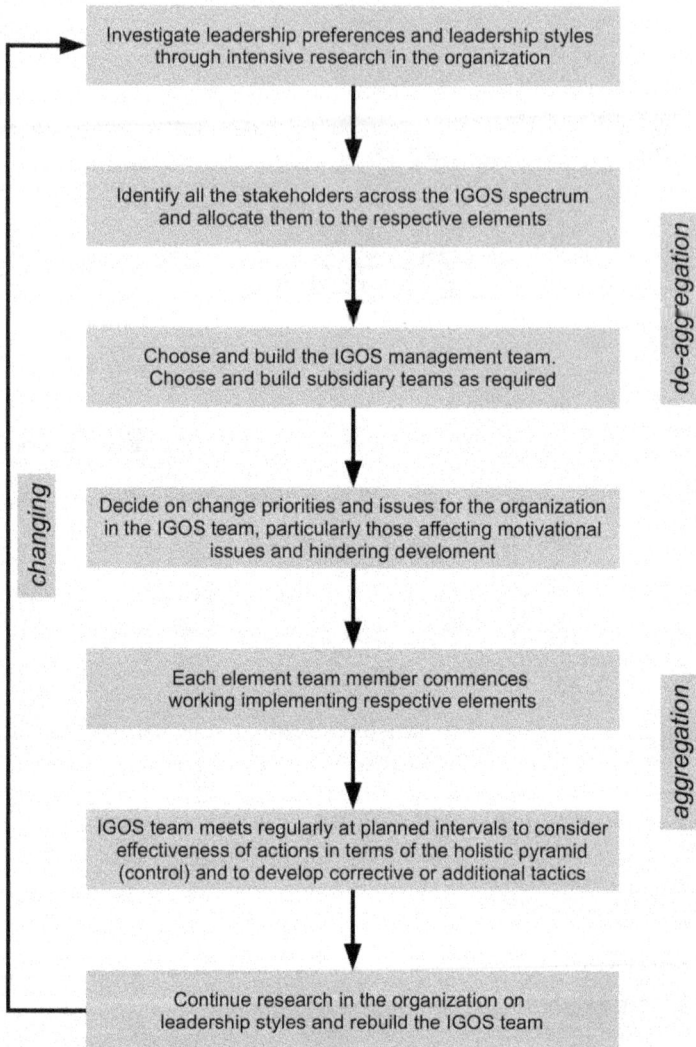

Fig. 83: The Seven Steps of Holistic Change

Change management should be planned in stages. Within these stages are specific processes and task which will need to be carried out. The proposed stages for a holistic strategic change are:

Investigation of leadership styles

This consists of testing of leadership preferences and correlating this with leadership self-assessment and peer-assessment. All individuals in the organization should take part in this irrespective of rank or position. This initial work may have to be carried out by an external agency in order to maintain impartiality and learning process. However trained change agent(s) from within the organization could be allocated to this providing there is the necessary support from the stakeholders.

Activity

Make use of the seven steps model above to construct a plan of how you would implement such a strategy in your particular organization.

Investigate Stakeholders and Allocate

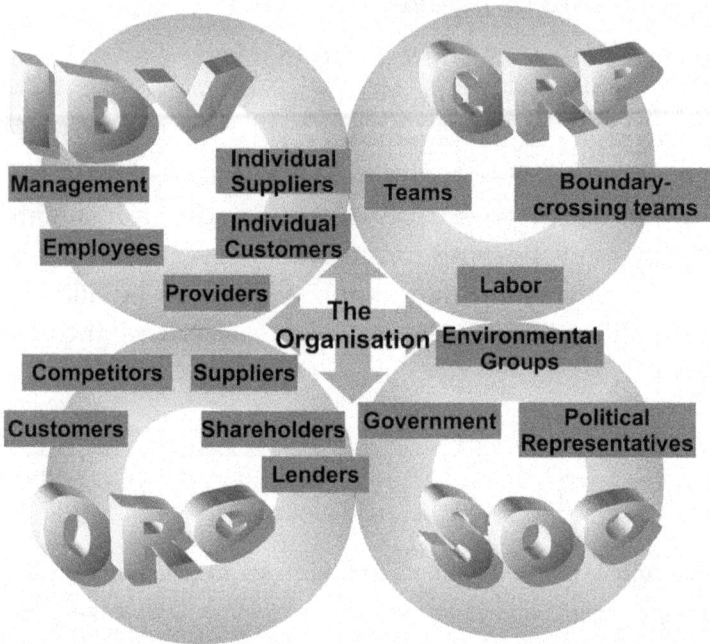

Fig. 84: A Holistic Approach to Stakeholder Analysis

To assist this process, an IGOS stakeholder analysis should be made. What we actually do here is to consciously split stakeholders into these IGOS groups so that they can be handled separately.

Activity

Take the above diagram and name names, putting the specific stakeholders of your organization into the diagram or making a table where appropriate.

Build the IGOS team

After determining the IGOS leadership qualities within the organization, a holistic change management team is developed with one person each responsible for one of the elements of the IGOS. These are referred to as **IGOS advocates**.

For the sake of simplicity, the four IGOS elements are abbreviated as follows:

IDV – Individual	**GRP** – Group
ORG – Organization	**SOC** – Society

These abbreviations will be employed in the text to avoid confusion with the letters designating the leadership types.

Each of these elements would require different management styles in order for the team work and implementation to work efficiently. These roles are themselves leadership roles and one possibility is to link this with Buber's leadership types mentioned in an earlier section which can be summarized as follows:

A	**Patriarch – At the beginning there are no people to lead. They are fathers and have to 'beget a people'** *This is often the role a leader plays in the early development of a firm. Often such leaders find it difficult to break away from this style of leadership and it may be necessary for the next generation to provide a new kind of leader which will create a new culture.*	**Abraham**

M	**The Leader in the original sense — one who literally leads the way** *A people in bondage who need to be led to freedom. This type of leader does not function as a king but may the precursor to a kingdom.* *This may be role played by a charismatic personality who leads people out of an existing stifling company environment to create a new company with those employees*	**Moses**
S	**The Judge** Based on voluntarism. Aim is to 'make right'. Often disappointing because men are what they are. Preparatory for the king leader. *This could be the type of leader who has his position due to charismatic power. He will often be disappointed when employees act on their own personal selfish motives rather than for the company as a whole. It may be that the employees see him as a weak leader and will also then call for a strong leader when they feel threatened*	**Samuel**
D	**The King — the founder of a dynasty** A king has to be anointed but also has to live up to the task. The failure of kings to do this gave birth to the idea of Messianism — the king who lives up to his anointing. *The tough leader who demands that things are done his way. Employees accept his decisions out of necessity and may fear to question them or to make suggestions, either out of fear or respect. Unfortunately, most of these leaders are privately criticized because they do not always have the interests of the employees at heart and may be exploiting the organization for their own interests. The stakeholders are also looking for the messianic kind of leader who only has their interests at heart*	**David**

	The Prophet
I	This leadership idea is contrary to history because he is appointed (from above) to oppose the king and even the people. Idea of the suffering servant because often rejected by king and people. Being a prophet means being powerless and his function is to remind those in power of their responsibility. *This is also a special leadership role to be found in business and may be the most important. This kind of leader accepts the current status quo but is critical and openly opposes the hypocrisy and self interest of the king as well as the dishonest and unfair ways of the stakeholders. If he is too loud in his protest, he is likely to suffer for it. He himself must be impeccable and have no interest in personal power. In a modern management setting, one could conceive a position in the organization derived for just this purpose with the necessary immunity.*

Isaiah

Fig. 85: Applying Buber's Leadership Roles

I have included a preference test so that you can see what type of leader people prefer in the appendix.

To try and discover the types of leaders people *are* you would need to get everybody to do a leadership preference test and you might have to try a 360 degree version of the test. You would need to adapt the test included in the appendix to accommodate those possibilities. The tests will be available for download on the www.ilbs.org website and you are free to make use of them for management and learning purposes.

Additionally, it will be necessary to allocate team roles within the team and, where a choice of suitable leadership types are available, to chose team members under application of a suitable team-building concept, such as Belbin's team roles.

The Individual (IDV) Advocate

This team member is the advocate for individuals. The first responsibility is for the individuals in the organization. This person is the one who has to represent the interests of each person as an individual and for their holistic development from the bottom to the top of the pyramid. He or she will make sure that possibilities and opportunities for this development exist and that individuals are encouraged to make use of this. In a sense, it is similar to Human Resources Management but is on a much more one-to-one basis. In a larger organization this team member may have a team of specialist working together with him responsible for various areas and functions but it is the leaders job to make sure that they operate within and share the complete IGOS vision and yet see each person in the organization also as individuals in their own rights. This IDV team has the task of discovering the individual needs of each member of the organization at each of the levels and doing their utmost to find ways of fulfilling those needs. No doubt, a team building model would be used to choose members. Some of the functions could be:

Functions

Training

Education

Mentoring

Motivational issues

Personal development

Spiritual needs

Reinforcing values and principles

Financial and material needs etc.

Of course, the word 'individual' can also be applied to other stakeholders than employees. These could include customers (which will be dealt with separately as part of holistic marketing) as well as, for example, students in a college or patients in a hospital, and the interests of individual investors or service providers outside of the professional core.

Leadership type

The question now occurs of what would be the best type of leader suited to this role. Leadership roles are allocated according to Buber's types of leader. The reader will find a detailed explanation of the leadership types in the first volume of this series, part of which is repeated here for the sake of completeness:

Martin Buber — Types of Leadership

In the fundamental thinking of the German philosopher Martin Buber (1928)[252] amongst his discussions of bible leaders, he comes to the conclusion that true leaders are chosen and that the term is reserved for those who actually begin something new. In the business context, the word leader for Buber seems similar to the meaning of the word 'entrepreneur'.

He identifies five basic types of leader. The leadership style is contingent and relevant for the particular time in history. We may be able to draw parallels between this idea and management leadership styles as they have developed over the last century or so. Whereas Taylorism, Scientific Management and the ideas of Henri Fayol may have been relevant in their era of industrial development, the knowledge society of today may require a different style of leadership. At the same time, we can apply this concept to the different types of leadership that may be required during the course of the development of an organization

Buber's 5 types of leader are:

The Patriarch (e.g. Abraham *A-Type*)

At the beginning there are no people to lead. Leaders have to be 'fathers' and have to 'beget a people'.

This is often the role a leader plays in the early development of a firm. Often such leaders find it difficult to break away from this style of leadership and it may be necessary for the next generation to provide a new kind of leader who will create a new culture. This issue is very much connected with the problems associated with a generation change in an organization. Understanding the role of leadership and recognizing leadership style can be an important tool in facilitating organizational change.

The Leader in the Original Sense (e.g. Moses *M-Type*)

This is the leader who literally leads the way for a people in bondage who need to be led to freedom. This type of leader does not function as a king but may the precursor to a kingdom. Haller (1990)[253] states that the Commandments and the

Law of Moses provided the basis for an economic and social order based on God's directive but that this can only be understood in the context of the freedom from the bondage of Egypt and later Babylon. And this fact is contained in the preamble to the Ten Commandments. This is both an inner and external freedom. As Haller, using non-religious language, expresses it: 'actually right from the beginning a society free from domination'.[254]

It may we worth reflecting at this juncture that freedom comes with duty, as Chappell (1993)[255] states, most people tend to think of absolute freedom as freedom from constraints but, he says: "I've learned that the most rewarding kind of freedom is *responsibility* – the duty to help others and the community" (Chappell, 1993, p. 161).

Thus this type of leadership role may be the one played by a charismatic personality who leads people out of an existing stifling company environment to create a new company with those employees (as Wilhelm Haller cited above, actually did).

The Judge (e.g. Samuel *S-Type*)

The idea of the Hebrew Judge is leadership based on voluntarism. The aim is to 'make right'. This can often be disappointing because 'men (and women) are what they are'. This type of leadership tends to be temporary and is preparatory for the king leader.

This could be the type of leader who has gained his position due to charismatic power. He will often be disappointed when employees act on their own behalf from selfish motives rather than for the good of the company as a whole. It may be that the employees see him as a weak leader and will also then call for a strong leader when they feel threatened. Such leaders have a strong sense of fairness and justice and are often respected for this.

In the Hebrew tradition, according to Haller (1990)[256], the demand made upon Samuel to appoint a king is seen as the first and greatest betrayal of the task set for the people. This had come about by the desire of the people to be 'like all other peoples'. A firm under this kind of leadership might have a strong call from employees to become a 'real firm'.

The King — the Founder of a Dynasty (e.g. David D-Type)

A king has to be anointed but also has to live up to the task. The failure of kings to do this gave birth to the idea of Messianism — the king who lives up to his anointing.

This is the tough leader who demands that things are done his way. Employees will except his decisions out of necessity and may fear to question them or to make their own suggestions, either out of fear or respect. Unfortunately, most of these leaders are privately criticized because they do not always have the interests of the employees at heart and may be tempted to exploiting the organization for their own interests. The stakeholders are also looking for the messianic kind of leader who only has their interests at heart.

Adair (2002)[257] quotes an example of this type of leader in an exemplary form in the person of King Alfred of England. According to Adair, this king changed the culture of England, combining strong leadership with spirituality and learning and was himself an intellectual, modeling himself on King David. In English legend, King Arthur is another messianic figure; who with his round table, where every member had the same status, there is no 'head of the table'. This seems to combine the idea of King with the ideal type of leader we discuss next.

The Prophet (e.g. Isaiah *I-Type*)

This leadership idea is contrary to history because he is appointed (from Above) to oppose the king and even the people. The idea of the 'suffering' servant because often rejected by king and people starts to develop, an idea we will further develop later. Being a prophet means being powerless and his function is to remind those in power of their responsibility.

This is also a special leadership role to be found in business and may be the most important. This kind of leader accepts the current status quo but is critical and openly opposes the hypocrisy and self-interest of the king as well as the dishonest and unfair ways of the stakeholders. If he is too loud in his protest, he is likely to suffer for it. He himself must be impeccable and have no interest in personal power. In a modern management setting, one could conceive a position in the organization derived for just this purpose with the necessary immunity. On the other hand, I am often asked by students, 'I haven't got any say in our organization—I have no power to change things'. Yet everybody can become a prophet leader and lead from the 'shadows'. This requires a deep understanding of power.

A Sixth Kind of Leadership—the Priest (*P-Type*)

However, the theocratic idea of Isaiah is the direct rule of God in men's hearts, not the rule of priests, which Buber states has been described as 'the most untree form of society' (ibid, p.157) because it abuses the highest known to man for the sake of power.

This form of leadership is often found in religious sects where the members are relieved of their own will to make decisions. Thus the members basically 'sell their soul' to the leader who claims to be able to interpret the will of God for the people. It has no justifiable use in business but will no doubt be found there all too often. None but the powerless can speak the king's will.

It can be considered that A characteristics should be relatively high because it is important that individuals can trust and respect the person responsible. Within the IGOS team, he or she would probably also have to display strong M qualities because of the necessity to stand up for the rights of individuals. The I type of leader would seem less suitable because this role is more to do with mediating between individuals rather than advocacy for individuals. The need for a IDV to remain neutral may in fact preclude him or her from this role. As a D is more a commanding type of leader, this role would also seem less suitable. An I has to work perhaps too undercover to be able to act as an IDV advocate. Thus it would seem expedient to look for stronger tendencies to A/M for this activity. Of course, we cannot use the P-Type at all in business but you may find them around, I am afraid.

The Group (GRP)

Advocate

The various groupings and teams within the organization will also require an advocate. This person will need to have a keen understanding of team working and be a good team worker him or herself. Understanding the needs of teams as opposed to individuals and understanding the differences is an important aspect as well as making sure that teams are able to work and communicate together. Also there will be issues that require close cooperation of IDV either in dealing with socialization problems or in team building. The main tasks would be:

Functions

Team formation and building

Building group knowledge sharing

Assisting in inter-team co-operation across organizational boundaries

Team resource advocacy

Communication – both at a human and a systems level

Team training and encouragement of team spirit

Co-ordinating team organizational accountability etc.

Leadership type

In this case, co-ordination is on a much more general level and the role player must ensure that he or she does not encroach on the role played by IDV. Therefore, a strong *A* type would seem to be less desirable because this is the type of leadership which individuals tend to look up to. There is a sense in which the qualities of an *M* type leader could be advantageous because this is likely to be a strong change agent and could act as a visionary bonding agent between teams. However, the leadership type *S* seems particularly suitable because of his or her inherent charismatic style and lack of emphasis on individuals. He is also able to mediate well and can ensure that teams do not act competitively, drawing everybody together for higher ideals. As the *S* type is in fact often seen as a 'weaker' type of leader, he or she could be better at ensuring that teams are not tempted to relinquish their empowerment. For this reason the *D* type of leader is not likely to be very suitable, whereas the *I* type would seem to display the type of characteristics most suited — especially his 'undercover' kind of role, often acting as a catalyst for change rather than a strong enforcer. As advocate for the groups, he or she may find themselves in the position of the Suffering Servant and it will often be a thankless task. To summarize, it is felt that *I/S* types are likely to be best suited in this team role.

Again, the group does not need only to apply to groups of employees but also groups of customers (segments), groups of shareholders, inter-organizational groups, etc.

The Organization (ORG)

Advocate

The ORG advocate's task is to stand up for the interests of the organization. This is a rather more virtual responsibility because the organization as such does not have a physical mouthpiece. This job entails keeping the interests of the other IGOS elements which may often appear to have a stronger moral case. One could see the task as maintaining the 'body and soul' of the company. This is a very essential function because the sustainable continuation of the company in good health is a prerequisite for the aims of the other IGOS elements.

Functions

Conserving resources

Financial interests of the organization — making profit, cash flow, value retention, etc.

Caring for the image of the organization as seen by outsiders and insiders

Maintaining organizational vision and mission

Managing culture

Quality

*Dealing with the interests of the company in the public
arena*

Building inter-organizational relationships

Benchmarking

Creative swiping

*Managing organizational knowledge, including patents,
trademarks and other intellectual capital*

Protecting against espionage, etc.

Leadership type

In considering the best type of leader for this team responsibility, it would appear that a more obvious authority is required. The SOC leader is more interested in strategy than tactics and is more like the traditional CEO or president, representing the company outside and interested particularly in the organization as a whole. Thus the *D* type of leader immediately springs to mind. This is the king who is going to "lead into battle and win wars". However, this would be a too simplistic view as in a holistic strategy, this leader is also required to work as a member of the IGOS team. In this role, he or she will have to be a good listener and able to be a constructive critic and is without real authoritative power within the organization. Thus strong *I* is likely to advantageous. At the same time, as inspiring visionary, it will also be necessary to have quite some *S*, particularly as powers of judgment and charismatic qualities are required. As this holistic change strategy is intended to lead the organization into the 'promised land', also *M* qualities will be necessary, especially as it will be necessary for others to trust his or her ability to do so. In conclusion, it can be said that this leader type has a good balance of the leadership qualities and this is more likely to be advantageous compared to having a strong tendency to any of the individual attributes.

The Society (SOC)

Advocate

The SOC advocate is likely to be a new approach in many organizations, although we are already seeing the functions appearing in forward-thinking organizations. This advocate stands for the interests of society — without compromise. It is like Schonfield's 'Me for Mankind'. This stance is without deference to any declared mission of the organization, as society's needs can change over time. His or her declared aim is to contribute to helping society reach societal enlightenment at the top end of the pyramid, while ensuring that the organization plays its part at all the lower need levels of society. Nevertheless, the SOC advocate is part of the IGOS team and has to be conscious that 'Rome was not built in a day' and that the interests of the other IGOS elements have to be considered. He or she will have to be co-operative and able to help constructing win-win solutions both within and without the organization.

Functions

Environmental issues

Helping the organization contribute to the local community

Sustainability in the macro environment

Political influence

Contributing to societal education

Drawing the rest of the IGOS elemental interests into the overarching holistic aim of the organization

Driving the organization forward as a motor for societal change

Interfacing the organization with society both local and global

Promoting the organization as an advocate of the better society etc.

Leadership type

This leader is faced by an endless (and seemingly impossible) challenge. Great tenacity of purpose is called for as it is a task which many will see as too vague and my be unpopular at times. As a very far-reaching vision is required, it would seem that a strong *I* type will be required here. The function within the organization will often be seen of one of criticizing and could easily be persecuted for his advocacy. Therefore there will also have to be a high level of immunity. The *M* type would be unsuitable here because this leader intends to 'enter the promised land'. A *D* would also be unsuitable because impartiality is required. The organization's interests are subordinate to the interests of society for this advocate. Some *A* qualities, providing they are not too strong, would perhaps be advantageous because in a sense it is about a people to be — a World People, a Servant Nation. However, too strong patriarchal tendencies could be misunderstood if displayed within the organization. The qualities of *S* are likely to be useful. The voluntary nature of the organization's societal contribution needs to emphasized. In this respect the organization is pro-active and does not wait for legislation before it acts. In representing the interests of society within the company, a charismatic style is likely to be of great assistance.

Team Spirit

Boundary Crossing

Accountability

GRP Group

Resources

Spiritual Needs

Education

Knowledge Sharing

Inter-Team

Motivation

IDV Individual

Team Formation

Mentoring

Training

Material Needs

Values

The Holistic Management Team

vision and mission

Motor for change

Societal change

Pushing holistic aims

SOC Society

Image

relationships

Benchmarking

Financial

Conserving resources

ORG Organization

Quality

Political influence

Creative swiping

Intellectual capital

Culture

Environment

Local community

Sustainability

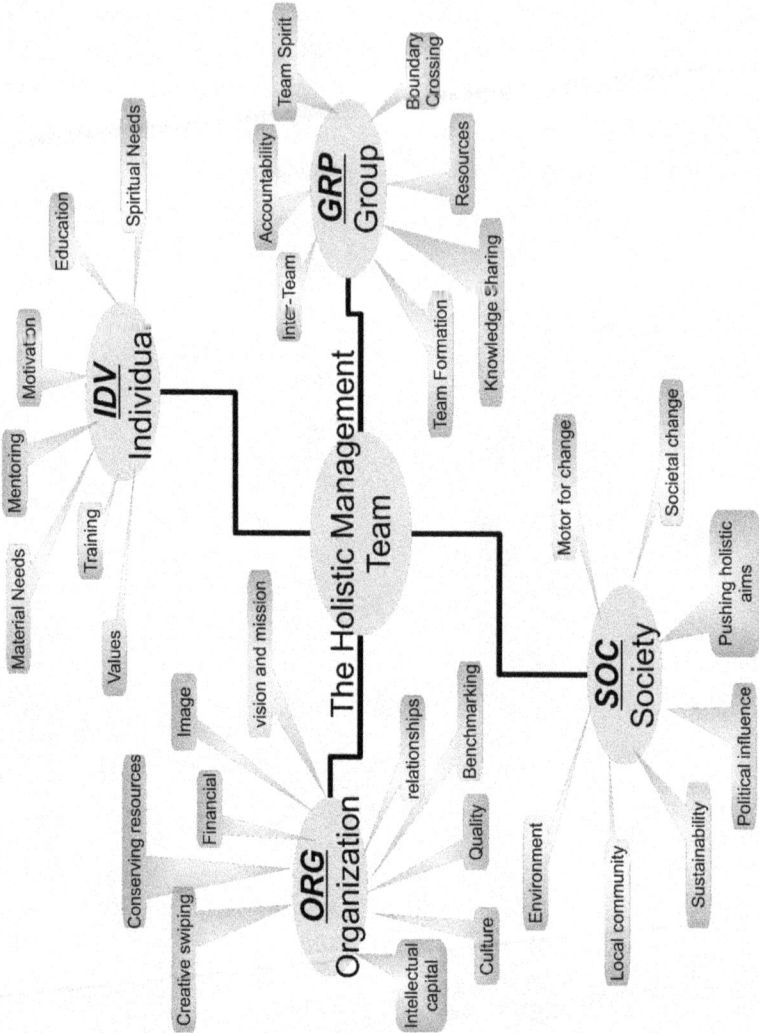

Fig. 86: The Four Advocates and their Areas of Responsibility

In the following section, we will explore how we can adapt conventional management theories in order to fit them better to a holistic approach to strategy.

The Importance of Strategy

Strategic issues can be characterized as developments inside or outside an organization that are likely to have an important impact on its ability to meet or determine its purpose or objectives. In applying a holistic approach to strategy we would have to be more specific in addressing the relevant areas, as described above. We have seen that strategy will always affect each element of the IGOS. This means making a closer scrutiny of the models and theories we traditionally employ in strategic analysis and planning.

Clausewitz, (ca. 1832): Tactics are for winning the battle, strategy for winning the war. For Clausewitz the war to be won or lost was pretty clear but what is the 'war' in relation to an organization which has to be, hopefully, won. Some would question whether the language used by Clausewitz is at all appropriate in this context and whether we should not be looking for a less violent explanation. However, assuming we take the word figuratively, the war to be won would be the one which achieved a four way win situation for all the members of the IGOS. One could think of each of the four advocates fighting the battles to achieve wins for their client areas, whereas, bringing this altogether in the IGOS team, they would be seeking for a four way win situation.

Win for Individuals

Win for Groups

Win for the Organization

Win for Society

The win-win-win-win solution!

This will require a lot of effort both on the part of the advocates as well as all the members of the organization and those affected by it. There has to thus be a clear commitment to consensus and inspiration by the vision.

Often strategy is confused with planning. Whilst we are proposing a certain structure in our approach to strategy, we need a very adaptive approach which takes full account of emergent strategies.

As a first step the strategist will be confronted with certain choices which tie in with the areas marked for change or development.

Strategic Choices

Firstly it will be necessary to decide on the type, area and scope of the activities to be undertaken. It could be anything from an entrepreneurial activity as discussed elsewhere or it may be more focused such as strategy to increase the size or profitability of the business. Seeing it holistically, it could be based on general feelings that certain stakeholder groups were not being considered sufficiently or even the introduction of such a holistic strategic change management system as described previously. Maybe a Human Resource (HR) department has become powerful and arrogant or a finance department is blocking progress for example. Maybe leadership qualities are seen to be not well matched after a leadership analysis.

The strategist would be keen to evaluate the success of current activities and if the way the organization was operating in the area under question was satisfactory. Such devices as benchmarking are often employed at this point as a comparison but even management gut feeling or customer response can be triggers as well as sources of evaluation. An experienced manager, for example, might just know that he is not gaining the maximum potential for his or her organization or that employees are not sufficiently motivated. Marketing could have become ineffective or maybe the organization has been getting bad press due to a scandal or environmental issues.

At the next stage it will be necessary to assess, acquire, allocate and commit a specific set of resources and capabilities needed to carry through the strategy. The use of such models as Hamel and Prahalad's (1994)[258] strategic stretch model, could be appropriate, especially if resources are particularly scarce.

A STEEP analysis will help the strategist to check for a match with the requirements of the environment but most important, there will be a need to manage the network of relationships with and between the stakeholder groups of the IGOS.

Levels of strategy

Traditionally there are three basic levels of strategic operation:

1. Corporate (whole organization)

2. Business (a business area within the corporation)

3. Internal unit (e.g. Department)

However, we might want to add the societal level added to this list. This would be opening the question of how the organization can have a societal strategy. Coming into line with our IGOS model, we might think of a particular strategy for the sake of individuals. In working with students who are working managers, I have often had to remind them to open the windows in their office and take a look outside. We are often are quite pre-occupied and have an unerring fascination for the walls of our office when we are thinking strategically and that is the meaning of seeking a holistic way to manage.

Strategic Fit

Kay (1993) states that corporate success is based on an effective match between external relationships and distinctive capabilities. Sustaining an effective strategic fit—fit between the organization and its environment is dynamic—not an averaging process where all competitors adopt the same strategies. This is sometimes also referred to as alignment theory.

According to Chorn (2007)[259], strategic fit is based on four logics:

1. Production

2. Administration

3. Development

4. Integration

These have to be aligned with the four elements:

1. Competitive Situation

2. Strategy

3. Culture

4. Leadership

And of course we would now wish to triangulate this so they also aligned with Individual, Group, Organization and Society.

However, Hammel and Prahalad (1994)[260] see things differently seeing change in the competitive milieu deriving from the following causes:

1. Deregulation and privatization

2. Structural changes to industries

3. Excess industry capacity

4. Mergers and acquisitions

5. Environmental concerns

6. Less protectionism

7. Changing customer expectations

8. Technological discontinuities

9. Global competition

10. Emergence of trading blocks

They pose the concept of strategic stretch—creating a chasm between resources and capabilities and bridging the gap by leverage as mentioned in an earlier section of this paper. Once again, we would like to go further, with each of our advocates considering these possibilities in each dimension.

Activity

How would you interpret Hamel and Prahalad's set of causes to ensure it fulfilled all the elements of IGOS? Is there anything missing in their list of causes in your opinion?

Strategic planning

Andrews (1971)[761] takes a more traditional approach and sees strategy as a sequential planning process. We made an attempt earlier to adapt his model to meet our holistic approach. Andrew's original concept is reproduced in the diagram below for the sake of completeness:

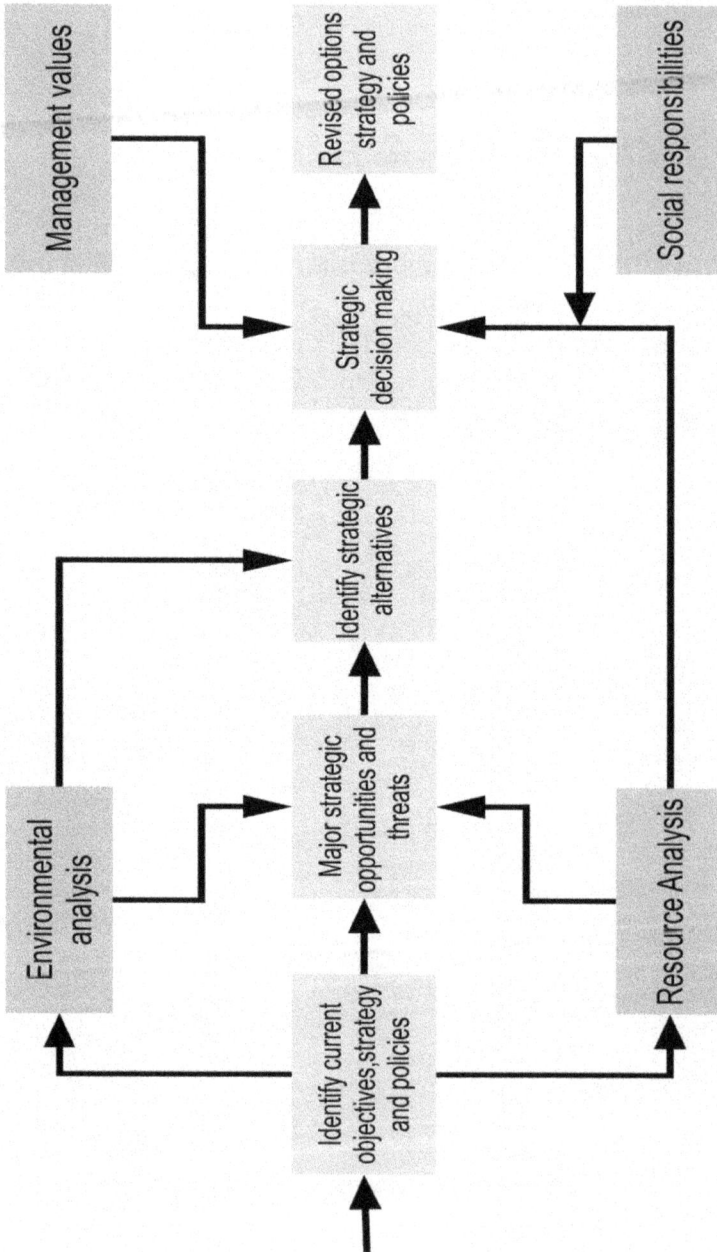

Fig. 87: Andrews Strategic Planning Process

Mintzberg (1990)[262] talks about two types of linear strategy differentiating between design (broad outlines—the whole picture) and planning (detailed steps to be taken) from which Mintzberg and Waters (1985)[263] develop the concept of deliberate and emergent strategies including pure deliberate or pure emergent strategies in their extreme forms and which is illustrated in the diagram below. This is an important concept because it emphasizes the point that 'life is what happens to you when you are busy making other plans'. In this example we show what can emerge when an organization decides to take up a holistic strategy to replace the intended atomistic strategy of shareholder value creation.

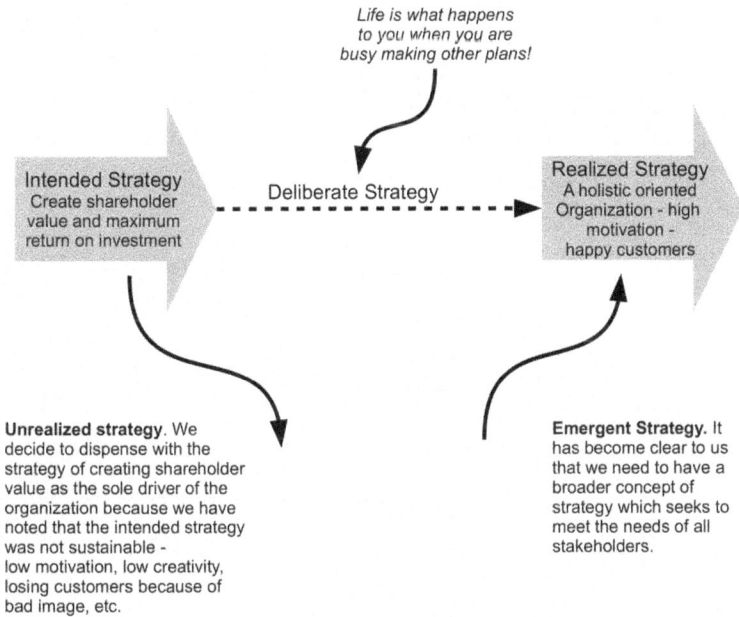

Fig. 88: Strategies Intended and Emergent and a change of heart

Porter (1987) makes the point that strategic thinking should not just be concerned with single management issues but involve all aspects of the business. To amplify this, Walsh (1995) talks of top-down / bottom-up information processing.

In order to assist the decision making process, it is necessary to employ the correct type of decision. This depends very much on the situation, especially in regard to the level of uncertainty. We can think of uncertainty in relation to what our objectives are and what the consequences of our actions will be. If we plot this on a matrix, as below by Earl and Hopwood (1980), we can define the type of decision making process required. It is quite clear that, on the one extreme, situations where outcomes and objectives are very certain, a computer may be best suited to solving the problem, whereas situations with considerable uncertainty of aims and consequences can only be solved using inspiration. Using the right method in the right situation is a key issue in decision making.

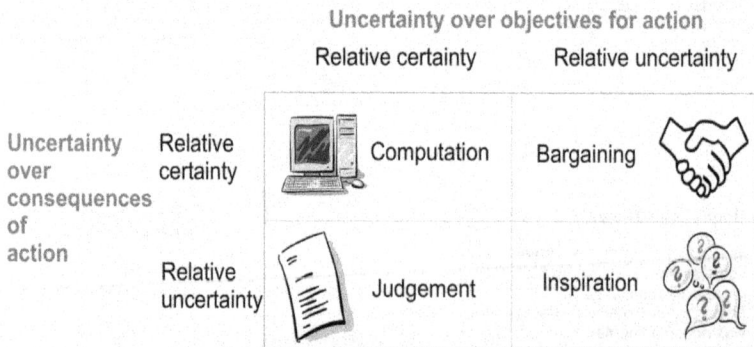

Fig. 89: Uncertainty

There is a danger that we can become bound with what is termed 'Strategic Recipes' (Spender, 1989)[264]. A Strategy can outlive its effectiveness as with the cheap goods retailer Woolworth's in the UK or Schlecker in Germany (a low cost drugstore chain, once the largest in Germany, collapsed as it was dominated by its authoritarian owner who treated staff badly and could not compete effectively against the DM chain, which is run by its Anthroposophic visionary leader Götz Woerner, able to motivate staff and gain loyal customers[265]). This thinking is driven from a manager's experience and provides principles to resolve problems without dealing with ambiguities and is thus less capable to react to change. Therefore there is a constant need for fresh thinking — doing something different from the industry recipe. This is where holistic thinking can help us because we can also enlist the creativity of our co-workers, customers and suppliers in the process. We might also glean ideas from family and friends outside of the organization.

Integration and complexity

Any strategic thinking is concerned with the following three fundamental questions:

> *Where are we now?*
>
> *Where do we want to go?*
>
> *How do we get there?*

Pettigrew (1988)[266] presents these elements formally as in the diagram adapted for our holistic strategy below:

Takes into account the whole environment

CONTEXT in which strategy occurs

PROCESS of strategic change

CONTENT of strategy

Process covers all aspects of the IGOS and uses advocates to ensure process runs holistically

Content is holistic and takes the whole picture into account

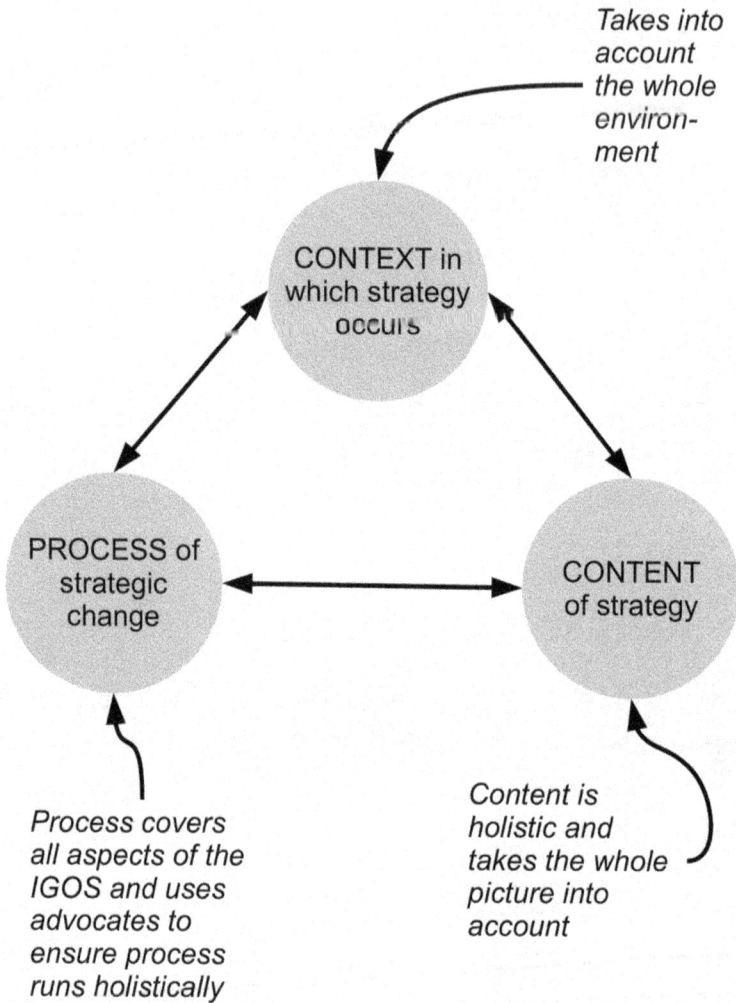

Fig. 90: Context, Process and Content

It can also be said that there are three basic dimensions to strategy:

1. Holistic or Atomistic. Whilst we are here propagating the introduction of a holistic strategy, we must remember that elements of running the organization will also

remain atomistic out of necessity. So, whilst our proposal has certain 'esoteric' elements about it, in the same way our feet have to be firmly planted on the ground in carrying out our day to day activities. It is being proposed here that the holistic strategy is the overarching driver of the organization whilst leaving room for individual strategies for specific purposes. However, having said that, there should in all cases be the full involvement of the advocate team in fundamental decision-making.

2. Current or Projective. We may still be moving from an existing atomistic general strategy of the organization to a holistic one. We need to keep the ship afloat as we gradually introduce the change process. The function of an advocate team might be purely projective in the initial planning stages.

3. Evaluative or Creative. Here again there is a place for both but we certainly will be wanting to encourage creative strategies as we aim at differentiating from the competition so that we can co-operate with them.

The W's and H of a Holistic Strategy

WHY?

Answer the question of *why* something should be done or changed. Can you be honest with yourself?

WHO?

Who is actually going to do the work? If you say the team should do it, you may be saying that other people should be doing it!

WHEN?

For everything there is a season. It may be better to carry out the plan at a later date. Timing is important.

WHAT?

A detailed idea of the steps to be carried out.

WHERE?

Where will it take place — including the discussions. What are the right communication methods?

WHOLE PICTURE?

Is the concept taking into account the whole picture and meeting the needs of all stakeholders, i.e. is it holistic?

+ HOW

How will you actually do it?

The SMART Framework

The SMART framework (Doran,1981)[267] is usually employed in assessing the feasibility of a strategy. We have slightly adapted it here to give it a more 'holistic' flavor:

SPECIFIC (to a holistic approach — what I mean is making **significant** difference across the board)

MEASURABLE (One often hears the adage — 'what gets measured gets done'. I am not sure if that is really true and I have not seen evidence to back that statement. It is often in the areas which are not subject to measurement where creative work actually gets done. So I would substitute **meaningful** here — does it carry meaning for those involved and society as a whole?)

ACHIEVEABLE (is it perhaps too other-worldly to be any earthly use?)

RELEVANT (not just to the task in hand but to the long term objectives of the organization and to building a sustainable strategy) You can add **realistic** here—is the project realistic? Also, will it **resonate** with people?

TIMELY (is now the right time for this or are there other priorities? Are the necessary resources available now and can one expect stakeholder support? Can it be achieved in a reasonable amount of time?)

You can make your SMART strategy even **SMARTER** by adding too more items:

ETHICAL and **ECOLOGICAL** (is what you are doing and the way there stick to ethical standards and the principles we discussed right at the beginning of this series?)

REWARDING (will doing the work and implementing the strategy be rewarding for everyone involved?)

Or you can make it the **SMARTEST** strategy ever by adding:

ETHICAL

STRETCHING stretching resources to bridge the chasm of your aspirations

TANGIBLE let everybody see what you propose in advance and where it could take you. Broadcast progress and build interest and motivation for your strategy.

Activity

Think of something requiring change in your organization. See if you can make use of these ideas by drawing a diagram based on them. Now see if you can add some ideas to the SMART acro-

nym or even try to make your own acronym which you think would help you to assess strategic validity.

Organizational Purposes and Objectives

Before embarking on a strategic plan it is essential to clarify the objectives and vision of the organization. In fact, one of the main reasons why companies fail may be due to just the fact that either the aims of the organization have not been clarified and understood or that the stakeholders are not in unison about them. There is an old saying that a house divided amongst itself cannot stand.

In the Ashridge Mission Model an attempt is made at logically defining:

1. Purposes and objectives
2. Policies
3. Public mission statements

The famous Ashridge diagram (see below) is used to clarify the elements of the mission. We may wish to ask ourselves at this stage, 'what is the purpose of a company'. This is a very difficult question to answer in general and will depend on our viewpoint. This can contrast from the simplistic notion that companies exist to make a profit through the entrepreneurial notion discussed earlier in this script which argues that an organization exists to fulfill its founder's dream. A marketer would argue that a company exists to meet customer needs while at the extreme end of the scale, we would take the holistic view, generally the thesis of this script, that organizations exist in order to change and improve society. This is the subject of the vision which lays behind the mission.

Activity

See if you can devise a mission for your organization using the framework of the Ashridge Model. If possible get colleagues to join you in this. After this exercise, discuss what difficulties you had and if and how you and your colleagues profited from the exercise. You might also try doing the same exercise with your family as organization.

Why the company exists

Purpose

I always suggest starting with the question, 'why do I exist?'. A good exercise is to get everybody trying to answer that question. Without knowing private agendas, you cannot design a purpose for the organization which people will buy into.

What the company believes in

Values

The same applies here – what do you and your colleagues believe in?

Behaviour Standards

The policies and behaviour patterns that underpin the distinctive competence and the value system

If you are introducing a holistic strategic underpinning for the organization, you are undoubtedly going to have to scrutinize these items

Strategy

The co-opetitive position and distinctive competence

I have changed the original 'competitive position' here to co-opetive position to come into line with our concept. A distinctive competence may be the bundle of things we can gain through a holistic organization

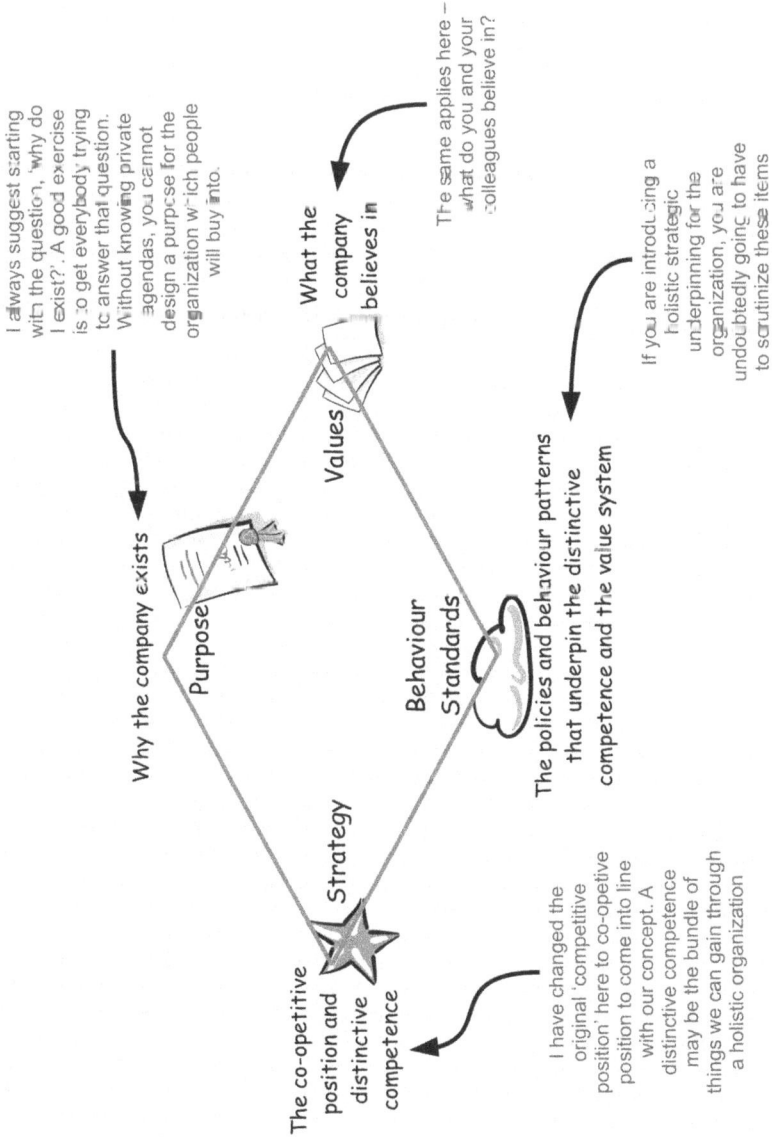

Fig. 91: The Ashridge Mission Model – adapted

Stakeholders

A stakeholder (do not confuse this word with 'shareholder') can be defined as 'Any group or individual who can affect or is affected by the achievement of the firm's objectives' (Freeman, 1984)[268] or as 'Constituents who have a legitimate claim on the firm' (Hill & Jones, 1992).

Stakeholder influence can be observed in the fact that:

> *Managers make choices dependent on a set of stakeholder expectations*

> *Organizations also have to react to multiple influences from a set of stakeholders*

> *This therefore requires a complex analysis of relationships in stakeholder environments (Rowley, 1997)*

Etzioni (1971)[269] identifies the reasons for Stakeholder participation as:

> *coercion*

> *mutual benefit*

> *Identification*

Stakeholder influence is shaped by:

> *The degree of influence of stakeholder power*

The balancing of stakeholder interests and finding compromises – 'Satisficing'

Managers may merely attempt to satisfy stakeholders while actually pursuing other goals (Pappas & Hirschey, 1989). This is the well known 'private agenda' unfortunately displayed by many managers which leads to a confusion between serving company interests and private motives.

The Stakeholder

Framework

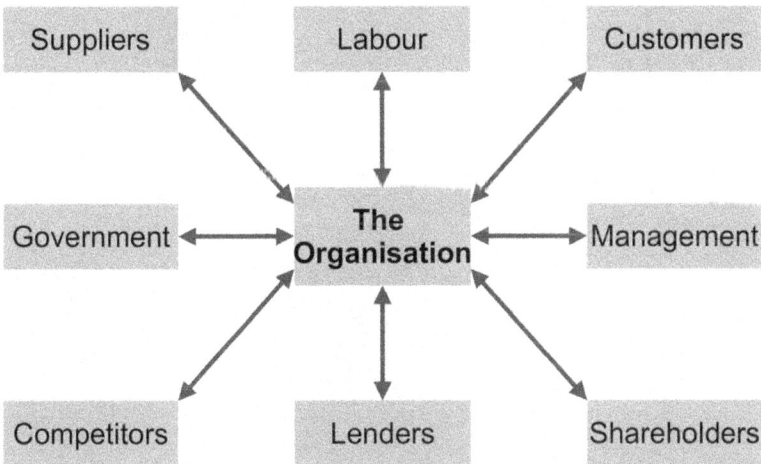

Fig. 92: Stakeholder Matrix

As argued above, not only shareholders and owners are involved in this. The stakeholders of an organization can be represented in a so-called 'stakeholder matrix'. We discussed stakeholders in the context of advocacy earlier but the diagram above shows a conventional stakeholder matrix included for the sake of completeness.

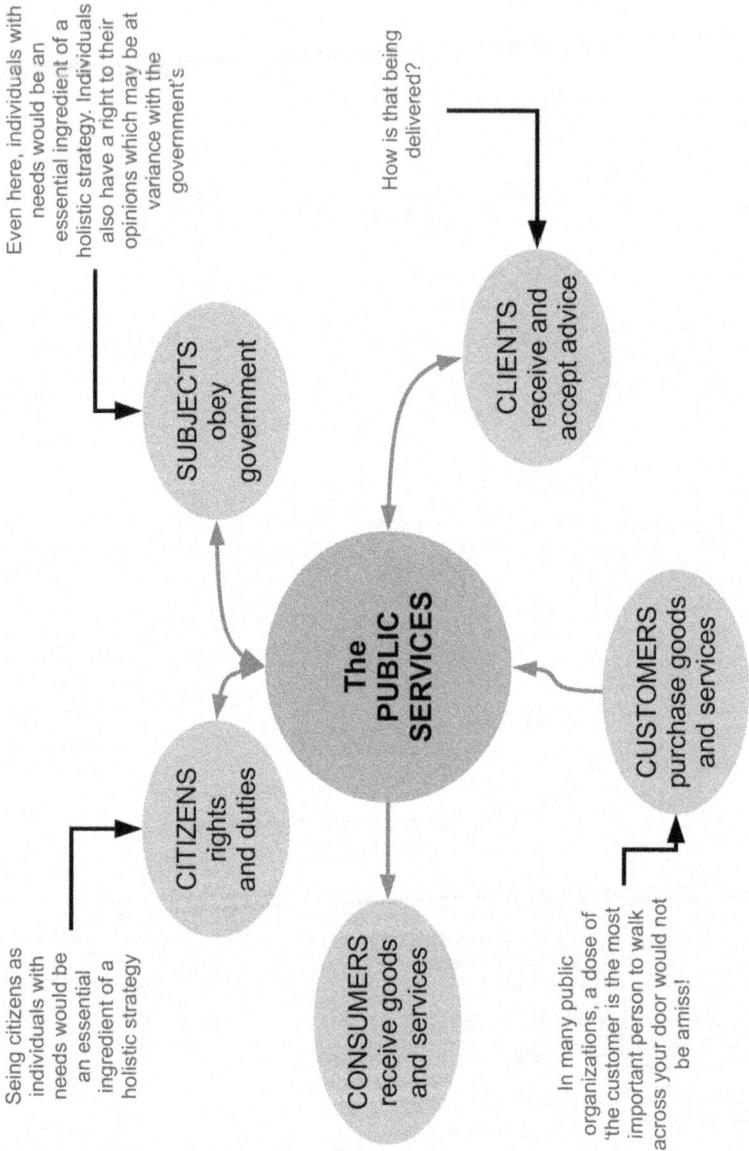

SUBJECTS
obey
government

Even here, individuals with needs would be an essential ingredient of a holistic strategy. Individuals also have a right to their opinions which may be at variance with the government's

How is that being delivered?

CLIENTS
receive and
accept advice

The
PUBLIC
SERVICES

CITIZENS
rights
and duties

CUSTOMERS
purchase goods
and services

Seing citizens as individuals with needs would be an essential ingredient of a holistic strategy

CONSUMERS
receive goods
and services

In many public organizations, a dose of 'the customer is the most important person to walk across your door would not be amiss!

Fig. 93: Stakeholders in the Public Sector

Public Services

The situation in public services differs somewhat because it may be difficult to define who the customer is and we find that the word 'customer' is not always adequate. Also, many services react to an assessment of public need rather than demand (Stewart, 1998). Relationships with the public also differ because the manger in public services is accountable upwards to citizens and accountable downwards to them as consumers (Elcock, 1995). The above diagram attempts to illustrate the five categories of users of public services.

Voluntary organizations

As with public services, voluntary organizations have the same accountability but also it can be said that:

> *Service users are increasingly perceived as consumers or citizens*

> *There is increased user involvement in government policy*

> *It is good practice to involve clients*

> *There is a greater influence of commercial management thinking*

> *Funders require user involvement*

> *Some beneficiaries question the right of campaigning charity to represent their interests*

Strategy as a quest for profit

You are probably aware of terms such as economic rent, EVA (Economic Value Added) and the Balanced Scorecard, for example and the issues of what the organization looks like to shareholders. While companies are required to make a 'profit', the term requires definition. What do we mean by profitability? Do we mean, for example:

Profits or accounting return?

Cash returns?

Economic profits or rents?

Shareholder value and share price?

Or, as in the case of voluntary or public organizations – profit to public, etc.?

There is a general confusion in the public mind about the term and often profit is confused with turnover. Actually, even not-for-profit organizations need to make a 'profit' in that they need to ensure that expenditure does not exceed income. Some corporations, like banks and universities for example, pay directors huge salaries and bonuses which are far in excess of what the owner of an SME might expect to earn. In public organizations, it could be considered as a way of concealing profits or used as a way of gaining political favors by offering highly paid posts to ex-politicians.

It would be ridiculous to condemn the making of profit per se but there may be a limit to what profit the public would consider to be reasonable. Bearing in mind that we also wish to serve society in our holistic approach, we will very much need to take great care on this issue.

Stakeholder Power

Morgan (1989)[270] defines various sources of power:

> *Formal authority – this is the kind of power a manager might have where you are expected to do as you are told.*

> *Control of scarce resources – people in organizations are often fighting for resources and this can become a source of power for those who have control of scarce resources.*

> *Organizational structures and procedures – most organizations have rules and procedures which have to adhered to and these are often used as a means of blocking or enforcing when perhaps others are not familiar with them.*

> *Control of decision processes – having a firm hand on meetings, insisting on committee discussions can be used as a way of exerting power for example. Those in authority can insist on signing for decisions or insisting that everything goes over their desk.*

> *Control of knowledge and information – the use of expert knowledge can be a way of making sure that certain things get done a certain way or by keeping back knowledge until the right moment, surprises can force decisions.*

> *Boundary management – probably everybody at some point in their career has crossed swords with a personal assistant in another department who blocks access to the boos or does not pass on information.*

> *Ability to manage uncertainty – some people are more risk averse than others and being willing to 'stick your neck out' where others are security conscious can be a way of getting ahead – as long as everything goes smoothly.*

Control of technology – if the IT manager does not want to do it, he may just say he has no time right now. You might need to have some special data and have to keep up good relations with the technology guys if you want to get it. In an engineering environment, one department's success may be totally dependent on the cooperation from another department who has access to special technology.

Alliances and informal networks – having strong connections and a good network can certainly be a valuable source of power. Sometimes you might need an ally in a meeting but that ally might expect favors from you too.

Countervailing power – opposing organizations like unions or works councils can hold a lot of sway. Making the right connections here can be a way of influencing their power.

Symbolism and the management of meaning – understanding how to make use of an organization's culture can also give power to the initiated.

Gender power – feelings of disadvantage can be exploited and of course sexual attraction or the differing way we treat the other sex can have an influence. Also, in some organizations, sexual persuasion can be a source of influence.

The Power one already has – our own character and style lend a certain art of persuasion which can be used to exert power. If people find us charming or charismatic even, they can often be persuaded to accept our ideas.

Activity

Think about the people you know both in your organization and amongst your acquaintances. How do they exert or express power? What about yourself? How do these approaches link to Morgan's ideas on power?

The market-led organization

Market-orientation and customer focus is the backbone of marketing theory and the domain of the marketer, as mentioned above. However, it has to be asked in how far this is compatible with balancing stakeholder interests. To conclude, it can safely be said that management specialists tend to support the interests of the stakeholders they represent. Some of the ideas used in a market-led organization are described below.

Analyzing External Relationships

Kotler, 1980[271] refers to the far and near environment:

1. Task—suppliers, distributors and final buyers

2. Competitive—organizations competing for scarce resources of all types

3. Public—regulating institutions

4. Macro—major societal forces, demography, economics, natural resources, politics, etc.

The Far (macro) Environment

Fahey and Narayanan (1986)[272] see the macro environment as a system which has come to be known as STEEP (sometimes referred to as STEP, PEST and PESTLE) analysis. Its elements are as follows:

Sociological

Demographics, income levels, social class, education levels, religion, etc.

Technological

Transport systems, energy supplies, telecommunications, technical equipment in households and businesses, etc.

Economic

Rate of inflation, spending power, percentage of people in pension, the general economy, bankruptcies, etc.

Environmental (this was added to STEP/PEST)

Prevailing ecology laws, green sensibility in the population, percentage of renewable energy and energy consumption, pollution controls and laws, etc.

Political

Taxes, unemployment laws and employment laws, social security contributions, customs duty and embargoes.

Legal (in STEEP, this is included in Political)

Industrial health and safety, advertising standards, product safety, legal system, company registrations and company law, etc.

Activity

By researching in Internet and elsewhere, gather as much information as you can about the external (macro) environment in your country or one where your organization is active. Make sure you keep this general and do not fall into the trap of relating it specifically to your organization or its products.

The Near (Micro) Environment

Influences on the micro environment are such things as resource rivals, supplier rivals and customer rivals. Sometimes emplyees, the public, media and so on are added to the list, depending on the area of business involved.

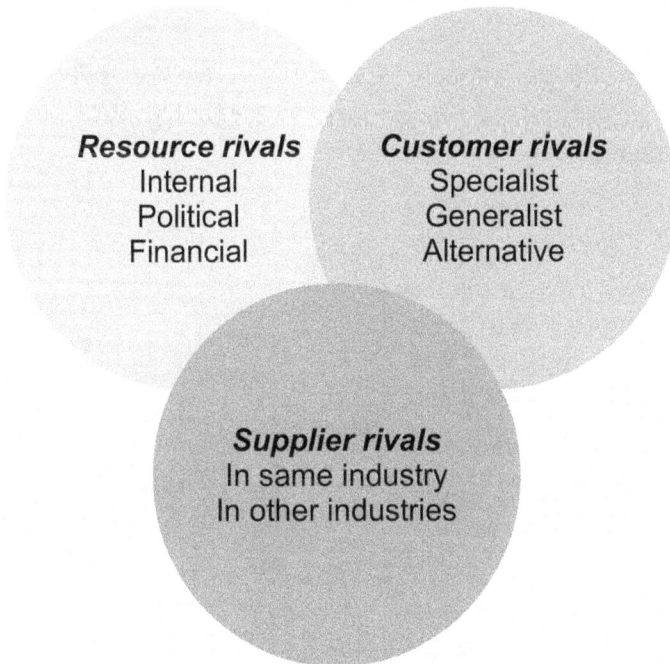

Resource rivals
Internal
Political
Financial

Customer rivals
Specialist
Generalist
Alternative

Supplier rivals
In same industry
In other industries

Fig. 94: Influences in the Near Environment

Activity

*Now analyze your near environment in the same way you did
with the macro environment above. This time, of course, this is
very much tied to your organization and you will need more internal information to do this exercise. You can also try doing the
same thing with one of your competitors. If you now have the
possibility to share your findings and discuss them with others,
this would be most helpful.*

Industry structure (Porter, 1979)[273]

The industry sector can be seen as a tension between the
threat of entrants/threat of substitutes/bargaining power of
customers/suppliers/industry rivalry:

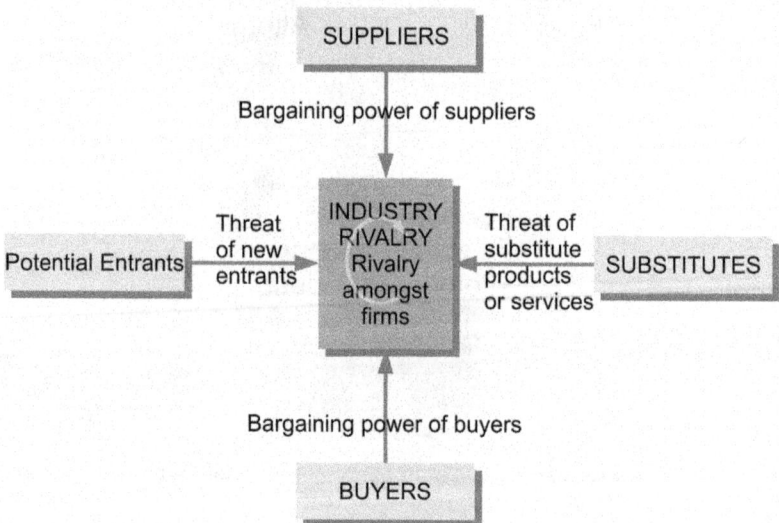

Fig. 95: Porter's Model of Industry Rivalry

Activity

Again, try your hand at an analysis of the industrial structure around your organization. What does it tell you?

Schumpeter (1942)[274] doubted whether the current industry structure is a reliable aspect to enable us to foresee the future and talks of a "Perennial gale of creative destruction" We are in a state of Hypercompetition — intense and rapid moves.

Game theory

At this point we should introduce the idea of co-opetition (Brandenburger and Nalebuff, 1997)[275]. In this scenario, the player is a "complementor" when customers value your product more when they have the other player's product also (e.g. Microsoft+Intel). The player is however a competitor when your products are valued less when they have the other player's product than when they have yours alone. Value Net recognizes these two types of relationship and the player can occupy multiple roles. There are fundamentally two Key success factors (KSF's):

1. What do customers want?

2. How does the firm survive competition?

Anybody who has tried introducing a new product into a market which has never as such been seen before, will be aware of how difficult and expensive it is without competitors to help build your market. At first glance, it would seem that having exclusivity is a real chance to make money and fix prices how one will but it soon will become apparent that competitors are in fact your best partners because they help you build markets. So do not fight your competitors — it is better to try and please your customers!

Activity

Do a brief survey in your organization. Ask colleagues and sales people how they see the competition. See if you can tie this up with the discussion here.

Prisoner's Dilemma

In the famous so-called 'Prisoner's Dilemma' (Flood, 1952)[276]:

Two men are arrested, but the police do not possess enough information for a conviction. Following the separation of the two men, the police offer both a similar deal — if one testifies against his partner (defects/betrays), and the other remains silent (cooperates/assists), the betrayer goes free and the one that remains silent receives the full one-year sentence. If both remain silent, both are sentenced to only one month in jail for a minor charge. If each 'rats out' the other, each receives a three-month sentence. Each prisoner must choose either to betray or remain silent; the decision of each is kept quiet. What should they do? If it is supposed here that each player is only concerned with lessening his time in jail, the game becomes a non-zero sum game where the two players may either assist or betray the other. In the game, the sole worry of the prisoners seems to be increasing his own reward. The interesting symmetry of this problem is that the logical decision leads each to betray the other, even though their individual 'prize' would be greater if they cooperated.

Decisions

There are different basic strategic decisions an organization can make and this will influence the way they concentrate their resources:

By Deciding to specialize

1. By pursuing strong branding. Be creating a strong brand image, it helps customers make choices as well as making a clear differentiation to others in the market.

2. Employing a highly specialized or skilled sales force. A technical orientation of sales people can help customers in their decision-making and create a certain bonding of customer relations.

3. By dominating niche markets. Particularly smaller companies are best advised to search for what others are not doing rather than going for a 'me too' approach.

4. By cultivating specialist knowledge or skills. The knowledge based company is going to be at an advantage long term but it may need considerable investment in early stages.

5. By investing in intellectual property. It is not enough to take out as many patents or registered trade marks as possible, the organization must also be in a financial

position to defend them, otherwise they can prove worthless.

6. By pursuing exclusivity in links to the distribution network. Whilst having exclusive contractual arrangements may seem advantageous, such contracts have to be enforced and may in fact not be the best long term approach. Good relationships are more valuable than contracts and trust is a better partner than law. Making sure to take care of distributor interests, ensuring a solid and honest attitude to business relationships and giving maximum support are all key issues in building a sustainable distribution network. Good partnerships can be more valuable long term than absolute control of markets. Good relationships will give you feedback from the market and drive you to become more competitive.

or by:

Deciding to seek lowest cost production (cost leadership — usually there is only room for 1 or 2 firms in a market)

1. Economies of scale. Keeping production and distribution costs down to a minimum are likely to be key factors for success with this strategy. Small companies may not find this so easy and off-shore solutions with currently cheap labor may also not be a sustainable strategy.

2. Accumulation of experience. This can hardly be beaten and may be harder to imitate but others may attempt through the use of cheap labor and momentarily disturb customer relations.

3. Superior technology or logistics. Amazon is one of the most famous examples of this. Changing the delivery

    chain and having superior IT solutions as well as gaining special terms with transport companies has helped them become market leader.

4. Establishing a cost-cutting culture. Getting everybody behind this in the organization can promote higher efficiency. If the only aim is increased shareholder value, it may be hard to realize.

alternatively by:

Deciding to focus (on customers). This is an important strategy where economies of scope are a possibility. Having a wide range of products to satisfy customer needs can be a helpful approach but it will be necessary to monitor costs carefully to make sure that losses are not incurred.

Deciding to radically go for a holistic strategy and to seek the greatest creation of value. This is my suggestion based on the ideas propounded in *The Beans and the Dreams*. By building a holistically oriented culture and a buy-in from all stakeholders with a common aim to create value rather than a cost and profit culture, may in the end in fact, lead to greater profitability in fact.

Activity

Which of these strategies are likely to fit best to your organization? Perhaps it will be a combination of a number of strategies listed here. How does this compare with your organization's strategy at present?

Capabilities

The actual capabilities of the organization have to be considered and it has to be decided whether the organization can:

Outperform its opponents. This could be in any area, technically, logistics, customer service, etc.

Generate significant customer-value. Will the customer have a strong feeling that the package you offer really creates value for him. This is another exercise at taking a customer focus rather than an internal view of the organization.

Reinforce its existing position. Sometimes this is referred to as 'tweaking' or fine tuning. Checking how one can increase customer-value again is a valid option. Checking for weak points in customer service and perhaps doing customer surveys to find out what needs improving.

Trying to ensure that competitors have limited capacity to respond to our moves. This could be about developing a culture of excellence in the organization. Who can serve the customer best?

Maximum output for minimum input. Efficiency is important and finding simple solutions to standard and recurring issues can be a key way to improve this. Doing everything in house might not always be the most efficient, for example.

Actions won't cause adverse reactions (e.g. price war). Remembering that your competitor is not your enemy but your ally on the market, it makes absolutely no sense to start dumping in order to gain market share. You should remember that dropping prices is the easiest way to copy your competitor but both suffer in the end – as well as the customer.

Interaction in the Industry

Strategists have to choose between competition and co-operation:

Competition:

On the basis of surprise. Doing the unexpected.

Making the maximum use of resources

Being more vigorous and skillful in the use of marketing tools and market drive.

Cooperation:_

Hamel & Prahalad (1994)[277] observe a number of reasons for coalitions:

No single organization has all the resources so it makes sense to share these where practicable.

Some industries are very much tied into political considerations. The oil industry is an example of this. We might note that cooperation may have gone too far in some cases with price fixing and political lobbying.

To help share risks. As mentioned earlier, the risks involved in completely new product concepts or inventions is considerable and it is better to share the market here.

Competing with Capabilities

A more resource based approach takes the view that organizations possess unique bundles of assets Hamel and Prahalad (1989)[278] talk of companies possessing **core competencies** whereas Kay (1993)[279] poses the idea that companies possess **distinctive capabilities** which must be hard to imitate and therefore call for a combination of resources. This has led to a debate over resource based vs. market positioning. The question is whether these ideas are complementary or substitute.

Activity

What do you think about these different approaches? What core competencies does your organization possess? Or does it have distinctive capabilities which are hard to imitate?

Value chain analysis

After making an analysis of the value chain of the organization, this is used to make a comparison with other organizations—so-called benchmarking which was a fashionable idea in the 1990's. In this analysis, the following aspects are considered:

The size and cost of each activity

The factors which are driving costs

Understanding the linkages and horizontal strategy opportunities

How best to create perceived value holistically (for all stakeholders)

The following diagram is an attempt to develop a value chain to meet our holistic strategy:

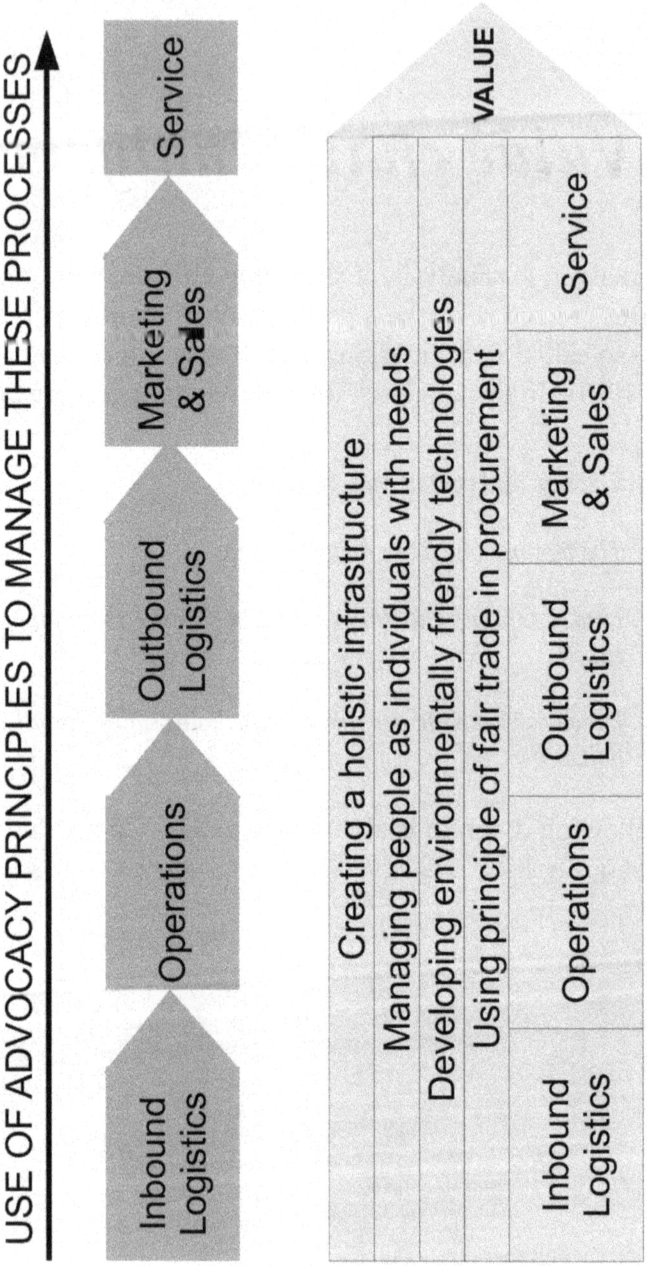

Fig. 96: Value Chain Analysis

These and other considerations can be be put together using Porter's (1985)[280] generic strategies matrix which was discussed in the chapter on holistic advocacy.

Activity

Try to put together a unique value chain for your organization – you can use the diagram above as a starting point but things are bound to be different in your organization. What activities could you undertake to make this happen in your organization?

The Sources of Cost Advantage

Up to now, we have been trying to bring over the argumentation for a value oriented organization rather than a cost-cutting one. However, in order to maintain efficiency, it is important to make sure that unnecessary costs are not incurred or develop over time. The important thing to remember is that you should avoid creating a culture which is cost-cutting oriented, where this is seen to be the main priority. Cost-cutting initiatives should never be carried out to the detriment of a particular stakeholder and intensive information and discussion must always take place. Failing to do this may destroy trust in the organization and eventually erode creativity and competitive advantage. As labor costs are a big factor in organizations, it is often here where the axe first starts to strike. There will be times when there is absolutely no alternative due to mismanagement in the past or because of drastically changed environmental conditions.

According to Grant (1995)[281] the main drivers of cost advantage are as in the following diagram:

ECONOMIES OF SCALE	Indivisibilities Specialization and division of labor
ECONOMIES OF LEARNING	Increased dexterity Improved coordination/organization
PROCESS TECHNOLOGY	Mechanization and automation Efficient utilization of materials Increased precision
PRODUCT DESIGN	Design for automation Designs to economize on materials
INPUT COSTS	Location advantages Ownership of low-cost inputs Bargaining power Supplier cooperation
CAPACITY UTILIZATION	Ratio of fixed to variable costs Costs of installing and closing capacity
RESIDUAL EFFICIENCY	Organizational slack

Fig. 97: Grant's Sources of Cost Advantage

Bowmann + Asch (1996)[282] criticize Porter's model as being too static. They rather point to innovation as a source of competitive advantage.

Activity

As we have pointed out, there is a big danger of becoming too cost-focused in an organization. Taking into account Bowmann and Asch's criticism and a holistic approach, how would you adapt Grant's diagram to convert it to 'value advantage'?

Strategic options for old and new markets

Below, I have reproduced the famous so-called 'Ansoff Matrix' (Ansoff, 1965[283]). This has been criticized by many particularly because it tells us nothing new. On the other hand, I have always found it a useful brainstormer because, especially in a group, it can provoke thinking:

	Present product	**New product**
Present market	Market Penetration/ Consolidation/Liquidation	Product Development
New market	Market Development	Diversification

Fig. 98: Ansoff Matrix

Testing Criteria

Any strategy needs to be tested for viability and a number of simple concepts have been developed by various authors, for example:

Johnson+Scholes (1988)[284] suggests the use of generic testing criteria:

Suitability

Feasibility

Acceptability

Rumelt (1995)[285] suggests the following four criteria pointing out that a strategy should show evidence of:

Consistency

Consonance

Advantage

Feasibility

Grant (1995)[286] has come up with the famous '4 E's':

Efficiency

Effectiveness

Economy

Equity (in the sense of fairness, particularly applied to non-profit organizations but increasingly considered a sustainability factor for all organizations)

Risk Analysis

A risk analysis should be made. According to Day (1990)[287] the risk is only acceptable if the three following criteria are met:

Superior prospects for profitability

Chances will be realized

Acceptability of risk-reward ratio

An interesting concept is that by Batsleer (2005, p.19)[288] — the so-called CATUR acronym:

Complexity — management is full of complexity and it is necessary to take this into account when calculating risk.

Ambiguity — nothing is ever as straightforward as it looks and there are always two sides to a coin.

Tension — there are always tensions between people, departments or between potential decisions.

Uncertainty — there is no such thing as a certain plan and most plans never come into fulfillment exactly as they were conceived. This element of uncertainty has to be taken into account as a risk factor.

Risk — there are all sorts of risks. One needs to revisit decisions to see if one has not overlooked a particular risk or perhaps preferred not to face it because one is determined to push through one's pet idea.

Activity

Take an example of a strategic move in your organization and apply the above concepts to it. See if you can come up with a fair

---

calculation of risks involved. Are there any risks involved which are not really fully covered in the models here? What are the risks of implementing a holistic strategy in your organization?

The Process of Strategy

One of the classical and most fundamental strategic planning models is Johnson and Scholes (1993)[289] overlapping process model as shown in the following diagram. This basic model is at the core of more complex ideas and all planning actually comes down to these three overlapping and continually rotating stages:

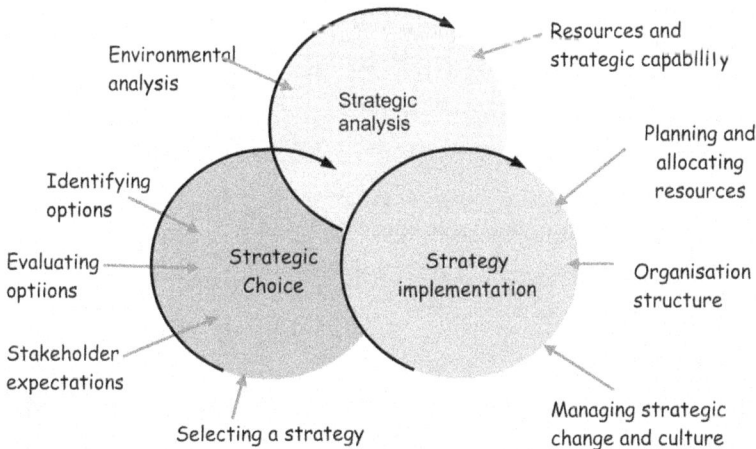

Fig. 99: Johnson & Scholes Strategic Process Model

Activity

Concluding this brief overview of strategy, take an issue where there is a need for change or a new project and build a strategic report based on the above Johnson & Scholes model or one of the change frameworks and integrate as many of the theories and aspects of strategic management from this paper as possible. Make a presentation to a tutor group or colleagues based on your findings. If you have the opportunity, this exercise could be carried out as a group exercise.

Conclusions

The intention of this series was to introduce the reader to the concept of holistic strategic management rather than providing an exhaustive presentation of all relevant management theories. The author wishes to provide this rather as an incentive for the student or manager to become reflective and to start their own research and develop their own ideas.

However good a theory may be, it is only of value if it can be put into practice and that is the task of the reader. We would very much appreciate any contributions to extending this work on holistic strategy and the author is always happy to hear from readers via the contact form on www.ilbs.org. I hope I am spared to continue developing the ideas and to gradually integrate business into the whole picture where it, in fact started — providing a service to society and humanity as a whole.

Devote thyself to My service, do all thine acts for My sake, and thou shalt attain the goal. Bhagavad-Gita, 12:10

Appendix

Books by the Author

Engelking, S. A. (2015) A Life for Mankind: The Biography of Hugh Joseph Schonfield.

ISBN: 978-1507528051
Kindle: ASIN: B00SU6HTOG.

Engelking, S. A. and Baermann, M. (2013) Creating a Nonviolent Culture in a Modern Organization.

ISBN: 978-1481965712
Kindle: ASIN: B00B2D6DPK

Engelking, S.A. (2012) Marketing for a Better World: A Holistic Approach to International Marketing.

ISBN: 978-1480049291
Kindle: ASIN: B009N3GQPS

Engelking, S.A. (2013) The Beans and the Dreams: Strategic Management from an International and Holistic Perspective

ISBN: 978-1492325819
Kindle: ASIN: B00944FYMM

Von Roeder, F. and Engelking, S.A. (Ed.) (2012) The Engelking Letters: A Collection of Letters Written by or Pertaining to Ferdinand Friedrich Engelking 1810-1885.

ISBN: 978-1481059992
Kindle: ASIN: B00AAK2E8G

Trenckmann, W. and Engelking, S.A. (Ed.) (2015) A History of Austin County: Edited and published in 1899 as a supplement to the "Bellville Wochenblatt"

ISBN: 978-1511991605
Kindle: ASIN: B00WXI50VQ

Engelking, S.A. (2012) Educating for Business in a Global Society: The Strategic relevance of Cooperative Education for Germany's Small and Medium Sized Enterprises.

ISBN: 978-1478297307
Kindle: ASIN: B008X7AC1Y

Leadership Preferences Assessment

The following test is to assess which type of leader you would prefer to work with.

We are all involved with those playing leadership roles in life at some time or other and to different degrees. The following questions are intended to categorize your leadership preference type. Please relate them to the type of leader you think best. This can be in any realm, such as business, voluntary service or the home and family. Please allocate a total of 10 points to each group of questions to indicate which answer is the nearest to your personal leadership style preference. You can give any score from 0 to 10 for each question but the total in a group must add up to 10. There are seven groups altogether from A to G.

Questions Group A	Score
1. It is good to have somebody around to consult whose opinions everyone considers fair.	
2. Power is less important in a leader than true principles and a reflective attitude.	
3. I would rather follow a charismatic leader wherever he or she goes than to stay put in a stagnating situation.	
4. Parents would do well to insist that their children accept and know their beliefs and if necessary punish them if they stray from the path of truth.	
5. It is better that we give all authority to a specific person, especially if he or she has everybody's interests at heart.	
6. 'Never change a winning leader' is the best strategy no matter what happens.	
Total Group A	

	Questions Group B	Score
1.	It is better to have a strong leader in authority and that people obey him or her—even if the leader's decisions are not always logical or seemingly fair.	
2.	If needs be, a leader should enforce his or her authority, particularly in terms of adherence to the rules of the organization.	
3.	Somebody has to pave the way for others to follow.	
4.	I do not like the kind of 'strong leader' who makes it clear to everybody what needs doing.	
5.	It is better to have somebody as leader who has proved him or herself over a long time.	
6.	Sometimes it is necessary to oppose your boss's ideas—especially if you think he or she is in the wrong.	
	Total Group B	

Questions Group C	Score
1. It is better to follow somebody who knows where they are going.	
2. It is important for any organization to have a clear mission and to insist on all members adhering closely to it.	
3. Most leaders are born to lead and it is therefore essential that people accept their authority.	
4. I feel it is better to have somebody inspiring in authority who leaves it down to individuals to make the right decisions.	
5. Often it is not the boss but somebody who takes the lead covertly who really leads an organization and I think this is good.	
6. Those who have an ordained position of authority should be obeyed without question.	
Total Group C	

Questions Group D	Score
1. People with an impeccable character are the ones that give the real direction in an organization.	
2. Our society would be a better place if our laws were more strictly enforced.	
3. When situations are new and just starting it is important to have a mature leader.	
4. I am quite happy to be led by somebody competent.	
5. Mothers and fathers can expect unquestioning obedience to their instructions.	
6. Leaders who do not set clear goals for everybody are not necessarily too weak.	
Total Group D	

Questions Group E	Score
1. It is less important for parents to teach children the difference between right and wrong than to help them understand basic guiding principles.	
2. I think it helps everybody understand authority when top management drive an executive class car and wear smart clothes.	
3. Organized religion should take a much firmer stance in forming the attitudes in society.	
4. It is more important for a person in authority to stick to their principles than do what those above them tell them to do.	
5. Although I can give strong guidance I am quite happy to be the one who prepares the way for somebody else who can take over complete control of a situation when it is running.	
6. I expect people to accept my authority because I have more experience.	
Total Group E	

Questions Group F	Score
1. I know what needs doing and can expect my subordinates to loyally follow me.	
2. I can convince others of my ideas and insist that they carry them out to the letter.	
3. I think I have a strong ethical stance and do not need to bow to those above me.	
4. After a leader has been running the show since the beginning, it is quite welcoming to have somebody afterwards with clear ideas to follow.	
5. I think everybody can be their own master when they follow their best instincts.	
6. I consider that it is necessary that people have somebody older or more experienced to look up to.	
Total group F	

Questions Group G	Score
1. A top manager who can control an organization efficiently is entitled to take a large salary.	
2. People should act in the interest of the organization, not from purely selfish motives.	
3. Parents should guide their children by good example rather than telling them what to do or appealing to authority.	
4. Others cannot always see the possibilities in new projects and it is necessary in that situation for someone to take the lead.	
5. It is better to accept the leadership of those who have been in authority for a long time.	
6. A strong manager can expect that his or her staff abide strictly to the rules he has set and if necessary to put aside any personal reservations they may have.	
Total group G	

Evaluation Sheet

Enter the scores you gave in each group against the respective question number which appear in each of the cells below (in italics). Then add up each column to find your leadership preferences.

Group	#	Score	#	Score	#	Score	#	Score	#	Score	#	Score
A	1		5		2		4		3		6	
B	4		1		6		2		3		5	
C	4		6		5		2		1		3	
D	6		5		1		2		4		3	
E	1		2		4		3		5		6	
F	5		1		3		2		4		6	
G	2		1		3		6		4		5	
Total												
Type:		Judge (S)		King (D)		Prophet (I)		Priest (P)		Leader (M)		Patriarch (A)

Notes and References

1   Engelking (2015) A Life for Mankind: The Biography of Hugh Joseph Schonfield, The Hugh & Helene Schonfield World Service Trust

2   Mintzberg (2004) Managers Not MBAs: A Hard Look at the Soft Practice of Managing and Management Development, Berrett-Koehler Publishers, p. ix.

3   I am thinking of the term 'bean counter' which describes someone pre-occupied with the financial aspects of business.

4   Clausewitz, Karl von (1982) On War, translated by Col. K. Graham 1908 from the 1832 original. New edition edited by Anatol Rapaport, London, Penguin.

5   Nonaka, I. & Takeuchi, H. (1995). The Knowledge-Creating Company. New York: Oxford University Press

6   Lovelock, James (1988) The Ages of Gaia — A biography of our living Earth, New York, W.W.Norton.

7   Goldratt, E. (1984) The Goal: Excellence in Manufacturing. Croton-on-Hudson, NY: The North River Press. Read more: Theory of Constraints — strategy, organization, system, style, examples, manager, model, company, business http://www.referenceforbusiness.com/management/Str-Ti/Theory-of-Constraints.html#b#ixzz1g2BM26if

8   Eli Goldratt is famous for his 'Theory of Constraints' (TOC) which is based on the convergence of cause and effect logic to a core problem, coordinating all local efforts towards a global or holistic system solution and implementation through the only sustainable competitive advantage of an organization – people. It fundamentally concentrates on education, helping understanding and concentration of critical constraints (hence the name of the theory) to gain fast improvement.

9   Knapp, Liahona-Holistic Enterprise Compass (1999) in International Symposium Measuring and Reporting Intellectual Capital: Experience, Issues, and Prospects Amsterdam Technical Meeting 9-10 June 1999 Holistic Measurement of Intellectual Capital.

10 Handy, Charles (1999) The Hungry Spirit: Beyond Capitalism: A Quest for Purpose in the Modern World, Doubleday.

11 Maslow, A. H., Frager, R., Fadiman, J. (1987) Motivation and Personality, Addison-Wesley Pub Co; 3rd edition.

12 Maxfield (2001) Result of a personal discussion between the author and Norman Maxfield. Norman Maxfield was a lecturer for Open University Business School and a dynamic octogenarian at that time as well as being an experienced businessman and academic. He was still very active at the time of writing this book and well into his 90's.

13 http://twocranesaikido.com/Community.htm, accessed 16.12.2011.

14 Packard, V. (1960) *The Waste Makers*, New York, David McKay.

15 Schumacher, E. F. (1975) Small Is Beautiful : Economics As If People Mattered, Harper Trade.

16 Brainard, W. C., Nordhaus, W. D., Watts, H. W. (Editor) and Tobin, J. (1991) *Money, Macroeconomics, and Economic Policy: Essays in Honor of James Tobin.*

17 Gallup International (2005) Voice of the People 2005 Report on Hunger and Poverty.

18 Csikszentmihalyi , M. (2002) 'Flow with Soul', *What is Enlightenment Magazine,* Spring-Summer, 2002. In an interview with Milhaly Csiksentmihalyi.

19 Flow with Soul, An interview with Dr. Mihaly Csikszentmihalyi, by Elizabeth Debold accessed at http://www.enlightennext.org/magazine/j21/csiksz.asp?page=2, December 9th 2011.

20 Ibid.

21 Ulrich D, Zenger, J and Smallwood, N. (1999) Results Based Leadership, Harvard Business School Press, Boston, MA.

22 Beck, D. and Cowan, C. (1996) Spiral Dynamics: Mastering Values, Leadership and Change, Blackwell Publications: Malden, MA.

23 Pugh, D.S. and Hickson, D.J. (1989) *Writers on Organizations,* fourth edition, Harmondsworth, Penguin Books.

24 The Open University (1995) *On Being a Manager,* Margate, Thanet Press.

25 Pardy, D. (2006) *Introducing Leadership*, Oxford, Elsevier.

26 Doran, G. T. (1981). There's a S.M.A.R.T. way to write management's goals and objectives. Management Review, Volume 70, Issue 11(AMA FORUM), pp. 35-36.

27 Rudyard Kipling in "Just So Stories" (1902), in a poem

included in the story "The Elephant's Child".

28 Kirton, M.J. (1989) *Adaptors and Innovators: Styles of Creativity and Problem Solving,* London, Routledge.

29 Henry, J. (2001) *Creativity and Perception in Management,* Sage, London.

30 Adapted from an idea by Open University Business School B800 etc., The Open University, Milton Keynes.

31 Handy (1991) 'Creativity in Management', Radio 1, B882 *Creative Management,* Milton Keynes, The Open University in Henry, J. (2000) *Managing Problems Creatively,* Sage, London.

32 Henry, J. (2000) *Managing Problems Creatively,* Sage, London.

33 http://www.orangepapers.org/What_Is_The_Oxford_Group.pdf accessed 12.12.2011

34 Rainer, T. (2004) *The New Diary, How to Use a Journal for Self-Guidance and Expanded Creativity,* Tarcher/Penguin, New York.

35 Mintzberg, Henry (1998) 'The Role of the CEO', *Design Intelligence, August 15th 1998.*

36 Adapted from an idea by Open University Business School B800 etc., The Open University, Milton Keynes.

37 Luthans, Fred (1988) 'Successful vs. Effective Real Managers' *Academy of Management Executive, 1988, 2(2): 127-132*

38 These ideas on time management are largely adapted from an idea by Open University Business School B800 etc., The Open University, Milton Keynes. Some useful additional information is to be found on Wikipedia.

39 Mintzberg, Henry (1973) *The Nature of Managerial Work,* New York: Harper & Row.

40 Hamel, Gary (2011) 'First, Let's Fire All the Managers', *Harvard Business Review,* December 2011.

41 Missildine, W. Hugh (1987) 'Your Inner Child of the Past', Simon & Schuster.

42 Handy, Charles (2002) 'Elephants and Fleas: Is Your Organization Prepared for Change?' *Leader to Leader, No. 24 Spring 2002.*

43 Handy, Charles. (1990) *The Age of Unreason.* London: Arrow Books.

44 Pinchot, G. 1985 Intrapreneuring: Why You Don't Have to Leave the Corporation to Become an Entrepreneur. New

York: Harper & Row.

45 Moss Kanter, R. (1983) *The Change Masters,* New York, Simon and Schuster.

46 Lawler, E. (1991) *High-Involvement Management: Participative Strategies for Improving Organizational Performance,* San Fransisco, Jossey-Bass.

47 Perkins, D. and Holtman, M. and Kessler, P. and McCarthy, C. (2000), *Leading at the Edge: Leadership Lessons from the Extraordinary Saga of Shackleton's Antarctic Expedition,* New York, Amacom.

48 Marcic, D. (1997) *Managing with the Wisdom of Love; uncovering virtue in people and organizations,* San Fransisco Jossey-Bass.

49 Hawley, J. (1993) *Reawakening the spirit in work,* Berret-Koehler, San Fransisco quoted in Marcic, D. (1997), ibid.

50 Torbert, W. and associates (2004) Action Inquiry. The secret of timely and transforming leadership, San Francisco, Berrett-Koehler

51 Senge, Peter M. (1990) *The Fifth Discipline: The Art and Practice of the Learning Organization,* New York, Doubleday, p339ff.

52 Shaw, George Bernard (1903) *Man and Superman,* London in ibid p. 352.

53 Ibid. p.360.

54 Buber, Martin (1928ff) in Glatzer, N. (1968) *On the Bible – Eighteen Studies, pp. 137-159,* Schocken, New York.

55 Haller, W. (1990) *Die heillsame Alternative: jesuanische Ethik in Wirtschaft und Politik,* Hammer, Wuppertal (author's rendering of the German text).

56 Ibid.

57 Chappell, T. (1993) *The Soul of a Business – Managing for Profit and the Common Good,* New York, Bantam.

58 Ibid.

59 Adair (2002) *Inspiring Leadership – Learning from Great Leaders,* London,Thorogood.

60 Fiedler, F. E. (1967) *A Theory of Leadership Effectiveness,* New York: McGraw-Hill.

61 Covey, S.R. (1991) *Principle Centered Leadership,* Free Press New York.

62 Gandhi, Mohandas K. (2001), *The Bhagavad Gita according to Gandhi,* Berkley Hills Books, Berkeley.

63 cf. Covey, S.R. (1991) *Principle Centered Leadership*, Free Press New York.

64 Deming, W.E. (1982), *Out of the Crisis,* MIT, Cambridge, Mass., p.99.

65 "My views on Christianity are directly influenced by a book, The Passover Plot by Hugh J. Schonfield. The premise in it is that Jesus' message had been garbled by his disciples and twisted for a variety of self-serving reasons by those who followed, to the point where it has lost validity for many in the modern age." John Lennon, The Boston Globe, reported on Dec. 12, 1980.

66 Lennon, J. (1971) the song *Imagine,* Apple Released: 9 September 1971 (US)8 October 1971 (UK).

67 Jesus of Nazareth – Luke 22:26.

68 http://neweconomicsinstitute.org/e-newsletters/role-money-new-economy, accessed 13.12.2011

69 Greenleaf, R. (1977) Servant leadership: A journey into the nature of legitimate power and greatness. New York: Paulist Press,

70 http://www.butler.edu/volunteer/resources/principles-of-servant-leadership/ accessed 13.12.2011

71 Tao Ti Ching

72 Thomas, M. (2006) (citing Mandela in) Gurus on Leadership: A Guide to the World's Thought Leaders in Leadership, Thorogood.

73 Weil, S. (1951) Waiting for God, Perennial; 1st Harper Colophon Edition, 1973 edition (September 1992), pp. 139, 143-146.

74 Harman, Willis (1978) *What are Noetic Sciences* IONS Newsletter, Vol 6, No. 1, Spring 1978 quoted in http://www.homepages.ibug.co.nz/noetic_sci.html, accessed 4.8.06.

75 Lewin K. (1943) Defining the "Field at a Given Time." *Psychological Review.* 50: 292-310. Republished in *Resolving Social Conflicts & Field Theory in Social Science,* Washington, D.C.: American Psychological Association, 1997.

76 Lewin K. (1943) Defining the "Field at a Given Time."

Psychological Review. 50:292-310. Republished in *Resolving Social Conflicts & Field Theory in Social Science,* Washington, D.C.: American Psychological Association, 1997.

77   Sacks, J. (2002) The Dignity of Difference, Continuum, London.

78   Bauman, Z. (1998) Globalization: The Human Consequences Columbia University Press

79   Whitehead, Alfred North (1942) *Adventures of Ideas.* Harmondsworth: Penguin.

80   Held, David (ed.) (2000) *A Globalizing World?* London, Routledge.

81   Brown, Gordon (2002) *Tackling Poverty: A Global New Deal,* London, H.M. Treasury.

82   Held, David and McGrew, Anthony (eds) (2000) *The Global Transformations Reader.* Cambridge: Polity Press.

83   Barber, Benjamin (1992) 'Jihad vs. McWorld', *Atlantic Monthly* (March – 2001), New York: Ballantine.

84   Schumpeter, Joseph (1947) *Capitalism, Socialism and Democracy.* London: Duckworth.

85   Havel, Václav (1998) *The Art of the Impossible,* New York: Fromm.

86   Clausewitz, Karl von (1982) *On War,* translated by Col. K. Graham 1908 from the 1832 original. New edition edited by Anatol Rapaport, 1982, London, Penguin.

87   Semler, R. (1993) *Maverick! : The Success Story Behind the World's Most Unusual Workplace,* Arrow, London.

88   Moss-Kanter, R., 1989. 'The New Managerial Work', *Harvard Business Review,* November-December, pp. 85-92.

89   Fayol, H., 1949. General and Industrial Administration. London: Sir Issac Pitman & Sons, Ltd.

90   For more information on Elliott Jaques, visit: http://www.requisite.org/biography.html (accessed 4th April 2012).

91   Bowen and Lawler, 1992 in Potterfield, Thomas A., 1999. The Business of Employee Empowerment, Democracy and Ideology in the Workplace, Quorum, Westport.

92   Bennis, W., 1997. *Managing People is Like Herding Cats.* Covey Leadership Center.

93   Thurow, L., 1995. "*Surviving in a turbulent environment*",
      Strategy & Leadership, Vol. 23 Iss: 5, pp.24–29.

94   Gallie and White, 1993. in Hendry, C. and Jenkins, R., 1997.
      "*Psychological contracts and new deals*", Human Resource
      Management Journal Volume 7 Issue 1, Blackwell
      Publishing Ltd

95   Acero, L., 1990. Microelectronics: T*he Nature Of Work, Skills
      And Training, An analysis of case studies from developed and
      developing countries*, International Labour Office, CH-1211
      Geneva 22, Switzerland.
      http://www.ilo.org/public/libdoc/ilo/1990/90B09_369_en
      gl.pdf. Accessed 4th April 2012.

96   Lawler, E. and Mohrman, S., 1985. *Quality Circles after the fad.*
      Harvard Business Review, January-February 1985. pp. 65-71
      cited in Webster, M. (2009)
      http://martinwebster.eu/2009/06/13/employee-
      participation/. Accessed 4th April 2012

97   Brazzel, M., 1991. "Building a Culture of Diversity in the
      Cooperative Extension System: A Paper to Foster Dialogue
      and Discussion About Pluralism in Extension." ECOP and
      ES-USDA National Diversity Strategic Planning Conference,
      Denver, Colorado, September, 1991. Accessed at
      http://ohioline.osu.edu/bc-fact/0014.html 4th April 2012.

98   Taylor, F.W. *Shop Management, The Principles of Scientific
      Management and Testimony Before the Special House Committee,*
      Harper & Row.

99   Sorensen, C. E. and Williamson, S. T., 1956. *My Forty Years
      with Ford.* New York: Norton.

100   Mayo, E., 1933. *The Human Problems of an Industrial
      Civilization.* New York: Macmillan.

101   Haller, W., 1990. *Flexible Arbeitszeit – Vorteile und Chancen für
      den Betrieb und seine Mitarbeiter.* München: Wilhelm Heyne
      Verlag,.

102   Blake, R. and Mouton, J., 1964. *The Managerial Grid: The Key
      to Leadership Excellence.* Houston: Gulf Publishing Co..

103   Haller, W., 1990. ibid,

104   Thompson, M., 1993. *Pay and Performance – the Employee
      Experience,* Report No. 258, Institute of Manpower Studies

105   Kohn, A., 1993. *Why Incentive Plans Cannot Work,* Harvard
      Business Review, September/October, 54-63

106 Deci and Ryan, 1985. *Intrinsic Motivation and Self-Determination in Human Behavior.* New York: Plenum Press

107 Chartered Institute of Management (2000)

108 Pfau, B. & Kay, I., 2002. Does 360-degree feedback negatively affect company performance? Studies show that 360-degree feedback may do more harm than good. What's the problem? *HR Magazine*, Jun 2002. 47, 6; 54–60.

109 Kohn, 1993. ibid.

110 Deci, E. L. 1971. The effects of externally mediated rewards on intrinsic motivation. *Journal of Personality and Social Psychology*, 18, 105-115.

111 Mullins, L.J., 1993, *Management and Organizational Behavior*, 3rd Edition. London: Pitman Publishing,

112 Mullins, L.J.. 1993, Ibid.

113 Maslow, A., Frager, R. and Fadiman, J., 1987. *Motivation and Personality*, Addison-Wesley Pub Co; 3rd Edition.

114 Handy, C., 1994. *The Empty Raincoat : Making Sense of the Future*, London: Hutchinson.

115 Greenleaf, R., 2002. *Servant Leadership: A Journey into the Nature of Legitimate Power and Greatness* (25th anniversary ed.). New York: Paulist Press.

116 Locke, E., 1996. Motivation Through Conscious Goal Setting, *Applied and Preventive Psychology,* 5:117-124.

117 Mullins L.J., 1993. Ibid.

118 Karasek R.A. and Theorell, T., 1990. *Healthy Work; Stress, productivity, and the reconstruction of working life.* New York: Basic Books.

119 Karasek, R. A., 1979. Job demands, job decision latitude and mental strain: implications for job redesign. *Administrative Science Quarterly*, 24, 285-308.

120 Warr, P., 1987. *Work, Unemployment, and Mental Health,* Oxford: Clarendon Press.

121 Karasek, J., Baker, D. and Marxer, F., 1981. Job Decision Latitude, Job Demands, and Cardiovascular Disease: A Prospective Study of Swedish Men AJPH July 1981, Vol. 71, No. 7, at http://www.ncbi.nlm.nih.gov/pmc/articles/PMC1619770/pdf/amjph00667-0024.pdf, accessed 2nd April 2012

122 Baldamus, W., 1981. Efficiency and Effort, International

Behavioural and Social Sciences Classics from the Tavistock Press, 44, *The international behavioural and social sciences library Band 1*

123 Cain, B., 2012. A Review of the Mental Workload Literature, Defence Research and Development Canada Toronto at http://ftp.rta.nato.int/public//PubFullText/RTO/TR/RTO-TR-HFM-121-PART-II///TR-HFM-121-Part-II-04.pdf. Accessed 5th April 2012.

124 Annual report of the Industrial Fatigue Research Board (1920) H.M.S.O., London.

125 http://www.legalcompensation.com.au/work-injury-impacts

126 Oldham, G. R. and Brass, D., 1979. Employee reactions to an open-plan office: A naturally occur- ring quasi-experiment, *Administrative Science Quarterly*, 24: 267-284.

127 Maher, A. and von Hippel, C., 2005. Individual differences in employee reactions to open-plan offices, Journal of Environmental Psychology 25 (2005) 219–229. http://www2.psy.uq.edu.au/~courtney/pdf/M&vHJEP.pdf. Accessed 5th April 2012.

128 Hackman, J.R. and Oldham, G.R., 1975. Development of the Job Diagnostic Survey, *Journal of Applied Psychology, 60.* 159-170.

129 Garg, P. and Rastogi, R., 2006. New Model For Job Design: Motivating Employees Performance. *Journal of Management Development*, 25(6), 572-587 in Kaymaz, K. (2010) The Effects of Job Rotation Practices on Motivation: A Research on Managers in the Automotive Organizations, *Business and Economics Research Journal Volume1*. Number 3. 2010 pp. 69-85.

130 Herzberg, F., 1959. "The Motivation to Work." New York: John Wiley and Sons

131 Haller, W., 1973. The Human Job, *The Mondcivitan Bridge 1973*.

132 Herzberg, F., 1964. The Motivation-Hygiene Concept and Problems of Manpower, Personnel Administration (January–February 1964), pp. 3–7.

133 Herzberg's Two-Factor Theory of Job Satisfaction, Defense Systems Management School, Fort Belvoir, Virginia. http://www.dtic.mil/cgi-bin/GetTRDoc?AD=ADA033814.

Accessed 5th April 2012.

134 Pearson CAL, 1992, 'Autonomous workgroups: An evaluation at an industrial site', Human Relations, vol 45, no 9, pp 905–37. in Mickan, S. and Rodgera, S. The organisational context for teamwork: Comparing health care and business literature. Accessed at http://www.publish.csiro.au/?act=view_file&file_id=AH000179.pdf on 5th April 2012

135 Herriot, P., 1993. "A paradigm bursting at the seams." Journal Of Organizational Behavior 14, no. 4: 371-375. PsycINFO, EBSCOhost (accessed April 2, 2012).

136 Mischel, W., 1968. Personality and assessment. New York: Wiley.

137 Noon, M. and Blyton, P., 1997. The Realities of Work. London: Macmillan.

138 Hunter, J. E., & Hunter, R. F., 1984. Validity and utility of alternative predictors of job performance. Psychological Bulletin, 96, 72–98.

139 Nisbett, R. E. and Wilson, T., 1977. "The halo effect: Evidence for unconscious alteration of judgments". Journal of Personality and Social Psychology (American Psychological Association) 35 (4): 250–256.

140 Creighton-University http://www.creighton.edu/fileadmin/user/AdminFinance/HumanResources/docs/Compensation_Performance_Mgmt/Errors_in_Performance_Evaluations.pdf. Accessed 16th April 2012

141 McDaniel, D., Schmidt F. and Maurer S., 1994. The validity of employment interviews: A comprehensive review and meta-analysis. Journal of Applied Psychology, 79, 599-616.

142 Swanson. J., 2005. accessed at http://www.articlesphere.com/Article/Handling-First-Day-Job-Anxiety/193910. Accessed 3rd April 2012.

143 Latack J., 1981. Person/Role Conflict: Holland's Model Extended to Role-Stress Research, Stress Management, and Career Development. Academy Of Management Review [serial online]. January 1981;6(1):89-103. Available from: Ipswich MA: Business Source Complete. Accessed April 3, 2012.

144 Wanous, J.P., 1992. Organizational Entry. Recruitment, Selection, Orientation and Socialization of Newcomers.

Eastbourne: Addison-Wesley.

145 Ruble, T. L. and Thomas, K. W., 1976. Support for a two-dimensional model of conflict behavior. *Organizational Behavior & Human Performance*, 16(1), 142-155.

146 Carnegie, D., 2009. How To Win Friends and Influence People. New edition Simon & Schuster (original edition 1937).

147 Rosenberg, M., 2003. *Nonviolent Communication: A Language of Life*, Puddledancer Press; 2nd edition.

148 Gandhi, A., 2003. *Legacy of love: My education in the path of non-violence*, El Sobrante.

149 Haller, W., 1983. Die Politik Jesu, http://ilbs.org/knowledge/die-politik-jesu. Accessed 16th April 2012. (Author's translation).

150 Etzioni, A., 1971. *A Comparative Analysis of Complex Organizations*. New York: The Free Press,

151 Etzioni, A., 1999. *The Limits of Privacy*. New York: Basic Books.

152 French, J.R.P. and Raven, B., 1959. The Bases of Social Power. In D. Cartwright (Ed.), *Studies in Social Power*, University of Michigan, Institute of Social Research, Ann Arbor, 1959.

153 Cook, K, Emerson, R, Gillmore, M, and Yamagishi, T., 1983. 'The Distribution of Power in Exchange Networks: Theory and Experimental Results', *American Journal Of Sociology*, 89, 2, pp. 275-305, JSTOR Arts & Sciences I, EBSCOhost. Accessed 24 April 2012.

154 Bass, BM., Wurster, C.R. and Alcock, W., 1961. "A Test of the Proposition: We Want to be Esteemed Most by Those We Esteem Most Highly", *Journal of Abnormal Social Psychology*, Vol. LXIII, 1961, 650-653.

155 Hamel, G., 2011. First, Let's Fire All the Managers, *Harvard Business Review*, December 2011.

156 Fisher, R. and Ury, B., 1981. *Getting To Yes: Negotiating Agreement Without Giving In*. Boston: Houghton Mifflin.

157 Belbin, M., 1981. *Management Teams*, London; Heinemann.

158 Kimball, L., 1997. Managing Virtual Teams. Text of speech given by Lisa Kimball for Team Strategies Conference sponsored by Federated Press, Toronto, Canada, 1997. http://www.groupjazz.com/pdf/vteams-toronto.pdf.

Accessed 9th May 2012.

159 Stated in an interview with J. Richard Hackman by Diane Coutu in the Harvard Business Review entitled 'Why Teams don't Work', May 2009. Accessed at http://hbr.org/2009/05/why-teams-dont-work/ar/1 on 23rd May 2012.

160 Willis,C., 2007. Critique of Teamwork http://tomjohny.articlealley.com/critique-of-teamwork-165430.html accessed 23rd May 2012.

161 Janis, I. L., 1971. "Groupthink". Psychology Today 5 (6): 43–46, 74–76 (November 1971).

162 Janis, I. and Mann, L., 1977 Decision Making: A Psychological Analysis of Conflict, Choice, and Commitment [p 132] New York: The Free Press in Aldag R. and Fuller, S., 1993. "Beyond Fiasco: A Reappraisal of the Groupthink Phenomenon and a New Model of Group Decision Processes", Psychological Bulletin 1993, Vol. 113, No. 3, 533-552. Accessed at http://liquidbriefing.com/twiki/pub/Dev/RefAldag1993/beyond_fiasco.pdf, accessed 24th May 2012.

163 Luft, J., Ingham, H., 1950. "The Johari window, a graphic model of interpersonal awareness". Proceedings of the western training laboratory in group development (Los Angeles: UCLA).

164 Irving, J. and Longbottom, G., 2007. "Team Effectiveness and Six Essential Servant Leadership Themes: A Regression Model Based on items in the Organizational Leadership Assessment", *International Journal of Leadership Studies*, Vol. 2 Iss. 2, 2007, pp. 98-113. http://www.regent.edu/acad/global/publications/ijls/new/vol2iss2/IrvingLongbotham/IrvingLongbothamV2Is2.pdf. Accessed 24th May 2012.

165 Goodman, L., 2008. The End of Management. Albuquerque: Bridgeworks.

166 Aldrich, H., 1979. *Organizations and environments*. Englewood Cliffs, N.J.: Prentice-Hall.

167 Pang, L., 2001. *Understanding Virtual Organizations*. http://www.isaca.org/Journal/Past-Issues/2001/Volume-6/Pages/Understanding-Virtual-Organizations.aspx. Accessed 13.3.2012.

168 You can find more detailed information on the Benetton organization at http://www.csus.edu/indiv /o/obriene/art7/readings/benetton.htm

169 http://www.ilbs.org

170 Morgan, G., 1986. *Images of Organization,* London, Sage Publications.

171 Powell, W.W., 1990. 'Neither market nor hierarchy: network forms of organizational research in organization behavior', in Thompson, G., Frances, J., Levacic, R. and Michell, J. (eds) (1991) *Markets, Hierarchies and Networks,* London, Sage Publications.

172 Ibid.

173 https://www.gema.de/en/

174 http://www.dihk.de/

175 http://www.gez.de/die_gez/index_ger.html

176 Ouchi, W.G., 1980. 'Markets, bureaucracies and clans', *Administrative Science Quarterly'* Vol. 25. pp 129-41.

177 Ouchi, W.G., 1981. *Theory Z: How American Business can meet the Japanese challenge,* Reading, Mass. Addison-Wesley.

178 http://www.buerokauffrau-online.de/arbeit-von-zuhause.html

179 Deal, T.E. and Kennedy, A. A., 1982. *Corporate Cultures: the rites and rituals of corporate life,* Harmondsworth, Penguin Books.

180 Ibid.

181 Deal, T.E. & Kennedy, A.A., 1982. Corporate Cultures, Addison-Wesley.

182 Ibid.

183 Peters, T.J. & Waterman, R.H., 1982. In Search of Excellence J. M. Shafritz & J. S. Ott, eds., Harper & Row.

184 Deal, T.E. & Kennedy, A.A., 1982. Corporate Cultures, Addison-Wesley.

185 Handy, C.B., 1985. *Understanding Organizations,* third edition, Harmondsworth, Penguin Books.

186 Bate, P., 1984. 'Impact of organizations' culture: approaches to organizational problem solving' *Organization Studies,* Vol. 5, No. 2, pp 43-66.

187 Johnson, G., 1992. "Managing Strategic Change—Strategy,

Culture and Action". *Long Range Planning* Vol 25 No 1 pp 28-36.

188 An important source of inspiration and information for this section was the excellent book by Philip A. Wickham which I would heartily recommend for further reading on the subject which can only be sketchily presented here: Wickham, P., 2001. *Strategic Entrepreneurship*, Harlow: Pearson Education Ltd.

189 Blaug, M., 1996. *Economic Theory in Retrospect* (Fifth Ed.). Cambridge: Cambridge University Press.

190 Kilby, P., 1971. "Hunting the Heffalump." Ch. 1 in *Entrepreneurship and Economic Development*, edited by Peter Kilby. New York: Macmillan.

191 Gartner, W.B., 1990. "What are we talking about when we talk about entrepreneurship?", *Journal of Business Venturing*, Vol. 5 pp.15-28.

192 Bygrave, W.D. and Hofer, C.W., 1991. 'Theorizing about Entrepreneurship', *Entrepreneurship Theory and Practice*, 16(2): 13-22.

193 Schumpeter, J., 1928. Unternehmer, in: Conrad, J.: *Handwörterbuch der Staatswissenschaften*, 4., gänzlich umgearbeitete Auflage, Band VIII, Jena, S. 475-487.

194 http://www.skollfoundation.org/about/. Accessed 16.7.2012.

195 http://www.bbc.com/news/magazine-31057308. Accessed 19.3.2015

196 McClelland, D. C., 1961. *The Achieving Society*. Princeton: Van Nostrand.

197 Backes-Gellner and Moog (2013) in Business Insider (http://uk.businessinsider.com/personality-difference-between-entrepreneurs-and-employees-2015-2?r=US. Accessed 19.3.2015

198 Webster, Frederick A., 1977. Entrepreneurs and Ventures: An Attempt at Classification and Clarification. *The Academy of Management Review*, Vol. 2, No. 1, pp. 54-61.

199 Landau, R., 1982. 'The Innovative Milieu' in Lundstedt, S.B. and Colglazier, E.W. , Jr. (eds), *Managing Innovation: The Social Dimensions of Creativity, Invention and Technology*, New York: Pergamon Press.

200 Jones-Evans, D., 1995. A typology of technology-based

entrepreneurs: A model based on previous occupational background in *International Journal of Entrepreneurial Behavior & Research*, Apr 1995 Volume: 1 Issue: 1 Page: 26 – 47, MCB UP Ltd.

201 Gartner, W.B., 1985. A conceptual framework for describing the phenomenon of new venture creation, *Academy of Management Review*, 10: 696-706

202 Wright, M., Robbie, K., Ennew, C., 1997. Serial Entrepreneurs, *British Journal of Management* 8, 251-268.

203 Czarniawska-Joerges, B. and Wolff, R., 1991. Leaders, Managers, Entrepreneurs on and off the Organizational Stage. Organization Studies (OS), 12(4), 529 - 546.

204 Wickham, P., 2001. *Strategic Entrepreneurship*, Harlow: Pearson Education Ltd, p. 28.

205 Luthans, F., 1988. Successful vs. effective real managers. *Academy of Management Executive*, 2, 127-132.

206 'The Global Entrepreneurship Monitor' was set up in 1997 as a joint research initiative between the Babson College in Boston and the London Business School and is a long-term project which aims to gather and analyze data on the relationship between entrepreneurship and economic growth. Ten countries take part including Germany under the auspices of the University of Cologne. Sternberg, R., Otten, Claus and Tamásy, C., 2000. *Germany 2000 Country Report Global Enterprise Monitor,* University of Cologne, p.12.

207 Verheul, I, Leonardo, G., Schüller, S. and van Spronsen, J., 1999. *Determinants of Entrepreneurship in Germany*, Erasmus University Rotterdam (Publication under Consideration) p.32.

208 http://www.uni-koeln/wiso-fak/szyperski/gruendung

209 Twardy, M and Esser, F., 1998. Entrepreneurship als didaktisches Problem einer Universität – aufgezeigt als Organisationsentwicklungskonzept "WIS-EX" der Universität zu Köln in: *Kölner Zeitschift für Wirtschaft und Pädagogik,* Vol. XIII, fasc. 24, pp. 5-26, especially p.18.

210 Schubert, R., 1997. *Lernziele für Unternehmensgründer. Dargestellt am Beispiel der Tourismusbrance*, Eul Verlag.

211 Szyperski, N., Nathusius, K. ibid, Brüderl, J., Preisendörfer, P., Ziegler, R., 1996. *Der Erfolg neugegründeter Betriebe, Eine empirische Studie zu den Chancen und Risiken von*

Unternehmensgründungen, Berlin, Duncker & Humblot. (Betriebswirtschaftlichen, Heft 140).

212 Ripsas, S., 1997. *Entrepreneurship als ökonomischer Prozess. Perspektiven zu Förderung unternehmerischen Handelns*, Wiesbaden, DUV/Gabler, pp. 178-192.

213 Günther, U. and Kirchhof, R., 1998. Paper presented at the Internationalizing Entrepreneurship Education and Training - 8th Annual Conference 26-28th July 1998

214 Harhoff, D. and Licht, G., 1996. *Innovationsaaktivitäten Kleiner und Mittlerer Unternehmen*, Baden-Baden, Nomos.

215 Pfirrmann, O., 1994. The Geography of innovation in small and medium-sized firms in West Germany, *Small Business Economics* 6 (1), 24-41.

216 Seymour, N., 2001. Entrepreneurship Education in American Community Colleges and Universities, *Digest Number 01-06*, CELCEE at http://www.celcee.edu/products/digest/Dig01-06.html

217 Drury, R. L., 2000, Fall. Measuring demand for noncredit entrepreneurship and small-business management education from Virginia's businesses: A review of the literature. *Inquiry: The Journal of the Virginia Community Colleges, 5*(2), 22-31. (c20012808), p.9.

218 Dunn, P., & Short, L., 2001. *An Entrepreneurship Major?* Retrieved October, 2001: http://www.sbaer.uca.edu/Research/2001/ASBE/27asbe01.htm (c20013680).

219 Greenleaf, R., 1970. *The Servant as Leader*, Robert K. Greenleaf Center.

220 Hugh J. Schonfield in 'The Politics of God' and many other writings. Schonfield was a leading historian of Jewish and Middle East history and a became famous when his controversial book 'The Passover Plot' became a best seller selling millions of copies. However, his main vision was that a Messianic nation without territory made up of people of all creeds and races should come into being in order to act as the spokesman of and mediator on behalf of mankind. He later joined others in the founding a constitutional republic in 1952 which also took over the life work of the Nobel Peace Prize winner Sir William Randolf Cremer. His thinking apparently inspired the later ideas of John Lennon.

221 'Everyone gives what he has. The soldier gives strength, the merchant goods, the teacher instruction, the farmer rice, the fisherman fish...... I can think, I can wait, I can fast' (Hesse, 1922 – translation by Peter Owen Ltd, 1954). In one of the stories in Hesse's book the following narrative is also found which further illustrates this point: Siddhartha, a Brahmin, is working for a merchant named Kamaswami who sends him to a village to buy the rice harvest. When he gets there the rice has already been sold to another merchant. Nevertheless, he remains in the village for a number of days, entertains the farmers, gives money to the children, attends a wedding and goes home afterwards completely satisfied. Kamaswami scolds Siddhartha for not returning immediately and wasting his money and time. However, Siddhartha states that he is completely happy with his journey and has done no harm because the people did not even take him for a merchant. On the other hand, he had made good friends in the village who would hold him in happy remembrance. Accused of only traveling for his own pleasure, Siddhartha seems proud of the fact, making the point that if he had left annoyed and angry the loss would be greater. This way he had made friends of the villagers who would be more likely to receive him friendly if he went again to negotiate a future harvest.

222 Wickham, P., 2001. *Strategic Entrepreneurship,* Harlow: Pearson Education Ltd.

223 ibid.

224 Manimala, M., 1999. *Entrepreneurial Policies and Strategies - The Innovator's Choice*, Sage.

225 Hamel G, Prahalad CK, 1993. Strategy as Stretch and Leverage, *Harvard Business Review* 2003 Aug;81(8):109-17, 142.

226 Wickham, P., 2001. *Strategic Entrepreneurship,* Harlow: Pearson Education Ltd, p. 98.

227 ibid., p. 99.

228 Handy, C., 1995. *The Empty Raincoat,* Random House.

229 Rummelt, R., 1995. *Inertia and Transformation,* Corporate Renewal Initiative Reprint Series, INSEAD, Paris.

230 Senge, P. M., 1990. 'The Fifth Discipline – The Art and Practice of the Learning Organization', Doubleday.

231 Cliff Bowman, 1995. "Strategy workshops and top-team commitment to strategic change", Journal of Managerial Psychology, Vol. 10 (1995) Issue: 8, pp.4 – 12

232 Lewin K., 1943. Defining the "Field at a Given Time." Psychological Review. 50: 292-310. Republished in Resolving Social Conflicts & Field Theory in Social Science, Washington, D.C.: American Psychological Association, 1997.

233 Rowlandson, P., 1984. 'The Oddity of OD' *Management Today,* November, pp. 91-93.

234 Bowman, C. and Asch, D., 1987 *Strategic Management,* MacMillan Education Ltd, London.

235 Hammer, M. and Champy, J., 1993. *Reengineering the Corporation: A Manifesto for Business Revolution.* HarperCollins.

236 Hammer, M., 1990. Reengineering Work: Don't Automate, Obliterate. *Harvard Business Review,* July-August, 104-111.

237 ibid.

238 http://www.12manage.com/methods_bpr.html

239 Davenport, T.H., 1993. *Process Innovation,* Harvard Business School Press, Boston, M.A.

240 http://www.dod.mil/comptroller/icenter/learn/reeng.htm

241 http://www.doc.ic.ac.uk/~nd/surprise_95/journal/vol2/tmkl/article2.html

242 Caron, J., Jarvenpaa, S. and Stoddard, D., 1994. Business reengineering at CIGNA corporation: experiences and lessons learned from the first five years, *MIS Quarterly,* 18, 3, 233-250.

243 Murphy, E., 1994. Cultural Values, Workplace Democracy and Organizational Change: Emerging Issues in European Businesses, in Coulson-Thomas, C. (Ed.) (1994) *Business Process Re-engineering: Myth & Reality,* Kogan Page, London, 201-210.

244 Senge, P. M., 1990. 'The Fifth Discipline – The Art and Practice of the Learning Organization', Doubleday.

245 Senge, P.M. ,1992. *The Fifth Discipline: the art and practice of the learning organization,* London, Century Business/Doubleday.

246 Grant, R.M., 1995. *Contemporary Strategy Analysis,* (2nd edn)

Blackwell, Oxford.

247 Kay, J., 1993. *Foundations of Corporate Success*, Oxford University Press, Oxford.

248 Porter, M.E., 1985. *Competitive Advantage: creating and sustaining superior performance*, The Free Press, New York.

249 Kotter, J.P. and Schlessinger, L.A., 1979. 'Choosing strategies for change', Harvard Business Review, March-April.

250 Mintzberg, H., 1979. *The Structuring of Organizations*, Prentice-Hall, Englewood Cliffs, NJ.

251 Andrews, K., 1971. *The Concepts of Corporate Strategy*, Dow Jones-Irwin, Homewood, II.

252 Buber, Martin, 1928ff. in Glatzer, N. (1968) *On the Bible – Eighteen Studies, pp. 137-159*, Schocken, New York.

253 Haller, W., 1990. *Die heillsame Alternative: jesuanische Ethik in Wirtschaft und Politik*, Hammer, Wuppertal (author's rendering of the German text).

254 Ibid.

255 Chappell, T., 1993. *The Soul of a Business – Managing for Profit und the Common Good*, New York, Bantam.

256 ibid.

257 Adair, 2002. *Inspiring Leadership – Learning from Great Leaders*, London,Thorogood.

258 Hamel, G. and Prahalad, C.K., 1994. *Competing for the Future*, Boston, MA, Havard Business School Press.

259 Chorn, N.H., 2007. *The "Alignment Teory": Creating Strategic Fit*. http://centstrat.com/wp-content/uploads/2008/05/strategic-alignment.pdf, accessed 16th August 2012.

260 Hamel, G. and Prahalad, C.K., 1994. *Competing for the Future*, Boston, MA, Havard Business School Press.

261 Andrews, K.R., 1971. The Concept of Corporate Strategy, Homewood, Ill., R.D. Irwin.

262 Mintzberg, H., 1990. 'The design school: reconsidering the basic premises of strategic management', Strategic Management Journal, Vol. 11, pp. 171–95.

263 Mintzberg, H. and Waters, J., 1985. 'Of strategies, deliberate and emergent', Strategic Management Journal, vol. 6, pp. 257–72.

264 Spender, J.C., 1989. Industrial Recipes, Oxford, Blackwell.

265 Götz Woerner is also campaigning in Germany for an unconditional basic income. Such an idea would change the face of employment and motivation. See: http://en.wikipedia.org/wiki/Basic_income

266 Pettigrew, A.M., 1988. The Management of Strategic Change, Oxford, Blackwell.

267 Doran, G. T., 1981. There's a S.M.A.R.T. way to write management's goals and objectives. Management Review, Volume 70, Issue 11, AMA FORUM), pp. 35-36.

268 Freeman, R.E., 1984. Strategic Management: A Stakeholder Approach, Boston, MA, Harper Collins.

269 Etzioni, A., 1971. *A Comparative Analysis of Complex Organizations,* The Free Press, New York

270 Morgan G, 1989. Images of Organisations, London, Sage.

271 Kotler P., 1980. Marketing Management: analysis planning and control, Englewood Cliffs, NJ, Prentice-Hall.

272 Fahey,L. and Narayanan, VK, 1986. *Macroenvironmental Analysis for Strategic Management, West St. Paul*

273 Porter, M.E., 1979. 'How competitive forces shape strategy', Harvard Business Review, March April.

274 Schumpeter, J., 1942. Capitalism, Socialism and Democracy. London: Routledge. p. 139.

275 Brandenburger,A.M. and Nalebuff, B.J., 1997. *Co-Opetition : A Revolution Mindset That Combines Competition and Cooperation : The Game Theory Strategy That's Changing the Game of Business,* Doubleday, New York.

276 Flood, M.M., 1952. Some experimental games. Research memorandum RM-789. RAND Corporation, Santa Monica, CA. Retrieved from a Wikipedia article: http://en.wikipedia.org/wiki/Prisoner's_dilemma

277 Hamel, G. and Prahalad, C.K., 1994. *Competing for the Future,* Boston, MA, Havard Business School Press.

278 Hamel, G. and Prhalad, C.K., 1989. 'Collaborate with your competitors – and win', *Havard Business Review,* January-February pp. 133-139.

279 Kay, J., 1993. *Foundations of Corporate Success,* Oxford University Press, Oxford.

280 Porter, M.E., 1985. *Competitive Advantage,* The Free Press,

New York.

281 Grant, R.M., 1995. *Contemporary Strategy Analysis: Concepts, Techniques,* Blackwell, Oxford.

282 Bowmann, C. and Asch, D., 1996. *Managing Strategy,* Macmillan, Basingstoke.

283 Ansoff, H.I., 1965. *Corporate Strategy,* McGraw-Hill, New York.

284 Johnson, G. and Scholes, K., 1988. *Exploring Corporate Strategy* (2nd edn), Prentice Hall, Hemel Hempstead.

285 Rummelt, R., 1995. 'The Evaluation of business strategy', in Mintzberg, H. Quinn, B.J. And Ghoshal, S. (1995) *The Strategy Process,* Prentice Hall, Hemel Hempstead.

286 Grant, R.M., 1995. *Contemporary Strategy Analysis: Concepts, Techniques,* Blackwell, Oxford.

287 Day, G.S., 1990. *Market-driven Strategy Process for Creating Value,* The Free Press New York.

288 Batsleer, J., 2005. 'Making a Difference - The Guide'. Milton Keynes, The Open University.

289 Johnson G. and Scholes K., 1993. *Exploring Corporate Strategy: Text and Cases* (3rd edn), London, Prentice Hall.